LITERATURE OF CRISIS, 1910–22

Literature of Crisis, 1910–22

Howards End, *Heartbreak House*, *Women in Love* and *The Waste Land*

Anne Wright

Reader in Modern English Studies
The Hatfield Polytechnic

St. Martin's Press   New York

St. Martin's Press, Inc., 175 Fifth Avenue, New York, NY 10010
Printed in Hong Kong
Published in the United Kingdom by The Macmillan Press Ltd.
First published in the United States of America in 1984

ISBN 0-312-48802-5

Library of Congress Cataloging in Publication Data

Wright, Anne, 1946–
    Literature of crisis, 1910–22

    Includes bibliographical references and index.
        1. English literature – 20th century – History and criticism.   2. World War, 1914–1918 – Literature and the war.   3. Forster, E. M. (Edward Morgan), 1879–1970. Howards End.   4. Shaw, Bernard, 1856–1950. Heartbreak house.   5. Lawrence, D. H. (David Herbert), 1885–1930. Women in love.   6. Eliot, T. S. (Thomas Stearns), 1888–1965. Waste land.   I. Title.
    PR478.W65W7 1984   820'.9'00912   83–40168
    ISBN 0-312-48802-5

Contents

Acknowledgements

The approach to writing of the early twentieth century which this book proposes has been framed in the light of experience of designing and teaching undergraduate and postgraduate courses in modern English literature. Accordingly, I register my appreciation to both students and colleagues for the critical dialogue – still continuing – which that process has involved. Much of the specific research for and some of the writing of the book took place during a year of sabbatical leave from the Hatfield Polytechnic, which I am glad to acknowledge here. I am also grateful for support received from the British Academy, in an award in 1979 from the Small Grants Research Fund in the Humanities which enabled me to visit and research the Shaw and Lawrence collections in the Humanities Research Center, University of Texas at Austin; and for the kindness and help of members of staff in the Humanities Research Center; the British Library, especially the Department of Manuscripts; and the library of the Hatfield Polytechnic. I wish to thank Professor Dan H. Laurence, for his advice and information; Miss Elizabeth Poston; Professor Stanley Weintraub, for continued interest and encouragement; Dr Dennis Brown and Dr Gill Davies, who read the various chapters and offered their comments; and Martin Wright, for his practical help at all stages.

The author and publishers wish to thank the following who have kindly given permission for the use of copyright material:

Edward Arnold (Publishers) Ltd and Alfred A. Knopf Inc., for the extracts from *Howards End* by E. M. Forster, copyright 1921 by E. M. Forster; and the extract from *The Manuscripts of Howards End*, edited by Oliver Stallybrass.

The Executors of the Estate of H. G. Wells for extracts from *Mr Britling Sees It Through* and *Tono-Bungay*.

Faber & Faber Ltd and Harcourt Brace Jovanovich Inc., for the extract from 'Little Gidding' in *Four Quartets* by T. S. Eliot; and the extracts from T. S. Eliot's 'The Waste Land' in *Collected Poems 1909–1962*, copyright 1936 by Harcourt Brace Jovanovich Inc., copyright © 1963, 1964 by T. S. Eliot.

Faber & Faber Ltd and Farrar, Straus and Giroux Inc., for the extracts from '*Ulysses*, Order and Myth' in *Selected Prose of T. S. Eliot*, edited by Frank Kermode.

David Higham Associates Ltd, on behalf of Ford Madox Ford, and John Lane, for the extracts from *The Good Soldier: A Tale of Passion*.

The Hogarth Press Ltd and the Literary Estate of Virginia Woolf, and Harcourt Brace Jovanovich Inc., for the extracts from *Mrs Dalloway* and *To the Lighthouse* by Virginia Woolf.

Mrs Laura Huxley and Chatto & Windus, and Harper and Row, Publishers, for the extracts from *Point Counter Point* by Aldous Huxley, copyright 1928 by Aldous Huxley, copyright renewed 1956 by Aldous Huxley.

Oxford University Press (New York) for the extracts from *The Sense of an Ending: Studies in the Theory of Fiction* by Frank Kermode.

Laurence Pollinger Ltd and the Estate of Mrs Frieda Lawrence Ravagli, and Viking Penguin, Inc. and the New American Library Inc., for various extracts from the published and unpublished works of D. H. Lawrence.

The Society of Authors on behalf of the Bernard Shaw Estate for extracts from published and unpublished works by Shaw.

1 Towards a Literature of Crisis

'while it hangs imminent and doesn't fall'

This book has arisen, in the first instance, from a felt need to draw a circle round a small number of texts which, according to received formulations, might not be susceptible to juxtaposition. It has seemed to me that the extraordinary similarities displayed by these texts – *Howards End*, *Heartbreak House*, *Women in Love* and *The Waste Land* – demand that they be read in conjunction as parallel articulations of a specific moment in history. This book seeks to establish a critical language which may recognise and express their affinities with each other; in so doing, it propounds a fresh configuration, and perhaps an alternative perspective. In an admittedly restricted focus, it reproblematises literature as it has been constructed in critical accounts of the period.

The texts – two novels, one play and one long poem – belong to different genres, and they have been variously placed and evaluated in relation both to each writer's work and to other authors. Written or published between 1910 and 1922, they are of the period surrounding the First World War: *Heartbreak House* and *Women in Love* have a common chronology, both largely written, and completed, in 1916–17. *Women in Love* was published in 1921, the year in which Eliot put together *The Waste Land* (which contains some material written much earlier). None of the texts is centrally or explicitly concerned with events at the Front; but each registers a response to the war, or to events leading up to or away from it. The period of their composition also spans the emergence and ascendancy of modernism in the arts: at one end, the Post-Impressionist exhibition, and Virginia Woolf's notorious remark that in or around December 1910 human nature changed;

and, at the other, the *annus mirabilis* of modernism, 1922, which saw the publication of *The Waste Land* as well as of Joyce's *Ulysses*.[1] Taking the four texts as a group, their chronology spans the crises of imperialism and liberalism, the First World War and its immediate aftermath, and the crucial years of the rise of modernism. Yet none of the four is usually considered primarily, or even substantially, as literature of the war; although it should be added that literary-critical constitution of 'war writing' has recently expanded to the point where one or more might be placed with reasonable ease in this category.[2] And, of the four, only *The Waste Land* is more or less indisputably labelled modernist. However, increasingly we find that two or more of the texts are compared, by critics seeking perhaps to characterise afresh literary production before and after the Great War. The grouping of all four together is still, nevertheless, an implicit challenge to the boundaries and delimitations of both literature of war and of modernist writing.

The texts have been, and are, subject to strongly argued debates as to their artistic value, as well as their place in literary history. In this respect, too, they are as it were *puzzling* texts. Moreover, adverse criticism of them shows a curious commonality of focus. *Howards End*, for example, has been condemned for an arbitrary or inadequate motivation of plot and psychology, or for awkward transitions from narrative realism to utopian vision, and embarrassingly obtrusive symbolism. *Heartbreak House* typically draws fire from those who expect of Shaw a realistic drawing-room comedy concerned with social problems, and who demur at its obliquity, obscurity and use of non-naturalistic characterisation and dramatic action. Even more than Forster or Shaw, Lawrence is charged with overt and excessive didacticism; and *Women in Love* is denounced either because of the prominence of Rupert Birkin as Lawrence's spokesman, or because of an imbalance which renders Birkin less sympathetic and attractive than Gerald Crich. In all these texts, characters and plot have been seen to be contrived in the worst sense, the endings as unconvinced and unconvincing, the mode of writing – realistic or symbolic – as wavering or uncertain. Even *The Waste Land*, paradigm of modernism, may be negatively described as discontinuous, fragmented, or nihilistic; or, alternatively, as exhibiting a naïve proto-Christian redemptive vision.

What my grouping of these texts proposes is, in effect, that such difficulties are misrepresented as individual and unconnected artistic failure: that they are, rather, defining features of a specific literary phenomenon within the period. These are, for example, texts or narratives which find it necessary to shift from realism into a non-naturalistic mode in order to achieve resolution; with *The Waste Land*, the shift becomes total. They also, as we shall see later in this chapter and in separate, detailed consideration, constitute a peculiar species of fiction. And, certainly, they do have 'difficult' endings: not merely open (indeed, not really open at all, in the sense that all legitimate dispute is permitted by the text); but problematic, ambiguous, fraught with tensions. I propose to attach to this group of texts the designation of a literature of crisis.

This said, in what sense do the texts I have chosen constitute a 'literature of crisis'? More specifically, for the moment, what precisely *is* their concept of crisis? Crisis is not merely the perception of change: each of the four texts is permeated by a sense of crisis, and disturbed by what is registered as an accelerating deterioration in the quality of life. Crisis is expressed as the fracturing or dismantling of personal relations, of social institutions, of civilisation. The dimensions of crisis are in fact questioned by each text, and actually vary: the site and the scope of the breakdown may be individual, national, cultural or cosmic, extending from sexual intercourse to the extinction of the species. Crisis is the distant or imminent threat of cataclysmic disruption of the familiar: total devastation, even if, as in *Howards End*, dimly perceived. In tendency, at least, all four texts are apocalyptic.

At this juncture, while apocalypse 'hangs imminent and doesn't fall',[3] modern life is perceived as both fevered and futile. Standing back a little from the texts, we may discern features which characterise their common rendering of the contemporary experience: madness, heartbreak and violence are endemic. The 'confounded madness' of a society in crisis may be located in personal behaviour – 'We all are [madder than usual]', observes Hesione Hushabye in Act I of *Heartbreak House* – or projected into the historical event of international conflict – war as a group madness – or internalised, again, in *The Waste Land* as neurasthenia: 'My nerves are bad to-night'. Heartbreak, too, is registered in both *Heartbreak House* and *Women in Love*: and the 'broken' world of emotional transactions passes into *The Waste Land*, where the 'heart of light' is negative, a silence. Alongside madness and heartbreak goes violence, latent or direct. All the texts display a marked violence of action and feeling: it is as if the fracturing of social stability generates a violence expressed in the killing of a Leonard Bast, a Boss Mangan or a Gerald Crich. In *The Waste Land* violence passes into the total environment, in a nightmare vision of destruction. Violence and violation, then – emotional cruelty, intellectual assault, physical attack, strangulation and suicide – are pervasive in these fictions: a barometer, perhaps, of anger or despair; certainly, indicative of a climate of tension and conflict. It is the act of placing the texts together which alerts us to the repetition from one to another of apparently casual or unrelated remarks, incidents and motifs. The grouping thus foregrounds images such as those of madness and violence; and we may then more easily, perhaps, make connections with other literature, and indeed other discourses. Scott Sanders has noted the level of rhetorical violence at home in the war years;[4] and 'war madness' is amply evidenced in essays, pamphlets and letters of the time.

On this broader scale we may also note the emphasis placed by the texts on sex, as locus of crisis in the sphere of interpersonal relationships, and as symptomatic, in its failures, of the larger, social crisis. This is not simply to be attributed to a greater frankness in writing about sex, or even, in the wake of a developing psychology of sex, to an increased awareness of the centrality of sexual drives to human motivation and behaviour. The point is that sexuality here is of a particular kind: the relationships are, on the whole, frustrated, inadequate, destructive and (literally) barren. Sex, we may conclude, is one of the problem areas in contemporary experience; yet the specific problem of the position of women and the struggle towards emancipation is exceptionally, and peripherally, an overt issue, except perhaps for Ellie Dunn in *Heartbreak House*. Certainly the female figures energetically initiate sexual relationships; and they reject conventional marriage, or motherhood, or both. But, with the exception of the typist in *The Waste Land*, and Ellie Dunn, we do not hear about them at work: they worry little about economic independence, trusting to unearned incomes or to male support. The 'feminist recriminations' which tired Captain Shotover are only intermittently registered.[5] They push at the edges of the narratives, but are deflected, as it were, into male anxieties and insecurities.

Returning a little closer to the texts, we find that each explicitly articulates the crisis as an acute split in society, as radical division, something that cannot hold together, to the extent that the epigraph of *Howards End* urges 'Only connect . . .', while *The Waste Land* 'can connect/Nothing with nothing', ll. 301–2. The split is expressed in the individual texts by a variety of dualisms or binary oppositions – materialism as against an enlightened humanitarianism, power versus wisdom, industrialisation as against nature – focused in representative characters or groups of characters, and in sharply contrasted environments. In each text there is the commercial or industrial magnate: Henry Wilcox, Boss Mangan, Gerald Crich (and, obliquely, the Bradford millionaire of *The Waste Land*). And there is the 'cultured' opposition, of the Schlegel sisters or Hector Hushabye, who register the problematic split with moral distress, and occupy a position closer to the authorial viewpoint.

The fracturing or split of society in these texts is a twentieth-century version of Disraeli's 'two nations', but concentrated within the middle classes. To Ellie Dunn, poverty is not being able to afford a new pair of gloves. But, to Leonard Bast, hunger and even starvation are real threats: the split between extreme wealth and dire poverty resonates in *Howards End*, in the 'abyss' familiar from Gissing's *The Nether World*, and from late Victorian and Edwardian sociological investigation. Leonard's horrified vision, from the edge of the abyss, of a torrid and destructive social mobility, may be glimpsed, if faintly, in Hector Hushabye's observation that survival is a miracle in the lion's den of a competitive capitalist society. The vertical fissure, the pit that opens in the smooth surface to reveal the stratifications beneath, is also registered in *Women in Love*, in the underworld of the colliers. This nether world, to which belong also Gerald, Gudrun and Loerke, is psychological as well as social; and here we seem closer, perhaps, to Freud or Jung than to the 'social explorers'. However, the division between the daylight world and the underworld is a potent motif, which may operate in many ways: as the descent into the underworld, it is one of the major informing myths of *The Waste Land*. Whether we perceive the underworld as a Freudian subconscious, a collective unconscious, or a social chasm, the very prevalence of the image in disparate areas of writing is remarkable. The various connotations of this slicing across experience suggestively coalesce in a text which predates by more than a decade those considered in this book. This is Wells's *The Time Machine*, where the two species of Eloi and Morlocks have an ambivalent symbiotic relationship. Here the motif is dynamic and emotive: the threat of falling into the pit, and dread of the night-creatures which emerge from it, are strongly felt. Here we reach an important point: in these texts it is a matter not only of their diagnosis of a split in society, but also of the accompanying sense of anxiety and threat. And it is not only the underworld that is to be feared: as we move forward to 1916–17, the thing from the air becomes increasingly the focus of dread, and takes shape as the Zeppelin or, later, as the Thunder of *The Waste Land*.

The split in society is also represented in terms of a temporal dualism, past and present. If the present is in flux and decline, the past is framed and perfected. There is an element of nostalgia in all the texts: each expresses regret at the loss of an integrated way of life, and rejects materialism, industrialism and philistinism in favour of this lost organicism. The nymphs have vanished, as in *The Waste Land*: pastoral and romanticism, the myth of the golden age, lurk behind the exposition of contemporary social problems. And, to an extent, these *are* elegies, recording with regret the passing of an era, as the sun sets on the perfected past.

Temporal pastoral is translated to spatial, in the familiar dichotomy of country and city.[6] In *Howards End* the rural ideal persists, if under threat. The normative country house adjoins a working farm, and is firmly rooted in native soil. Both *Howards End* and *Women in Love* discriminate *between* country houses; in both, however, the city is summed up, and abhorred, in London. *Heartbreak House* is less comprehensive than these, focusing on just one, 'cultured', country house, although it envisages others, such as the colonial household of Lady Utterword, or the Horseback Hall of the Preface. It is from this perspective that the city is viewed; and here the City, as in *The Waste Land*, is represented by the activities of the financier. Moreover, Mangan does not stand alone. We feel that his 'mutual admiration gang' provides a strong economic and political back-up, from the citadel. In *The Waste Land* the respective positions of city and country are reversed: the city becomes the main focus, while both temporal and topographical contrasts serve to heighten the sense of urban and cultural decay.

These texts reach back, then, to the line of country-house fictions, as well as to, say, *The City of Dreadful Night*. But to say this is not at all to reduce their status and significance as vitally *contemporary* writing: indeed, all firmly 'place' themselves, as it were, in their world, addressing contemporary events and issues. In this sense each – and I do not exclude *The Waste Land* – records the moment of crisis. In some sense, of course, all literary discourse may be seen as integral to the contemporary process; but the engagement of these texts with the world beyond the fiction is more than simply a matter of belonging to the historical moment. In *Heartbreak House* and *Women in Love*, for example, the war is more central and meaningful than might be inferred from the obliquity of treatment. There is more than a common chronology of composition here: the war is at the heart of both texts; and similarities of theme and stance are striking through-out, and in some passages extraordinarily close. Both *Heartbreak House* and *Women in Love* try to make sense of the crisis of which they see the war as symptom. Both attempt to give the war a shape and significance, and, finally, to affirm its necessity in the scheme of things. Their respective attempts to affirm the 'necessity' of crisis will be discussed more fully in the chapters which follow.

A similar worrying at the meaning and significance of crisis characterises the texts which precede and follow the war: *Howards End* and *The Waste Land*. Not only does each speak for and about the world which the writer engages in, but that world presents a problem which must yield a meaning. These are all fictions which are concerned both to provide a descriptive model of society, and to project an outcome: they predict, exhort and warn. What they offer is, in effect, a 'cultural statement': 'cultural' in the sense of a shaped and shaping view (which is in the broadest sense a moral view) of society and civilisation; and 'statement' in the sense both of descriptive analysis and of polemic. Their cultural statements shape the crisis: they also seek its 'solution' – mending the split, or replacing a false dualism by a true one. Their fictive worlds, then, are neither wholly fictional nor wholly descriptive: these are purposive narratives, whose prescriptive aspect obtains most obviously in the projected, normative solutions.

This is, of course, to admit a didactic, or rather an ethical drive: at the very least, to see a moral imperative at work. Returning to *Heartbreak House* and *Women in Love* as literature of the war, we might say that the war broke in on Lawrence (as it did for Shaw), adding a further dimension to what was already to be a 'Condition of England' novel, of the twentieth century. It was Graham

Hough who said of Lawrence that 'perhaps the best way of looking at some of his works is to regard them as works of mixed purpose like *Sartor Resartus*'.[7] Lawrence, and indeed all these writers, offer us in fictive mode what is essentially a cultural statement of 'mixed purpose'; in the case of Lawrence, with a base in the discourse of historical and political philosophy. And the reference to Carlyle is particularly apt: one can look back, to compare Carlyle's vehement denunciation of a materialist society, his prophetic strain, and his moral fervour; and further forward, to cyclical systems of history such as that of Spengler.

This book is not centrally concerned with tracing lines of intellectual influence or development; but one name, or rather one theory, stands out pre-eminently in the statements which these texts make, in their attribution of a meaning to crisis. The impact of Darwin, and the theory of the evolution of species, constantly confronts us: the ubiquitous abyss, for example, may be a manifestation of the complex phenomenon of social Darwinism (and, incidentally, Carlyle was himself a proto-evolutionist). But the more one looks the more one finds Darwin, or, more precisely, post-Darwinian (and, largely, anti-Darwinian and non-deterministic) evolutionism, underpinning all the images and articulations of crisis. As we shall see in separate discussion of the texts, what emerges in the confrontation with a crisis such as that represented by the war, and following the theories of Bergson, is a willed and purposive evolutionism, which can still postulate a force making for good in the universe. As it happens, both *Heartbreak House* and *Women in Love* strive for meaning in a conflation of a post-Darwinian progressive evolutionary ethic, and a consoling salvationism. In this way the writers may gain a precarious optimism which can entertain any dimension of crisis – even the cosmic – as tending ultimately for good, or as a necessary stage in the evolutionary process (and so, ironically, themselves constitute a Darwinian adaptation to the social, political or ideological environment).

Even so broad (but intricate) a 'statement' as social Darwinism is, however, less a programme explicitly formulated within the text than a way, for us, of grasping and characterising what it is that the text has to say. The point to take here is that, despite shared diagnoses of crisis – such as that of sexuality as the site of the breakdown, or the warping effect of the modern industrial machine – each text constitutes in itself a cultural statement, as well as making or containing one. That is to say, each can speak to us of a moment of crisis in more than the ideas voiced by the characters, or by 'authorial' commentary. As we shall see, the cultural statement is carried more importantly by the plot or narrative sequence, the concatenation of events in the novel, play or poem. But narrative, although plotted by the author, is in a sense autonomous, and we may perceive its processes as other than a conscious, intentional construct. It is in this area, in particular, that the text may operate as a statement; and, possibly, one that articulates a crisis beyond, or other than, what the 'authorial' stance admits to. Here we are dealing with what a materialist criticism might call the 'silences' of the text, the *'not-said'* by which the work is separated from itself, and by which it puts ideology to work.[8] The discrepancy or disjunction between the dimensions of crisis as gauged by the author, and by the text, will be immediately pertinent in the next chapter, in discussing the peculiar tensions of *Howards End* and, in particular, the way in which the novel is 'plotted'.

The shaping of the plot, in the sense of narrative sequence, is of paramount significance. And the texts with which we are concerned are notable for their 'shared' plot-elements: the parallels between representative characters, groupings of characters, and situations are numerous. Moreover, each plot – including, by an extension of the term, *The Waste Land* – shapes itself in a particular relation to the genres of tragedy and comedy, using and exploring the narrative structures and plot-expectations conventional to each genre. Plot-expectations are geared to the conventionally comic or tragic endings of, respectively, marriage or death. As both marriages and deaths constitute, conventionally, plot-resolutions, both are also envisaged as potential 'solutions' to the problems thrown up in the preceding narrative. Death, we might say, is the negative solution, eliminating the undesirable; and each text covertly or overtly refers itself to the genre of tragedy by embracing death in its narrative. Weddings and births signify the positive solution, and provide for an affirmative resolution: these denote the possibility of harmony and regeneration, investing hope in one or more bearers of the vision of a redeemed future.

Each text opts, then, in its plot-decisions, for a generic attachment; but a simple choice or division between comedy and tragedy does not apply here. *Howards End* aims at comedy, but narrowly escapes tragedy. *Women in Love* may be a 'barren tragedy', as Gudrun describes Gerald's death. Each narrative strives to connect, to mend that radical split, by a marriage: the comedic solution. Each also embraces a death. The text seeks, still arguably in the comic tradition, to expel one or more characters in order to consolidate and ratify the selected social group. The sudden, violent or premature death of a central figure is the climax of each text, and we may discern a particular congruence in these plot-decisions. There is, too, a remarkable similarity between the figures who are killed off by the plot, or who are left physically maimed, or without power. But there is more to it than this: death is an ambivalent signifier in these texts, and occupies a shifting position in the articulation of the plot. I say this partly in that death is the prelude to and precondition of regeneration – either literally, as in *Howards End*, by property and inheritance, or symbolically, as in *The Waste Land*, by a process of metamorphosis and salvation – and, accordingly, constitutes a positive solution. But in part, too, death operates as an inclusive experience for each text, and so complicates the plot-resolution. The 'expelled' figures refuse, as it were, to be dismissed; their death or elimination threatens to decentre the narrative and disturb both its closure and the total signification. These deaths tip the narratives towards a symbolic statement of an entire society in decay.

The ambivalence does not apply only to deaths. As was noted earlier, sexuality in these texts is problematic: marriages also operate equivocally as tokens of a positive solution. In each case a marriage, or a sexual connection, is central to the direction of the plot; but each proves difficult, and usually unfruitful. Women are virgin or childless, and perversely so: the only child brought forth in these texts is conceived and born outside marriage. Yet, despite the overall infertility, the motif of the child is strong. Predominantly, however, it is the adult who is seen as a large child, and the image is not regenerative, but one of immaturity and inadequacy. The men of *Heartbreak House* are infantilised; and Gerald Crich, the Don Juan of *Women in Love*, is an infant crying in the night. As in Yeats's 'The Second Coming', some creature in these texts is labouring to be born; but the actual delivery, and indeed the nature of the creature to be born, are uncertain.

There is a further point. Each text centralises a marriage or an act of sexual intercourse, and each kills off or eliminates one or more characters. These features – birth, copulation and death –

are the linchpins of the narrative, as it strives to connect and regenerate. But in each case there was for the writer some doubt as to which character should be killed, and which characters should marry. The difficulty which Forster, Lawrence and Shaw experienced in deciding which should die and which survive is demonstrated, outside the texts, by the evidence of working-notes, draft manuscripts and letters; and, internally, by stages of revision. Forster and Lawrence both juggled, in drafts and notes, with various alternatives, only to change their minds in the final versions of their books. Shaw apparently arrived very late at the decision to kill off Mangan, and 'marry' Ellie Dunn to Captain Shotover. (Even in *The Waste Land*, 'Death by Water' was extensively revised by Eliot in collaboration with Ezra Pound: only the translation of an earlier poem survives in the final version, and the connection of Phlebas the Phoenician with other figures and 'events' in the poem is subject to dispute.)

It is not, I think, reductionist to take account of discarded drafts: in the complex process of composition one can unravel something of the text working itself through, and sometimes against the author's initial instincts of its direction. As for the final text, the ingredients of a disturbed closure may be detected in the alternatives envisaged before the text was finalised, as well as in the tensions within it. And it is, as it happens, a fascinating if vexing coincidence that Forster, Lawrence and Shaw all worried over whom their end-directed plots should eliminate: what, in other words, was the desired and necessary final configuration, the blueprint for survival. We have here a curious and important area of uncertainty: curious, again, in the common ground of these texts, here with respect to making plot-decisions, working themselves through; and important, in that the uncertainty is located in that area, crucial to this special kind of fiction, of the resolution of the plot, its final, normative configuration.

Each text reaches towards what I have called, in dealing with them separately, a normative configuration: it is this concluding tableau towards which all characterisation and plotting are directed. But the final configuration has itself a multiple aspect and purpose, which may produce a sense of unease. The denouement, to use a more traditional term, encodes, in the interrelatedness of the characters, and in what the plot has done to them, what are perceived to have been all along the dynamics of the representative picture of society, the tensions and stresses inherent in the situation as it is gradually uncovered. In this aspect the final configuration, like the closing chord of a piece of music, resolves and clarifies: it gathers in what will be heard as an expected and inevitable harmony. In retrospect the cumulative, diachronic experience of the narrative will reveal or uncover all the events, intrigues or complications as discord, whose referent and epiphany is the final accord. But, as these texts are also purposive narratives, the final configuration also operates as a moral recommendation. It is in this sense that the normative configuration offers a projected 'solution'; and it will seek also to dislocate itself from the descriptive analysis, to superimpose another model. In working through to both a realisation and a recommendation the text tries, as it were, to have it both ways. There is, further, the predictive aspect, according to which the final configuration may be an apocalyptic or a millennarian vision. The relation between these several aspects is complicated and intricate, and may itself indicate the problematic status of the text, its internal conflicts and tensions, which are disclosed, rather than resolved, by the ending.

However, these texts are so substantially end-directed that to understand how they operate one can indeed work backwards from the final configuration. As we work backwards we may well go beyond the texts themselves to earlier drafts, witnessing the struggle for narrative closure. Not only, however, do we find alternatives outside the texts; but the texts may disclose, internally, multiple (and possibly incompatible) 'endings', in a disclosure. In fact what we discover, paradoxically, about these end-directed narratives is that they do indeed reach for a particular, normative ending which, when reached, 'troubles' the preceding narrative in a way which suggests that more than one progression has been at work. Less problematically, but characteristically, the endings are also multiple in the sense that they offer us several successive closures before the final page. In each of *Howards End*, *Heartbreak House* and *Women in Love* we are waiting for the end for a considerable time, as the extended finale unfolds: beginning in *Howards End*, I think, with the death of Leonard, three chapters before the end. In *Heartbreak House* the end is signalled by Hector Hushabye, before a succession of 'closing' sequences. And in *Women in Love* we might, perhaps, have stopped with the death of Gerald, although we would then of course have had a different novel. (It is a little difficult to speak of narrative closure in *The Waste Land*: not, as we shall see later, because narrative is a concept alien or irrelevant to the poem; nor even because another writer had some hand in assembling the final version. Eliot, too, wrote another 'ending', in the Notes which he appended to the published book. Whatever the 'reason' for their inclusion, they cannot, in my opinion, be ignored; and, in contradiction perhaps of the doctrine of impersonality, they not only seal off the poem, but also mark it as the writer's own, with a personal signature.)

The point to take is that, of the several endings, any or all might be valid and sufficient. And there are, apart from those endings which the text gives us, those which it withholds, but which are clearly alluded to, even while being rejected or omitted. An example is Lady Utterword's reminder, in *Heartbreak House*, that Ellie Dunn might be expected to produce a baby: others are discussed in the chapters which follow. And the point does not only apply to the endings: at numerous stages in the narrative progression, we register a *selecting out* of alternatives. The reader is invited to recognise, at these junctures, other conceivable progressions, and to confirm the one that is chosen as being both possible and necessary. However, the reader may accept the 'invitation', but disagree with the concatenation of events. The net result of this relentless impulse towards the 'promis'd end', together with the paradox stated earlier, that the ending may not, after all, be the one which the text has expected, is to suggest a crisis. It suggests a crisis surrounding, and complicating, the intended statement, so that we perceive some distance between narrative and author, which foregrounds a certain dilemma for the latter. In all the texts, both the negative and the positive solutions present difficulties of interpretation and evaluation: they are variously schematic, tentative or ambiguous. The openness of the ending may be a measure of the writer's uncertain stance or divided sympathies: documenting change, and warning of catastrophe, but hoping for minimal loss. Moreover, the limitation of the *realised* vision is felt in intimations of further catastrophe, of larger and *unrealised* dimensions of crisis.

These texts are, then, eager for closure: they exhibit strongly, and with some anxiety, 'the sense of an ending' – the title of an elegant and persuasive study in the theories of fiction by Frank Kermode.[9] This work explores the relation between theological responses to apocalypse, and literary endings. Professor Kermode's starting-point is a consideration of the End of the World as it is represented in biblical narratives: from the theological and the eschatological, he then proceeds to examine the workings of narrative in fiction. The 'End-feeling'[10] of the apocalyptic passes, demythologised, into the processes of secular narratives. The inevitable fate of all detailed eschatological 'fictions of the End'[11] is disconfirmation, and the End is immanent rather than imminent. Kermode finds that this model can be extended; and that the basic paradigm of much fiction is also 'a disconfirmation followed by a consonance'.[12] The sense of an ending settles on the middle of things; and on a peripeteia which centrally but subtly disconfirms, without discrediting, apocalypse.

Professor's Kermode's study is pertinent to the concerns of this book; and not least in that it identifies, and provides a terminology for, 'end-determined fictions'.[13] Kermode uses the term 'end-directed' to describe a paradigm of crisis derived from a theological way of thinking about the present.[14] Moreover, he focuses on the persistence and prevalence of the myth of crisis; its apocalyptic base and eschatological tendency; and the coincidence of apocalyptic doctrines with contexts of crisis, decadence and empire. All fictions, including fictions of the End, provide models for the world, what he calls 'shapes which console the dying generations'.[15] The consoling shapes must rest, ultimately, on that final consonance which satisfies our sense of an ending; and indeed Kermode emphasises the undeniability of narrative closure: 'We cannot, of course, be denied an end; it is one of the great charms of books that they have to end.'[16] A great charm, perhaps; but one whose charming aspect may well be discomfited by problems of closure. There is a degree of consonance between what Professor Kermode says of the self-defining nature of literary endings, and what, from a very different perspective, Terry Eagleton writes of the problems of apparent dis-closure and 'non-solution': 'No text lacks a resolution in the sense of merely stopping: if it is to be a "finished" text – and strictly speaking there are no others, for that the text is complete as we have it is part of its definition – its "non-solution" must signify.'[17] In looking at a small group of 'end-determined fictions', and in adopting the term 'end-directed', this book is concerned both with how those fictions proceed towards closure, and with how the closures signify. Kermode quotes from *King Lear* (v.iii.263–4): 'Is this the promis'd end? Or image of that horror?' These questions draw our attention to the End of the World, and the ending of the tragedy. But the main point, in this context, is whether or not we have the *promised* end, the necessary destination of the narrative progression: what I have called the final configuration which the text yearns for.

What was not immediately relevant to Professor Kermode's study, with its base in theological apocalypse, but which is crucial here, is the dual connotation of end-direction, as both predictive and purposive. Certainly the texts are apocalyptic in tendency, and display the predictive or prophetic features suggested by the term 'end-directed'. However, they are also teleological and purposive: the plot is the working through of an argument; and the ethical drive is towards establishing the meaning and purpose of life in society. This dual aspect or 'mixed purpose' is expressed in the epigraph, taken from Ruskin, which C. F. G. Masterman prefixed to *The Condition of England*: 'Whether in general we are getting on, and if so where we are going to.' Another expression of the duality comes in *Howards End*, which asks both 'to what end' and 'for what end' events tend. In this case the dual aspects come together, as the ending of the fiction will axiomatically demonstrate its purpose. And in a particular sense all the fictions we examine here are end-directed, in that it is the ending, the final configuration, which is to define and confirm the preceding narrative.

These texts belong to the early twentieth century, and to the period of what Kermode in chapter 4 of his book calls 'The Modern Apocalypse', seen in the context of imperialism, of turn-of-the-century millennarianism, and the Great War. The modern apocalypse, in writers such as Yeats and Lawrence, elevates the interstitial period of crisis – crisis as transition – into an 'age' in its own right. We are left with 'eternal transition'[18] and perpetual crisis, which accordingly focus not only on the End, but also, peculiarly, on the endless. Endlessness is a recurring and characteristic phenomenon; but apocalypse remains, as the 'permanent feature of a permanent literature of crisis'.[19]

This book does not look for the permanent features of a permanent literature of crisis. Rather it identifies, within a circumscribed area of writing, what constitutes a literature of permanent crisis, or, more exactly, of persistent and continuing crisis. As we proceed, we shall see these texts increasingly characterised by what I term 'end-anxiety'. Like 'end-directed', this term alludes both to the End and to ending: it is both apocalyptic and eschatological, and literary. End-anxiety is the way in which the text yearns for, and at the same time dreads, the end: the texts direct themselves towards an End, which may not after all be the 'promis'd end', but only, in some sense, a refracted image of that horror. And the real horror, equivalent to the terrors of apocalypse, is that there may be no end. The texts are waiting for the end; but, when they achieve closure, it has a particular quality of endlessness. Moreover, finality and endlessness themselves become an issue for the texts, overtly discussed. Kermode noted that one of the semantic components of crisis was 'judgement': to a greater or lesser degree, all the texts suspend judgement and remain in crisis. What we are dealing with, then, is a literature not simply *about*, or *of*, crisis; but one which is arguably *in* crisis.

Professor Kermode associates the modern apocalypse with war. This book is also concerned with the orientation of the texts in relation to the Great War, which was both the war to end war, and the war which could not end. It was at the point at which it was felt that the war could not end that two of these texts were written. Written and completed before the outcome of hostilities, *Heartbreak House* and *Women in Love* are marked by irresolution and ambivalence. It is in these texts that the literature of crisis, as perceived in this book, is exemplified. We shall see, in *Howards End*, that a normative configuration may be determined, or reached towards, by selecting out the undesirable, and thereby putting a seal on the positives of society. But the literature of crisis, held *in media res*, is thwarted in its end-direction: it strives for meaning, in a normative configuration which cannot be definitive or unambiguous, and an ending which cannot, in a sense, be finalised or achieved.

End-anxiety is crucially *not* resolved or consoled by *Heartbreak House*; in *Women in Love* the narrative closure is more finely controlled, but still anxiously, and with some disturbance. Where end-anxiety leads to, in this book, is the achieved poise of *The Waste Land*: here is not only a paradigm of modernism, but the culmination of the cultural statement, in which we see a mode confirmed for the literature of crisis. 'Freed' from plot, linearity and the diachronic, and using a symbolic landscape which invests relationships and environment with signification of cultural decline, this poem of crisis proceeds by a 'narrative' which is synchronic, discontinuous and non-discursive. Here we find, supremely, the persisting crisis of suspended judgement, in a continuous present of apocalypse. *The Waste Land* speaks to us of crisis in a vision of repeated, recurring, immanent *and* imminent apocalypse. There is, however, a sense in which *The Waste Land* dissociates itself, as it were, from the other three texts. As we shall see, what Eliot termed the 'mythic method', and the self-reflexive nature of the poem, permit it to escape engagement in the immediacy and historical specificity of the moment of crisis; and to arrive at the permanence and aesthetic completion of a universalised condition of crisis. Nevertheless, the comparison does, I think, stand: not only in the shared themes and concerns, the stance of the cultural statement; but also in the acute sense, and strenuous denial, of an ending.

The chapters which follow offer a reading of each text. Although the aim is as much to discriminate as to draw parallels, the perspective provided by this close reading may well invite additions to the initial grouping. Some extension is suggested at the end of the book, by way of conclusion to this attempt to delineate a literature of crisis.

Before turning to these texts of crisis, however, we might pause over another book, published in 1916, which attempts in fictive mode to establish the significance of the Great War, and its impact on life in England. This is H. G. Wells's *Mr Britling Sees It Through*, parallel in date of composition to both *Heartbreak House* and *Women in Love*, but engaging more directly than these with contemporary events and issues, and bringing the war more overtly and centrally into focus. Here Wells writes a semi-documentary war fiction which brings the war up to date at the time of composition (the book closes at November 1915). This, too, is a novel of mixed purpose: its socio-historical and political details is full, and the commentary sharp (in some ways the book reads as a novelistic parallel to Shaw's Preface to *Heartbreak House*); but the shaping purpose is clear. This is a demonstration, from the limited hindsight of 1916, of what the outbreak and continuation of war meant in terms of everyday experience; and an attempt by Wells to grasp its course, direction and overarching 'meaning'. In this latter respect the omniscient narration, and the interpolated historical information and authorial commentary, are crucial. In one such interpolated passage, which comes well into the narrative, the book propounds its own framework:

> This story is essentially the history of the opening and of the realisation of the Great War as it happened to one small group of people in Essex, and more particularly as it happened to one human brain . . . only by slow degrees did it and its consequences invade the common texture of English life.[20]

The purpose, then is clear; and so, up to a point, is the signification of the events which the novel documents. But the direction and outcome are, as they must be in 1916, uncertain; and this uncertainty has implications for the normative and predictive aspects of the narrative. What this novel is concerned with is to explore the meaning of the war, and to offer a shaped solution. It is this which, in 1916, effects a crisis. Here, in a more transparent and diffuse manner than in the texts to be examined later, we find the effect of problematic closure in a succession of multiple endings. *Mr Britling Sees It Through* situates itself boldly in the midst of things; but what it comes up with, by way of solution and resolution, is a number of faintly absurd plot-reversals, followed by a broadening of the ethical perspective to permit an optimistic and cosmic evolutionary statement.

The novel focuses on 'one small group of people in Essex', using representative figures in a representative environment to provide a panorama of contemporary society. This small group comprises relatives and friends gathered at the Dower House, in the village of Matching's Easy, on the eve of the war. The 'one human brain' which operates as centre of consciousness is that of Mr Britling. As his name suggests, Mr Britling epitomises in little the Condition of England before and during the war; and, significantly, he belongs to the dominant group of the Edwardian plutocrat. This self-made man occupies the large old country house; drives (very badly) an expensive new motor-car; and holds house parties which consist mainly of eating, talking politics and playing games. The visitor to the house is the American Mr Direck, whose response as naïve outsider to the unfamiliar English class-structure throws it into sharper focus. The household includes Mr Britling's eldest son Hugh, his secretary Teddy and his wife Letty, and the young German tutor Herr Heinrich. The figures are chosen not only to represent English society before the war, but also to experience its changes. Mr Britling himself is a naïve centre of consciousness, but invested with sufficient intelligence and imagination to register progressively the actuality of war, and its disturbance of the way of life he has assumed to be stable. The movement of the book matches his expanding awareness. The course of national and international events, as well as what happens to the small group of characters, serve to feed into and guide Mr Britling's quest for meaning.

We begin before the outbreak of war, in the pregnant pause before August 1914. Wells can juxtapose with ironic ease the leisure of 'Matching's Easy at Ease', and the tensions leading to the declaration of war. The war is, in fact, parenthetical: the 'loud report' (p. 76) from Sarajevo is interpolated between breakfast and lunch at the Dower House, and followed by a family hockey match played on an English lawn on a glorious summer afternoon. The ethic and strategies of the game are made clear, both for Mr Direck's instruction, and as an ironic but apt gloss on the historical moment. Wells permits himself, as narrator, a more informed insight than Mr Britling could achieve. Whereas, from the hindsight of two years on, the narrator perceives that 'A whole generation had been born and brought up in the threat of this German war' (p. 123), Mr Britling anticipates civil war in Ireland, and problems from the suffragist movement, but is almost deliberately negligent of the possibility of war with Germany. He suspends belief for a considerable time, managing, by the 'doubly refracting nature' of his mind (p. 114), not to think about Germany while at the same time registering the build-up to war.

Book II shows us 'Matching's Easy at War': the chapters move, suggestively, from 'Onlookers' to 'Taking Part', and on to 'Malignity' and 'In the Web of the Ineffective'. Here the novel documents the response to the war. 'Taking Part' bears witness to the survival and force of old concepts of heroism and patriotism: Hugh enlists, followed by Teddy; and Herr Heinrich returns home to fight for his country. At this stage Mr Britling hopes that the war 'may be a tremendous catastrophe in one sense, but in another it is a huge step forward in human life. . . . It is crisis and solution' (p. 196). Moreover he supposes that 'it is only through such crises as these that the world can reconstruct itself' (p. 198). Against this positive outlook are set other possible characterisations of events: 'Was Huxley right, and was all humanity, even as

Mr Britling, a careless, fitful thing, playing a tragically hopeless game, thinking too slightly, moving too quickly, against a relentless antagonist? Or is the whole thing just witless, accidentally cruel perhaps, but not malignant?' (p. 119). Malignity comes, however, in the form of anti-German hatred, and in the 'immediate horror' of slaughter (p. 291). When a Zeppelin passes over Essex, with resultant carnage, Mr Britling muses, 'Is the whole scheme of nature evil? Is life in its essence cruel?' (p. 294). This spectrum of alternative models of the universe waits for an answer from events. Events take a turn towards the madness, absurdity and futility of the war. Hugh's letters home from the trenches describe life and death at the Front: to him 'War is an exciting game' which has soon turned to 'dirt and muddle and boredom' (p. 328). Caught 'In the Web of the Ineffective', Hugh cries out, 'What is all this for? When is it to end?' (p. 338). The shape of the crisis – its purpose and direction – engages this book, as it does *Heartbreak House* and *Women in Love*. Here too, we find the sense of an ending, and acute end-anxiety.

The 'endings' consist in part of the fates of the several characters: taken separately, each might constitute a statement of the significance of the war. Together, they exhibit an uncertainty of stance. Hugh is killed, and his death itself has an uncomfortable ambivalence: his heroism was 'unutterably silly' (p. 367). Here is one 'ending', as 'the generation of 1914' is wiped out.[21] Teddy is 'wounded and missing' (p. 329), and subsequently listed as 'missing, since reported killed' (p. 375). This, again, could provide an ending; but the narrative emphasis has already passed to those who survive and wait at home, and particularly Teddy's wife Letty. Unable to cope with loss, Letty becomes an 'assassin dreamer' (p. 383), too disturbed to face the truth. Here is yet another 'ending': widow and orphan bereft, and life at home irrevocably shattered. This is 'The Testament of Matching's Easy', in the aftermath of bereavement. But the book has yet another go at closure, and the plot a further twist. In a further and double reversal, 'Mrs Teddy Goes for a Walk' during which, first, she breaks through to recognition and acceptance of her husband's death. Secondly, just at this point, she meets Teddy, alive after all, in a joyful reunion. This further, discrete 'ending' is modulated yet again to a sober realism when we learn that the returning hero is maimed, his left hand severed.

The effect of these successive reversals is to disperse and dilute

the direction and conviction of the narrative. The problem for
Wells is not only to make these separate resolutions signify, but to
opt for an inclusive or indeed selective signification. He must turn
to fictive resolution, or to vision or exhortation. In effect, he does
all of these; and the text has it all ways. The final closure is
reserved for the central figure, when 'Mr Britling Writes until
Sunrise'. Writing in November 1915 to the parents of Herr
Heinrich, now also killed, Mr Britling faces the problem – which
we will find in other texts – of identifying the Enemy. He
contemplates the irreconcilable facts of Hugh and Heinrich as
protagonist and antagonist, and both lamented. As he struggles to
write the problematic letter, his perception expands. He questions
what the fighting is for – '*Do you know? Does anyone know?*' (p. 422) –
and his hostility against Germany fades, in an acknowledgment of
larger historical processes at work. Moreover, a new phase has
been reached: '*Now we need dread no longer. The dreaded thing
has happened.*' This finality would represent to Rupert Birkin,
who hates the End of the World 'while it hangs imminent and
doesn't fall', a welcome release from dread and end-anxiety.

But Mr Britling undergoes a further personal crisis. His notes
'became more fragmentary. They had a consecutiveness, but they
were discontinuous' (p. 426). The last sheet of his manuscript is
represented in facsimile, as a collage of juxtaposed scribbles:
'Hugh Hugh My dear Hugh'; 'Lawyers Princes Dealers in
Contention'; '*Honesty*' (underlined); 'Blood Blood' (p. 431). The
fragmention and discontinuity may throw us forward to *The Waste
Land*: certainly they are a measure of the crisis in which Mr
Britling, and possibly the book, find themselves. In this lapse of
reason, however, faith floods in, to a climactic vision in which Mr
Britling finds God, 'who is the end, who is the meaning' (p. 432).
Both end and meaning, purpose and direction, are thus solved for
Mr Britling. But his God is a 'limited' person (p. 399) struggling
to become; and this God of progressive evolutionism can encom-
pass the immediate crisis of the war. Here, war becomes – as in
Heartbreak House and *Women in Love* – neither nuisance, nor
stupidity, nor anarchic disruption, but a stage in the divine
evolutionary struggle. And so, in the midst of things, Mr Britling
Sees It Through. Wells settles for an optimistic exhortation by
which Mr Britling, and the book, adapt to the environment of
crisis.

The coda is a glimpse of morning and sunrise, as Mr Britling steps away from his desk to look out of the window. Finally, the book draws away from the struggle, to take refuge in pastoral consolation: 'From away towards the church came the sound of some early worker whetting a scythe' (p. 433). That symbolic gesture of hope in social renewal and natural continuity is curiously similar to the rural idyll with which *Howards End* closes. Both Forster and Wells, we may think, endorse the pastoral vision, and at some cost to their novels. But *what about* that scythe?

2 *Howards End*

'Life's going to be melted down, all over the world'

As an Edwardian 'Condition of England' novel[1] *Howards End* connects with contemporary non-literary discourse, and most obviously perhaps with C. F. G. Masterman's *The Condition of England* (1909).[2] There is much to compare in these two pieces: Masterman's 'dispassionate' sociological analysis is in fact informed by strong political conviction and a passionate moral concern, and is both predictive and speculative. The epigraph, from Ruskin, is particularly telling: 'Whether in general we are getting on, and if so where we are going to.' Masterman challenges the 'illusions' of progress and security, but opts finally for a state of hopeful uncertainty. This stance, and much of the detailed commentary, closely parallel *Howards End*. The essential difference is that Forster, observing the same scene, and charged with a similar passion, casts his survey and prognosis in a fictive mould.

In writing a Condition of England *novel* Forster connects with the line of utopian writing from Butler to, say, Wells, but his chosen base is firmly that of fictive realism. There are problems here, even in principle: his narrative is at once descriptive social analysis, situated in a contemporary context and dealing with specific problems, and a purposive and speculative treatise. His apprehension of England as radically *split* – between Wilcox capitalist imperialism and Schlegel humanitarianism – is itself a model, and on this he must superimpose an alternative model, suitably adjusted, to provide a socio-political corrective and a narrative resolution. The novel aims at defining and rejecting what is wrong with England, and establishing a positive configuration: the ending is to provide a configuration which the narrative sequence has carefully moved towards by a process of selection and rejection. The configuration – a particular grouping of characters in a specific location, that of Howards End with its house, garden and meadow – is the 'England' which fully realises, as specific concrete scene, the exploratory landscapes which precede it. This grouping is the culmination of the plot, in its normative quest for resolution. Plot is itself normative here: this is in effect an end-directed and purposive narrative.

The manifest problems of the novel stem in part from the hybrid of the purposive fiction in itself; but, even granting this, we find *Howards End* uneasily poised between realism and symbolism. It is, very often, awkward transitions or shifts from one mode to the other – together with the issue they raise of whether a novel can or should abandon an apparently psychologically motivated narrative in midstream – which draw critics' attention. So the very episodes which draw fire – the 'seduction' of Helen, Leonard Bast's sudden death, the utopian ending – are, precisely, not realistic, psychological narrative, but plot-motivated or end-directed. It makes more sense of *Howards End* (and particularly when this is placed alongside similar modal disjunctions in the other texts we are to consider) to read these not as flaws in an imperfect realistic novel, but as evidence of what the text reaches towards in its effort to articulate a perceived crisis. There is, in fact, an embarrassment about the whole novel, rich and subtle though it is, which settles in the narrative 'voice' – at its most rhetorical and most richly ironic at the crucial junctures (or disjunctions). Forster attempts, without total success, to control his unwieldy material by a coping irony.

The irony, however, adds to the problem of what it is that this normative and purposive fiction actually endorses, the exact constitution of its final configuration. The plot-imperatives deal with such questions as who should die and who survive, as the text searches for its answer to the Condition of England question. 'Searches' is appropriate, given both the internal tensions of the ending (which will be examined at the end of this chapter) and its variation from the resolutions tentatively considered by Forster in his working-notes. The line was clear enough to begin with, but split into multiple progressions with Margaret's child:

M's life at Howard's End. – her child; Mr W. offended that it does not nail her down.
L. & Helen.

'She must be rescued.'
Then I think that Charles ⟨goes⟩ is sent by his father to horse whip Leonard, and is killed by him, and L. flings himself out of the window.
Or it may be that Helen & Leonard die.
Or perhaps Leonard lives.[3]

The single idea disperses into several alternatives, none of which is adopted by the final text. These particular possibilities are envisaged only to be rejected in the process of writing. It may seem perverse to begin examination of a novel with the endings that never were, but there is more here of critical significance than curiosity over deleted drafts. For one thing, it is evident that, in whatever specific configuration, and by whatever mechanisms of plotting, what mattered to Forster was continuity as embodied in the birth of a child; and that, correspondingly, he desired a certain finality in the elimination by death of one or more characters, 'selected out' of the final grouping. The second point is that the range of possible progressions and resolutions embraces moral and fictive conventionality – the vile seducer killed, the sinning couple atoning by death – but that the novel is unable to remain within these parameters. Indeed, the area of unclarity focuses, revealingly, on the figures who pose most problems for and in the novel, 'L. & Helen', and specifically on the fate of Leonard: 'Or perhaps Leonard lives.'

When we turn to the completed novel we find, in the closing tableau, Margaret at Howards End with her sister Helen, and Helen and Leonard's child. Several characters are absent from the scene – Leonard Bast is dead, Charles Wilcox imprisoned for manslaughter – but these are significant absences which actually contribute to the configuration (and in any case Leonard is 'represented' by his child, and Dolly Wilcox speaks for Charles). Here we see the Wilcox family in decline, with Henry weary perhaps unto death, Charles in prison, and Paul truculently alienated. The goodbyes have a ringing finality, as Henry has announced the transfer of the property to Margaret, and after her to Helen's child. This is the end, in the novel, of Wilcox rule – it is also, one might add, total male defeat, with male power and sexuality thwarted and exhausted. (In both *Heartbreak House* and *Women in Love* female sexual dominance is symptomatic of societal breakdown. Here, on the other hand, the movement towards a

female line of inheritance, together with the symbolic emasculation of the male figures, points to an endorsement of female power.
Howards End is perhaps closer, in chronology and sympathy, to the
suffragist movement and wider implications of female emancipation.)

A closer examination will reveal in this ending (the closing
scenes from chapter 41, and the death of Leonard, onwards)
tensions which are tantamount to a compression, within the text,
of several disjunctive closures. There is a very real problem in the
shrugging off of Margaret's failed marriage, which has been a
major focus of the narrative development, by the idyll of the
haymaking and the unnamed baby heir. However, problems of
psychological conviction or simplistic symbolism should not blind
us to the dense fabric of social observation and documentation.
Howards End rests on perceived problems of Edwardian life,
painted on a broad canvas as the split between philistinism and
culture, but rendered in lively and sensitive detail in such areas as
urban development, social mobility and the rise of the plutocrat.
What Forster has to tell us about his society bears comparison –
despite its obviously partisan stance – with contemporary and
subsequent sociological enquiry, as well as with Masterman.
Even more than this, though, the very *roughness* of *Howards End*
suggests a crisis beyond what the novel feels it has to deal with.
The artistic unevenness, the shifts from realistic to non-realistic
modes, signify a deeper crisis, social and artistic, than Forster will
admit to. *Howards End* seeks to make things right by internal
adjustments, in the face of a major upheaval which hovers at the
extreme limit of its vision. This pushes the novel closer to the
literature of crisis in *Heartbreak House*, *Women in Love* and *The Waste
Land*; it also anticipates, both in and despite its liberal humanism,
the greater firmness and clarity of George Dangerfield's vision, in
hindsight, in *The Strange Death of Liberal England 1910–1914*.

The Condition of England posited by the novel is one of division
and disunity, which Forster articulates by multiple dualisms. The
two main sets of oppositions employed are those of characters, or
groups of characters, and those of environments. Both sets direct
or motivate the movement of the narrative: they are not static
contrasts. What is happening is that the book is mapping out for
us, by its narrative, the limitations and possibilities of life in
England now, and in doing this it tries out and discriminates
between various 'views' of England as embodied in people or in

landscapes. This characterisation of the novel's dualisms points to its schematic and non-realistic dimension: what must also be grasped is its unremittingly ironic method. Each element of a given dualism provides a perspective on the other, to produce a complex ironic cultural statement. 'England' in the novel is not a geographical, political or demographic entity to be recorded objectively. It is rather a series of disparate possibilities for a definition of England as community or way of life.

However, before it can be normative or prescriptive the novel has to provide a descriptive model, and that model rests to a large extent on the main dualism of the grouping of characters. 'England' divides itself into the Wilcoxes and the Schlegels. The Schlegel sisters, Margaret and Helen, are the repository of cultured liberal humanitarianism (their brother Tibby is idle, but often shows more genuine sensitivity and judgement; Aunt Juley is conventional but has common sense). The girls are well educated, intelligent, with private incomes inherited from their father, who left Germany on intellectual and ethical grounds. Margaret and Helen (and, ultimately, Margaret alone) are the focus of growth and development in the novel, and it is they who voice the values of the 'inner life' and the supremacy of personal relations. (We catch here and there in their conversations cadences of the speech of the sisters in *Heartbreak House* – Hesione and Ariadne – and *Women in Love* – Ursula and Gudrun. This 'Bloomsbury' flavour may not be totally fortuitous: there may well be actual influence from the Stephen sisters, Vanessa and Virginia.)

Against the Schlegel ethos is set Wilcox materialism, seen most fully in Henry Wilcox and his eldest son Charles, but extended into the daughter Evie, the second son Paul, and the daughter-in-law Dolly. The Wilcoxes embody what Margaret Schlegel terms the 'outer life' of 'telegrams and anger' where personal relations do not count. They are the Edwardian plutocracy, with its premium on high finance. Millionaires were increasingly common at this time, as the wealth resulting from late-nineteenth-century commercial and imperialist expansion produced a cluster of rich families, with a concentration of economic power held by the male head of family. We see Henry Wilcox in his offices (the Imperial and West African Rubber Company), which represent the heart of Empire; and in his various houses, which he regards as investments. Henry is efficient, he makes decisions, he controls.

As Margaret realises, his strength is that of a limited vision, of seeing life steadily rather than seeing it whole. Henry's son Charles is both more extravagant and more anxious about money: he typifies the second or third generation of the plutocratic family. In the difference between Henry and Charles there is an echo of Masterman: 'The first generation accumulated these great possessions, in a fierce hand to hand conflict. . . . To the second generation is given the spending of it.'[4]

There is something to be said for the Wilcoxes, but it is Margaret who has to say it. She comes to see them as the force which made and maintains the Empire: 'their hands were on all the ropes'.[5] But the novel finally renounces its imperialists (Tariff Reform is an issue which clarifies the position), and it has already pointed to the price paid for such control in the lack of an inner life. Helen calls it 'Panic and emptiness' (ch. 5, p. 31), and the 'blank wall' (ch. 11, p. 89) of Henry's forehead speaks frighteningly for itself. As in *Heartbreak House* later, the dichotomy of power and culture works – although not without its ironies – largely in favour of the latter. Boss Mangan, the financier in *Heartbreak House*, is also a City plutocrat. The two texts offer us a similar indictment of the power-men, in terms of emotional inadequacy. Mangan, like Henry Wilcox, crumbles: he has totally invested his identity in the status which the City gives him, and, once deprived of this, he collapses inwards. Gerald Crich, too, in *Women in Love* becomes a hollow man, a mask hiding internal chaos, in direct proportion to his material success as colliery manager. The indictment is clear: material power – economic, political, industrial – is a sham in human terms.

And yet *Howards End*, like the other texts, confronts the issue of the relative merits of each 'side', as well as the possibility of their fusion. The problem is faced by the Schlegel sisters, who articulate the central 'debate' between materialism and the claims of the 'unseen'. Helen simply flees from 'panic and emptiness' and concludes that the inner life has paid. Margaret, more thoughtfully, declares early on, 'This outer life, though obviously horrid, often seems the real one – there's grit in it. It does breed character. Do personal relations lead to sloppiness in the end?' (ch. 4, p. 25).

That question will reverberate through the novel. In Margaret's case it is intimately related to the need to connect Wilcox and Schlegel, and the inadequacy of such connection. 'Only connect . . .' is not enough, partly because the meeting-ground for Wilcox and Schlegel is very thin ice, but more because the dualistic model is insufficient. The novel recognises that the binary opposition of Wilcox and Schlegel, the neat dualism of the inner and outer life, is untrue to the complexities of the social fabric. Accordingly, simple connection is abandoned in favour of synthesis and assimilation. A third 'element' is introduced in the shape of Leonard Bast.

The second main dualism which the novel employs is that of country and city, an opposition well established in pastoral, and in the country-house tradition in literature. The contrastive environments of *Howards End* contribute to the 'debate' of the novel: however, although, as we know, Forster cared deeply for the English rural heritage, this is not a matter of a straight preference for the country over the city. The point is that societal relations operate in a context, a setting: so Forster insistently and concretely situates his characters and incidents in an environment, whether rual or urban, natural or man-made. We see people in houses, and moving through landscapes, and we need to be alert to the significance established for each separate location. The objective is to 'select out' the undesirable, in order to establish the novel's normative environment: this is a *paysage moralisé*.

Oniton Grange in Shropshire, one of the novel's country houses, has been bought on a whim by Henry Wilcox, who now uses it rarely and wants to get rid of it. The Wilcox habit of acquiring residences is characteristic of the Edwardian plutocracy (and Boss Mangan, in *Heartbreak House*, also has plans to buy a house and settle in the country), who might have several country houses. New building (such as Crest Hill, in H. G. Wells's *Tono-Bungay*) became less common: more usually, it was the old country estates that were passing into the hands of millionaires, who rapidly adapted them to their requirements. Oniton Grange, an 'unintellectual but kindly' (ch. 25, p. 209) grey mansion, set in societal landmarks of houses, church and ruined castle, is deprived of its function within the community: it is simply decorative, and exists for pleasure. Oniton is placed in the country-house tradition of literature by the house party which is held there: we might compare it to Peacock, or to Jane Austen's *Mansfield Park*. There is no need, though, to turn to a literary tradition to capture the essence of this house party, a common-

place of Edwardian moneyed licence. Its significance is very
evident: Oniton can be summed up, in the famous phrase from
Thorstein Veblen's *Theory of the Leisure Class* (1899, repr. 1908) as
'conspicuous consumption'. Margaret Schlegel muses, 'Certainly
Oniton would take some digesting. It would be no small business
to remain herself, and yet to assimilate such an establishment'
(ch. 26, p. 219). The image of 'digestion' is apt, in an episode
whose main focus is the wedding-breakfast. The provision for the
breakfast far outstrips a real need to eat: 'They moved to a long
table behind which a servant was still standing. Iced cakes,
sandwiches innumerable, coffee, claret-cup, champagne,
remained almost intact: their overfed guests could do no more'
(p. 225). Jacky Bast's hunger, as she munches the left-overs,
emphasises the extravagance. This food was a 'conspicuous'
display. In the Edwardian period, however, actual 'consumption'
in the form of elaborate overeating was widespread, with vast
menus for such feasts. *Howards End* satirically registers the
phenomenon, and its accompanying social etiquette. Margaret
does not, after all, 'remain herself': confronted with the crisis of
the arrival of the Basts she copes by withdrawing to the role of
society hostess, as she begs, 'Do try a sandwich, Mrs Bast.'

   The flaws of Oniton go deeper, though. The novel 'rejects'
Oniton partly by introducing the black farce of Jacky's reunion
with Henry Wilcox. But, more alarmingly, the focus of the episode
is a wedding, emblem of social harmony in the tradition of comedy
and fiction. Oniton is *chosen* as 'setting' for Evie's wedding from
the range of possible venues in the numerous houses owned or
occupied by the Wilcoxes: 'She had a fancy for something rural'
(ch. 25, p. 206). The lack of a settled family home reduces the
ritual base of the marriage. A remark made by Raymond
Williams is apposite: 'The houses are places where events
prepared elsewhere, continued elsewhere, transiently and intri-
cately occur.'[6] Yet the house offers a potential community of
work-relations in the servants who provide for the occasion. We
go 'below stairs' in Margaret and Henry's visit to the kitchen and
wine-cellar. There is, however, a marked anonymity. The small
boy who meets them on the stairs shows no deference, because he
does not recognise Mr Wilcox. In any case, Henry doesn't know
the servants and, more importantly, they don't know each other:
'the servants were so new that they did not know one another's
names' (ch. 26, p. 219). This lack of real connection condemns

Oniton as a stage-managed backdrop, despite indications of a
potentially vital work community in such details as the band
(already drinking beer), the wedding-dish boiling over and the
butler's pride in his wine-cellar.

The Ducie Street house, in London, is in one sense a
contrastive, city, environment – but this too is pure Wilcox. The
point is made not only in the rooms themselves, although these are
characteristic enough (the dining-room is big and over-furnished)
but in what the house reveals of its owners. To Henry Wilcox,
Ducie Street is a commodity, and accordingly, when he takes
Margaret, as prospective tenant, to view the house, he describes it
in business-terms and exaggerates its virtues. This visit has
however a double purpose: here Henry proposes marriage to
Margaret. Marriage too is a contract, and Henry's efficient
business mind collapses the two projects of securing a tenant and
a new wife. He hedges his bets: if the proposal of marriage had
been refused, he might still have succeeded in letting the house.

The psychological territory of Ducie Street extends beyond the
house, although not, in this case, to garden and landscape. The
smoking-room, a male preserve ('Here we fellows smoke' – ch. 18,
p. 160) is explicitly linked by its shiny leather furnishings to
Charles's motor-car: 'It was as if a motor-car had spawned.' The
car is emblematic of the Wilcox way of life, and Henry sees it as
important and inevitable: 'The motor's come to stay. . . . One
must get about' (ch. 23, p. 195). Getting about is essential to
Wilcox supremacy, which is heavily dependent on rapid com-
munications – telegrams, as well as cars and trains. The Wilcox
car belongs to the eldest son, Charles, keener on money and
leisure than his father, and anxious to inherit power. His car,
which he drives daily for pleasure, is experienced by Aunt Juley as
a 'luxurious cavern of red leather' (ch. 3, p. 14), but it shakes her
about. Margaret reacts even more adversely. Motoring to Howards End she 'lost all sense of space' (ch. 23, p. 196), and the
landscape of England 'heaved and merged like porridge' (p. 195).
When she jumps out of the moving car her protest is against the
car as emblem of male domination and imperialist power
(Charles Wilcox rightly suspects her to be a 'woman in revolt' –
ch. 25, p. 211), and against its potential for harm. A cat has just
been killed, but this is not the only death to be brought about by a
car journey in the novel: as we shall see, Leonard Bast's death is
consequent on his being overtaken, as he walks to Howards End

from Hilton, by Charles in his car. It is not only Margaret's sensibilities that are affected. And the car damages the rural environment, depositing on the village a layer of pollution in its cloud of dust: 'Some of it had percolated through the open windows, some had whitened the roses and gooseberries of the wayside gardens, while a certain proportion had entered the lungs of the villagers' (ch. 3, p. 16).

In an important sense Ducie Street and the car are linked, because it is the car that carries the urban plutocrat into the country. This was the decade which saw the impact of the car (the Rolls-Royce partnership was formed in 1907, the same year that a small book entitled *The Joys of the Road* was published). 338,000 cars were bought in 1913 as opposed to 15,000 in 1901.[7] To an extent, in the early years, the car was the toy of the millionaire, and a fresh example of conspicuous consumption (compare Mr Britling's new car). The chauffeur has a significant role: not only are the rich seen to have their own private and speeded-up transport, but they pay people to drive them around. The problems presented by the popularity of this new invention related primarily to the condition of the roads: to Charles Wilcox, contemplating the cloud of dust, the solution was simply to tar the soft surfaces. But funding for such action was introduced only gradually, although as early as 1905 a Royal Commission had recommended an overall road policy.[8] But for Forster (who is clearly partisan in *Howards End*), Masterman and others this is not merely a matter of adaptation to the new mode of travel. Antagonism is in part directed against the worship of the machine (and the car as emblem of mechanistic power is used more ominously in *Women in Love*, where Gerald Crich literally forces his way in his car through the ranks of his colliery workers). It is symptomatic, however, of a wider anxiety over the nature of modern life: life was certainly speeding up in Edwardian England, and it leads eventually, in literature, to Lucy Tantamount's 'Living modernly's living quickly.'[9]

Like the car which emerges noisily and conspicuously from it, the city, in *Howards End*, connotes change. *Howards End* does not crudely oppose city and country, but it does draw on the literary tradition of pastoral which sees in the growth of the city the destruction of an old order. The way of life substituted is one of rootlessness and transit, a 'civilization of luggage' (ch. 17, p. 146), in 'continual flux' (ch. 13, p. 106). The plot-focus for treatment of the city in the novel is the expiry of the Schlegels' lease on Wickham Place, their move from the house, and its demolition to make way for flats. Thus the experience is one of loss: to Helen and Tibby 'the modern ownership of movables is reducing us again to a nomadic horde' (ch. 17, p. 146). In the London of *Howards End* demolition and rebuilding are endemic, as is moving house: as in *The Waste Land*, the urban vision is of 'Falling towers' (373) and 'hordes' (368) of people in transit.

In depicting the city in terms of destruction and loss the novel must concede to it something of value that *can* be lost and lamented; and indeed the city can be a nurturing environment, as is evidenced by Wickham Place. When this is demolished it is described as a corpse, and its fall denotes the passing of an order hitherto preserved in the city. Wickham Place is under threat from the opening of the novel, exposed by contrast to the flats which surround it. Even these flats 'would be swept away in time, and another promontory would arise upon their site, as humanity piled itself higher and higher on the precious soil of London' (ch. 2, p. 5). This anticipates Eliot's multi-layered London of *The Waste Land*, city upon city, with church after church designated for demolition.

The flux of continual demolition, of new as well as old, extends to the poorer areas. The urge to pull down and rebuild is found too in Camelia Road, where Leonard Bast rents a furnished basement flat in Block B. These flats, unlike Wickham Mansions, are not dignified with a name, and the block was cheaply built: the author comments on 'that shallow makeshift note that is so often heard in the modern dwelling place. It had been too easily gained, and could be relinquished too easily' (ch. 6, p. 45). Block B is soon to be relinquished by Leonard Bast, who, like the Schlegels, is desperately in quest of a home for most of the novel. Here too we sense change and decline: 'Further down the road two more blocks were being built, and beyond these an old house was being demolished to accommodate another pair' (p. 44).

Again, Forster registers a contemporary problem, that of housing and town-planning. The building-boom of the Edwardian period failed to satisfy the need for massive provision of cheap accommodation for the city workers, despite rapid development of the northern and eastern suburbs, and increasing efforts to build model blocks of flats by philanthropic trusts and the London County Council. Crowding intensified in the 1900s, and the 1909 Housing and Town Planning Act dealt with the development of new suburbs, not existing built-up areas.[10] Forster registers arbitrary and ill-considered development as an all-encompassing feature of London. Indeed, the account of the fate of Camelia Road goes on to generalise, 'It was the kind of scene that may be observed all over London, whatever the locality – bricks and mortar rising and falling with the restlessness of the water in a fountain, as the city receives more and more men upon her soil'. The authorial condemnation is clear: 'bricks and mortar' are far from the full experience of a house as a home, and 'restlessness' suggests a perverse desire for change. The novel makes a concession to what London has to offer – 'Certainly London fascinates' (ch. 13, p. 106) – but this is, on balance, an environment of insecurity, weariness and depression. To Mrs Wilcox the fog is a 'darkening of the spirit' (ch. 10, p. 82), and she escapes to the country. London is presented as an animated landscape, a kind of creature in itself, 'a tract of quivering gray, intelligent without purpose, and excitable without love' (ch. 13, p. 106). This looks forward to Eliot's urban wasteland, vibrating though unconscious (in a draft passage deleted by Pound).[11] Both writers present the city as metaphor for the modern experience, and we may detect here, in the unindividuated and unpleasant characterisation of the 'animal' of London, a common element of alienation and distaste.

Against the city environment of *Howards End* is set the country, with the cyclical stability of its natural rhythms. Certain key passages assert this positive vision of landscape and the mode of life it signifies. In chapter 33 Margaret, at the farm, sees that 'The sun was shining without. The thrush sang his two syllables on the budding guelder rose. Some children were playing uproariously in heaps of golden straw' (p. 266). There is a notable vitality in the chosen images, but also an unqualified totality, by contrast with the discriminating delineation of households and city vistas. The signification is simple and undivided: it is that of a wholly endorsed pastoral myth. The centrality of the assertion appears in what immediately follows: 'In these English farms, if anywhere, one might see life steadily and see it whole, group in one vision its transitoriness and its eternal youth, connect – connect without bitterness until all men are brothers'. The imperative felt in these lines takes on an authorial weight, despite its ostensible situation in Margaret's consciousness, as the syntactic disjunction at 'connect – connect' indicates. At this point there is a shift from meditation to exhortation. This imperative is pushing us towards a normative environment for the novel.

Parallel to this passage, in chapter 41, is the description of Leonard Bast's walk from Hilton to Howards End. Here too the country is locus of utopian transfiguration: 'Here men had been up since dawn. Their hours were ruled, not by a London office, but by the movements of the crops and the sun. . . . They are England's hope. Clumsily they carry forward the torch of the sun . . .' (p. 320). Again the narrative transcends character-boundary, but this in itself is not the problem. The problem is one of catching the exact tone or stance. This passage is one of the points at which the affirmative vision of the novel is seriously strained. There are ironic concessions, in such saving gestures as 'clumsily', but on the whole it seems that this is what the novel has been aiming at. It is in and immediately following these comments that the city and the imperialist are finally rejected. But in favour of what? One feels that despite its qualifications and self-ironies the statement glosses over difficulties. Its gauche hyperbole rests on a disturbing lack of specificity: ('men . . . they'). The rhetorical strategy here is identical to that of the earlier description of the farm: both passages proceed apparently innocently towards a central declaration of faith. In each the inference ('They are England's hope') is based on a preliminary generalised idyllic description. In the earlier passage there was the sun, the thrush, the golden straw. Just before the lines quoted above, Leonard has noted 'Over all the sun was streaming, to all the birds were singing, to all the primroses were yellow, and the speedwell blue'.

The primitivist vision of these passages is not an index of authorial naïveté. As I have indicated, the narrative in each case carefully leads up to the normative statement, which is, after all, hopeful rather than definitive. What may make us pause is not the generality of description, nor the hopeful speculation, but the essential conventionality and literariness. The problem is more acute, but similar, in the final haymaking scene of chapter 44. The novel draws on a reservoir of conventional imagery of the 'rural heritage' and gives it moral weight. But to place such imagery beside a minutely observed contemporary scene begs the question of its relevance. There is, too, the issue of narrative mode: these are just the points at which the narrative shifts into non-realistic

fable. That shift may well be essential to invoke a vision which is
beyond the scope of realistic fiction.

Against this deliberate simplicity, however, can be set the
paysage moralisé of the opening of chapter 19 (pp. 164–5), in which
the panorama of England is viewed from the hills above Swanage
near the south coast. This chapter, in which Margaret announces
her engagement to Henry Wilcox, is framed by two parallel views
of the landscape, balanced by the ebb and flow of the tide. The
difference between the opening of chapter 19 and the snatches of
pastoral is that this is a sustained and explicit landscape of the
mind, an attempt to grasp the socio-political map of England. The
process is exactly described in the closing sentence: 'the imagination swells, spreads and deepens, until it becomes geographic and
encircles England'. This is a significant tableau for the 'trained
eye', and its elaborate rhetoric foregrounds it as an authorial
essay, a sketch in miniature for the novel's full-scale painting of
England.

The view encompasses country, coast, suburbia and the 'City's
trail': it sets, with the sequence of parallel exclamations 'How
many . . .', the sound stability of the old community of 'villages',
'castles' and 'churches' aginst the pressure for change implied
by 'ships, railways, and roads'. The exploratory analysis of the
passage is more sharply indicated in 'What incredible variety of
men working beneath that lucent sky to what final end!' The
exclamatory mode disguises a question that is both purposive and
directive, and central to the novel: to what final end? The
problems of integrating this incredible variety are suggested in the
tidal imagery of 'double and treble collisions'. The marriage of
Margaret to Henry Wilcox – the main plot-movement – will
indeed cause double and treble collision of Wilcox, Schlegel and
Bast.

This opening passage is complemented, at the close of the
chapter (p. 172), by a parallel meditation which registers Helen
Schlegel's distress at the news of her sister's engagement: 'One
would lose something'. Helen's distress may also be detected in
the sense of oppression and constraint, as the incoming tide
'forced inward' England 'against' itself. But the narration transcends Helen's viewpoint by echoing the authorial rhetoric of the
opening passage, and in such a way as to press further the earlier
questions – 'What did it mean? For what end . . . ?' – with a more
emphatically purposive concern. '. . . fair complexities' ironically

restates the 'double and treble collisions', and we might bear in mind that Margaret's marriage will separate the sisters until the latter stages of the novel. The issue opens out more widely in the final question of the passage, which relates to the rightful 'ownership' of England. Here again is a question central to the novel: the contenders are apparently the imperialists, and those with vision, such as the Schlegels, who have 'somehow seen her'. The allusion to the patriotic fervour of *Richard II* ('jewel in a silver sea'),[12] and the image of the ship of state, invoke the issue of the fate of England as a nation, among 'all the brave world's fleet'. In the manuscript of *Howards End* Forster originally made direct reference to Germany and France: the final version is a heavily disguised allusion to the growing prospect of international conflict (which may also refer us back, in another sense to those 'double and treble collisions').

Both of these speculative meditations attempt to grasp the 'meaning' of the landscape in its entirety. What strikes one in both is the conjunction of a prospective connection, in the marriage, with a sense of unease, contradiction and threat. Here perhaps is a hint of crisis which goes beyond internal realignment, as 'over the immense displacement the sun presided, leading it to triumph ere he sank to rest' (p. 172). That 'immense displacement' suggests profound crisis, and the juxtaposition of 'triumph' and 'sank' puts in question the presiding sun. This visual image of the decline of empire is comparable to the fading of the late afternoon of *Heartbreak House* into deep night, and the angry apocalyptic sunset of chapter 26, 'A Chair', in *Women in Love*. These passages in chapter 19 of *Howards End* are both finer in their discrimination, and more suggestive, than the unqualified idyll of the 'solved' vision. When we come to assess the adequacy of the solution offered we should bear in mind the troubled conjectures of this chapter, as well as the ratified pastoral. The questions raised in *Howards End* are more far-reaching than can be answered by the narrative, and at points such as these the novel takes the measure of the problem, although it cannot finally admit it.

Certainly the novel does provide an environmental norm: it is in Howards End and its rural setting that the true 'England' is finally identified. Howards End is old and little, delightful to some but poky to others. A comparatively modest house, it is firmly rooted in a landscape. There is the wych-elm which stands on the boundary between garden and meadow. There was a paddock, until Henry sold the pony and built a garage. Adjacent is the farm, and close by the village and church. The topography is as sharply defined as at Oniton, but endorsed by contrast.

What is valuable about Howards End is its history and function. It is a family house, embedded in a community, and it represents continuity. The house belonged to Ruth Wilcox, who was the last of the Howards (Miss Avery had refused to marry Tom, Ruth's brother, which would have preserved the family line). Both the house and Ruth Wilcox embody the spirit of place and desire for connection with the earth (and according to Miss Avery the Wilcoxes aren't very keen on Howards End just because it lies too much on the land). The novel and Mrs Wilcox insist on the value of house as home, and home as centre of a stable society. Margaret's depression and anxiety in the first part of the novel stem from having to move house, and Mrs Wilcox sympathetically compares moving house to dying: 'To be parted from your house, your father's house – it oughtn't to be allowed. It is worse than dying. . . . Can what they call civilization be right, if people mayn't die in the room where they were born?' (ch. 10; p. 81). Ironically, Mrs Wilcox herself is removed to die in a nursing-home. Dying, she is unwilling to leave her home to the Wilcoxes (she regrets the 'improvements' already carried out by Henry), and looks outside her family for an heir. There is some indication that she should establish a female line of inheritance: although the house transcends sex it is amenable to female sensitivity, and it is implied that the spirit of place and desire for permanence are 'female' qualities, opposed to 'male' movement and change. We might test this against *Heartbreak House*, where the house operates a dominant 'female' symbol in the dramatic action, and the ship as 'male' symbol, attached respectively to the figures of Hesione and her father, Captain Shotover, between whom ownership of the house is disputed. *Heartbreak House* is noticeably female-dominated. For Shaw this 'mothering tyranny' and 'slavery of men to women' are indices of subverted or displaced power:[13] for Forster (who, one remembers, was deeply but ambivalently devoted to a dominating mother) in *Howards End*, female control can still be posited as an ideal.

We know, of course, that Howards End is modelled on Rooksnest, the house near Stevenage (Hilton) in Hertfordshire where Forster spent ten years of his childhood, and for which he had a lasting affection.[14] In later life he often returned from

Cambridge to the house, then occupied by Miss Elizabeth Poston, and obviously regarded it as a store of childhood innocence and stable values. He insisted that the house remain, as far as possible, just as it had been, and even brought there old toys. Visitors to the house anxiously count the windows, which actually number eight, not nine, to the front elevation (the 'ninth' window looks out over the back of the house).[15] In modifying this detail Forster was not seeking symmetry for its own sake: the 'missing' ninth window of Rooksnest is that of the nursery in Howards End, the room directly above the hall where Miss Avery pointedly places Tibby's old bassinette, and where Helen's baby is born – the 'central room of the nine' (ch. 44, p. 337). There is deep nostalgia in Forster's use of his childhood home, and a profound significance: birth, and the nursery, are indeed at the heart of *Howards End*'s concern for continuity.

The novel moves towards the normative environment of Howards End, and the chosen configuration, by directing its characters to connect, as the epigraph, 'Only connect . . .', suggests. Connection is sought in Margaret's balancing perspective, her capacity to forge and sustain relationships across the boundaries of the 'split' society. Specifically, it is her marriage to Henry Wilcox which is to connect and reconcile Wilcox and Schlegel, and provide a 'solution' to the problem of the condition of England. This central event is surrounded by other weddings and other couples: Charles and Dolly Wilcox, Evie's wedding at Oniton, Leonard and Jacky Bast, memories of Henry's marriage to Ruth, the brief encounter of Helen Schlegel and Paul Wilcox, and Helen's sexual encounter with Leonard.

The emphasis on marriage places the novel firmly in the comedic tradition. Forster decides on comedy (although he will admit some admixture of tragedy) and accordingly establishes marriage as the major narrative expectation (although not its resolution, and death will creep in too). The comic figure of Aunt Juley acts as guide to these narrative expectations, ever alert to marital possibilities. Her stream of conventional social enquiries – 'How old would the son be? She says "younger son". Would he be in a position to make Helen happy?' (ch. 2, p. 6) – comically echoes the central questions of the differences between Wilcox and Schlegel, and the possibility of a satisfactory mutual

relation. The novel's marital expectations are signalled by the
'false start' of Helen's engagement to Paul Wilcox, a comic
prelude which provides a basis for subsequent discrimination.
Against Helen's impulse we shall set Margaret's restraint; but we
shall also set Helen's later rejection of the Wilcoxes against
Margaret's permanent connection with them; and Helen's total
abnegation of marriage against Margaret's childlessness. The
story might be said to hinge on the sexual development of 'The
Sisters' (an early title for *Women in Love*). The main focus is
Margaret's marriage, by which we are to gauge the success of
'connection' in the novel. Margaret's progress towards 'thinking
conjugally', with its blend of maturity and compromise, is
carefully delineated, but the process involves disturbing features:
an increasing dishonesty to her self, and some damage to others.

The sisters' first conversation (ch. 4), in which they discuss
Helen's involvement with Paul Wilcox, is also the first stage in the
long debate which the novel conducts about love and marriage,
personal relations and social contracts. Helen avers personal
relations to be the 'real life, for ever and ever' (p. 25), but already
Margaret concedes their alternative, public meaning to the
Wilcoxes: 'There love means marriage settlements, death, death
duties.' This issue will divide the sisters, and their reconciliation
near the end of the novel is an important factor in its resolution.
Between them, Margaret and Helen accommodate both Henry
Wilcox – the sustained settlement of the outer life – and Leonard
Bast – the moment of passion or passionate error. (What the novel
does not accommodate is a sustained sexual and emotional
relationship between a man and a woman.)

The moment of passion has to be accommodated. That is the
point of the encounter between Helen and Paul, and the
implication of Mrs Wilcox's uncritical comment on its end: 'They
do not love any longer' (ch. 3, p. 20). Their kiss, which is both
'inevitable' and a chance collision, is an impersonal biological
imperative: 'the embrace of this boy' is reinforced by the
impersonal sexuality of 'A man in the darkness' (ch. 4, p. 23). The
embrace scarcely connects for Helen with Paul's 'slender personality', and is more a measure of her fascination with the entire
Wilcox family. But even so slight a contact must be accepted in its
necessity, rather than condemned as a failure because it does not
last.

Besides prefiguring Helen's later relationship with Leonard

Bast, this episode marks the starting-point of the development of Margaret's sexual attitudes and activity. Unlike Helen, she will enter into the sustained partnership of marriage. That sexual relationship is measured against Helen's, and even the embrace of Helen and Paul is explicitly recalled when Margaret and Henry first kiss, after they have become engaged (ch. 20). They have been discussing business-matters, and Henry simply kisses her goodnight; but this is a parallel to the moment of passion in the darkness, and it does not look well by comparison. Margaret is displeased in hindsight, and her immediate response is mixed: she nearly screams at the sudden and clumsy embrace, but responds with genuine love. It is because she does love him that the quality of their married relationship, its combination of passion and respect, comes under scrutiny. Sexually, this first kiss doesn't promise much: the lips pressed against hers are detached from body or personality, and she feels acutely the disconnectedness of the event. Although Forster's narrative effectively sidesteps the issue, pulling down with a saving irony the 'astonishing glass shade . . . that interposes between married couples and the world' (ch. 19, p. 171), there is sufficient indication of Henry's sexual and emotional inadequacy. He regards this marriage as a moral chastity-belt, and soon forgets his first wife. Moreover, his 'simultaneous' embrace, in the past, of Ruth and Jacky confirms his conventionally compartmentalised sexual code, projected onto women as wife or whore. It is this split in him between the Monk and the Beast that Margaret hopes to heal by 'tenderness'. It seems improbable that she succeeds. Failing evidence of sexual fulfilment, it is all the more vital to assess the effect of the marriage on Margaret in other ways. When she overtly opts for a limited emotional investment in romantic love, she is virgin still not only in sex, but in the 'social pressure' (ch. 19, p. 171) of marriage. The main pressure on her will be to 'think conjugally'. In the frequent clash of their directly opposed attitudes, Margaret learns to adapt to Henry and to marriage by submission and deviousness. She herself later redefines thinking conjugally as 'the methods of the harem' (ch. 26, p. 227). The process is gradual but relentless, and reduces her at times to a burlesque figure. When she has created a difficult situation by jumping from the car on the way to Oniton, she takes the line of feminine weakness, confessing to Henry (who is, not surprisingly, bewildered), 'I have been so naughty. . . . Your poor Meg went such a flop' (ch. 25, p. 212). Increasingly we

find her apologising, yielding, obeying: learning to influence
Henry by anticipating his responses. Gradually she expects less of
Henry and surrenders more of herself. Her concessions are not,
however, always rewarded by events: when, at Evie's wedding,
she goes forward 'smiling socially' to greet the Basts, it is to be
confronted with the revelation that Jacky was at one time Henry's
mistress. Yet she still thinks conjugally, making Henry her priority
even over her sister or her aunt: she protects him, deceives him,
and allows him to deceive her.

But there are doubts. After finding out about Henry's past
infidelity to Ruth, she herself asks the question that the reader
would otherwise ask for her: 'Was he worth all this bother?' (ch.
28, p. 237). The issue is now not passion but respect. She does
surrender again, but this time we see the process graphically as, in
revising the letter which she writes to Henry, she progressively
deletes her own judgements (because 'comment is unfeminine'),
thereby deleting herself. Her acquiescence is complete yet
conditional: 'Henry must have it as he liked, for she loved him,
and some day she would use her love to make him a better man'
(p. 240). These conditions – her love, and his improvement –
become the reader's criteria for consent to the marriage.

Both criteria are to be tested by the second crisis for Margaret
and Henry. This comes when she attempts to force on him moral
connections, the equivalence of the sexual facts of Helen's
unmarried pregnancy and his own liaison with Jacky. In chapter
38 Helen, heavily pregnant, has arrived at Howards End, and
Margaret asks Henry's permission to sleep with her at the house,
against all propriety. Henry's refusal is 'the crisis of his life'
(p. 302), as Margaret confronts him with his double moral
standards. In a sense, Margaret finds herself again in the
'criminal' inadequacy of his response, recognising the inevitability of this breakdown between them. But her central realisation
is followed by a scene of reconciliation which mixes comedy and
melodrama in a melancholy satire. When later, after Charles's
arrest, Henry mutters 'I'm broken – I'm ended' (ch. 44, p. 331),
Margaret's triumph could be complete, and the novel could
redeem her from a dishonest relationship. In fact the alternatives
open to her are suggested in the curious compression and negation
with which her reaction is expressed: 'No sudden warmth arose in
her. She did not see that to break him was her only hope. She did
not enfold the sufferer in her arms'. This syntactic and semantic

complexity suggests alternative and opposed narrative progressions, with a revealing uncertainty. In the event she does, in effect, break Henry precisely by folding him in her arms, as she takes him down to Howards End, where we find him reduced and maimed. The end-directed nature of the narrative is relevant here: according to the plot-imperative, Margaret cannot leave Henry at this point, as he has not yet conceded ownership of Howards End to her. The problem of the fictive mode employed by the novel focuses on psychological conviction: on an unease as to whether this failed marriage, so painfully depicted, can or should be retrieved, and the novel drawn back into comedy.

In the final chapter Margaret has assumed control of Howards End, Henry, Helen, infant and all, and we find her acknowledging after all that she loves Henry, and that he has a kind heart. There is a kind of grotesque simplicity about this, with Henry a cipher, Margaret platitudinous, and Helen enthusing. But there is, too, a bitter self-irony in the narrative. The potential crack in its smooth closure comes when Henry tells Margaret that Ruth Wilcox had bequeathed Howards End to her in the first place: 'Margaret was silent. Something shook her life in its inmost recesses, and she shivered' (p. 340). She might still, at this point, reject him. But Margaret reassures Henry, and he smiles. What Forster has done is to reveal the incompatibility which brings this marriage to the point of breakdown, and to present Margaret at several junctures with alternatives. We might condemn the retrieval as an authorial failure or nerve, or conclude that the psychology of the characterisation is simply abandoned. There are indeed plot-imperatives at work here (and it is interesting that Henry must be in, and contained by, the final configuration, even if redundant now that Margaret has come into her possession). But the narrative closure, and its earlier progression, are actually more complex than a focus on Margaret and Henry might suggest. This marriage cannot 'solve' the novel, and we need to move Margaret Schlegel further from the centre of the novel to see where the narrative emphasis rests. To do this, we must approach the novel differently.

The narrative sequencing of *Howards End* rests on two questions: Who should inherit Howards End?; and 'How ought I to dispose of my money?' (ch. 15, p. 123). Both questions concern inheritance, which is the focus of the three Wilcox family-gatherings in the novel: the funeral breakfast after the burial of Mrs Wilcox; Evie's wedding, when Charles is worried about his father's prospective remarriage; and the closing scene, when Henry announces his intentions to the assembled 'heirs'. Both questions, moreover, are end-directed, and point us to the purpose and ending of the narrative.

Who is to inherit Howards End? This is a question of real concern to the Wilcox children, as Howards End was Mrs Wilcox's personal property, which she might dispose of as she wished. The question is also consonant with the problem of the Condition of England: the establishment of the 'true' heir is the crucial plot-decision of this normative and end-directed narrative. The extended passage of authorial commentary (ch. 12) which accompanies Charles and Henry's dismissal of Mrs Wilcox's deathbed bequest draws attention to the complexity and elusiveness of the issue: 'To them Howards End was a house: they could not know that to her it had been a spirit, for which she sought a spiritual heir' (p. 96). But despite the Wilcoxs' efficient disposal of her wishes, the problem does not go away. Charles, potentially disinherited, sees Margaret as a rival, and his suspicions are 'confirmed' by her engagement to his father. There is some sympathy for Charles's position. His plight is felt most keenly when (ch. 25) he looks in from outside 'enviously at the Grange, whose windows poured light and laughter' (p. 213). As Margaret climbs the mound he watches remaining concealed, anxious lest the gleam of his cigar 'betray' (p. 214) him. His anxiety is projected into suspicion: 'that woman means mischief'. And, although Margaret does not *intend* 'mischief', her marriage does *signify* damage to his prospects, and those of his family. Charles will later confront another rival heir in Leonard Bast, also converging on Howards End. In the melodramatic climax (ch. 41) he literally races Leonard to the house: he wins the race, but loses the property (although he will still inherit money).

The rejection of Charles Wilcox as heir to Howards End is a rejection of the imperialist type. His father's concern about Tariff Reform was earlier condemned by Margaret's tacit disapproval, and the Schlegels, in so far as they are political, inherit their father's idealism and liberalism – a stance which, on balance, the novel endorses. The characterisation of Tibby admits as much. Tibby is cultured, effete and inactive, but his judgements, although moderate and seldom voiced, are sound. The tolerance which the novel displays towards Tibby is index of a liberal humanism which can – just – remain intact and impervious, by self-irony.

This stance declares itself too in the nomination of Margaret Schlegel as heir. The machinery by which Margaret is named as heir is as 'mysterious' – and non-realistic – as the question 'Has the soul offspring?' (ch. 11, p. 96). When she and Henry come to Howards End he finds the door 'locked' and returns to the farm for a key. With Henry gone, the door 'unlocks' to Margaret. She finds herself alone, downstairs: 'she would double her kingdom by opening the door that concealed the stairs' (ch. 23, p. 198). What is concealed is the female spirit of the place, which descends in the erect, impassive form of Miss Avery. She, guardian of Howards End, awaits a second Mrs Wilcox, whom she recognises in Margaret. Margaret herself grows into the assigned role, adopting the title and even the manner of the first Mrs Wilcox. By the end of the novel she has become absorbed into the cycle of renewal which Howards End embodies: 'Margaret still stopped at Howards End. No better plan had occurred to her' (ch. 44, p. 333). This is indeed a change for Miss Schlegel, and there is a touch of comedy as she removes her pince-nez to observe the scything. She has managed the transition by the 'mystery' of spiritual inheritance (which shows the plot-imperative at perhaps its least convincing) and by the self-effacement, sharply reversed into self-assertion, of her marriage. It is to the novel's credit that it goes beyond the vision of Mrs Wilcox to recognise that Margaret is not enough: the next heir will not be Margaret's child. The crucial plot-decision is that the inheritance passes through Margaret to the child of Helen Schlegel and Leonard Bast. The future of 'England' lies neither with the Wilcoxes nor, exclusively, with the Schlegels. Into the configuration and the legacy is drawn Leonard Bast: his anonymous and illegitimate infant is England's hope, connecting the disparate groups of the novel.

The second main narrative question, 'How ought I to dispose of my money?' (ch. 15, p. 123), links the motifs of inheritance and money. It is the title of a paper – the speaker being a hypothetical millionaire – given at a discussion-club attended by Margaret and Helen, and the debate addresses itself to the issue of the distribution of wealth. The debate is abstract and unsituated, but it does not remain so, as Leonard Bast figures with growing insistence in the argument, at first as the generalised and hypothetical man in need. But 'Mr Bast' will become the actual case on which the debate will bite: subsequent events will hinge on his financial ruin, and attempts to rescue him. And the novel will end with the near-millionaire Henry Wilcox's 'disposal' of his money to Wilcox heirs, while his property passes to Leonard's child. This discussion focuses the preoccupation of the novel with money, and the preoccupation passes into the plot, generating impetus for the remainder of the action. It is pivotal.

The placing of this debate is somewhat ironic, after dinner at a ladies' gathering. But concern over inequities of income was, with the development of methods of sociological inquiry, increasingly manifest in surveys based on forays of researchers into that second nation inhabited by the poor. The seventeen volumes of Charles Booth's *Life and Labour of the People in London* (1889–1903) were followed by a complementary study of York in B. Seebohm-Rowntree's *Poverty, a Study of Town Life* (1901), L. G. Chiozza-Money's *Riches and Poverty* (1905), Masterman's *From the Abyss* (1902), *In Peril of Change* (1905) and *The Condition of England*, and Maud Pember Reeves's *Round about a Pound a Week* (1913). The subject drew both Liberals and socialists, and was a particular concern of the middle-class intellectual Fabians, who numbered the Webbs and Shaw among their ranks, as well as Mrs Pember Reeves.[16]

In *Howards End* the moneyed classes divide into the Wilcox plutocracy, who make money, and the Schlegel intellectuals, who worry about it. The Schlegel money is unearned income, a legacy of nineteenth-century investment. For the Schlegels, unlike the Wilcoxes, money is not a given creed, but connects with the 'ethics of salvation', and is a potential source of anxiety and guilt. The Schlegel sisters work through money-guilt in the course of the novel.[17] Margaret's personal development involves an awareness that money underpins her position: 'Money pads the edges of things', 'I began to think that the very soul of the world is economic' (ch. 7, p. 58) and – a brave but shrill cry – 'Hurrah for riches!' (p. 59). In the discussion it is Margaret who proposes the radical alternative of giving cash instead of charity or commodities – or rather, distributing the interest on the hypothetical millionaire's capital to provide as many people as possible with a reasonable (unearned) income. It is here, in a sharpening and clarification – rather than change – of her attitudes, that she declares money to be the 'second most important thing in the world' (ch. 15, p. 125) – second, presumably, to personal relations. Margaret's programme is a modest one, of redistribution within the current system: she neither yields the supremacy of 'culture', nor envisages fundamental change.

Helen Schlegel takes the issue literally to heart, and acts on it in her attempt to rescue Leonard Bast, 'to have raised one person from the abyss' (ch. 30, p. 251). Her desperate impulses lead her to confront Henry Wilcox directly with their shared responsibility for Leonard – 'We upper classes have ruined him' (ch. 26, p. 222) – in the face of Henry's *laissez-faire* concept of 'great impersonal forces' (ch. 22, p. 188), which discounts individual blame. Helen attempts both sexual consolation and financial rescue: after sleeping with Leonard she flees, but offers him half her capital. This private, *ad hoc* redistribution of wealth – which Leonard refuses – is, apparently, sufficient to dispel her hysterical sense of guilt. After a suitable interval Helen reinvests her money, and is 'rather richer' (ch. 30, p. 253) than before. Both sisters are working out their salvation in their dealings with money, but neither effects much change for the better.

Howards End expresses the dilemma of combining a perception of an economic base with a continued premium on cultured values. The narrative registers the impulse to spend, by conspicuous consumption, and to atone, by some form of conscience money. Like *Heartbreak House* it deals with the anxiety of comparative poverty and the guilt of comparative and actual wealth, and both Forster and Shaw are of, and concerned with and for, the 'comfortable' middle classes. *Howards End* expresses to an extent Forster's personal ambivalence: he thought money dangerous, but admitted that the £8000 left to him by his great-aunt Marianne Thornton was his 'financial salvation'.[18] However, *Howards End* is not merely an interesting social document; nor need it be referred to a biographical genesis. The novel uses money as an iterative motif and a plot-motivator. Money is at the core of the novel, as is Leonard Bast. Both are central to the confrontation of Wilcox and Schlegel: Leonard is the point of collision between two worlds, having neither money nor 'culture', and striving for both. Leonard, the urban clerk, is the modern focus of the Edwardian novel. For him, money is a practical problem, and he is a problem for liberal humanism, and for the novel.

In moving Leonard Bast closer to the centre of *Howards End* we must take account of how the novel treats him. Leonard's progress is from the relatively stable condition of his job as a clerk and his domestic life with Jacky, to an involvement with Schlegels and Wilcoxes which precipitates change and eventual catastrophe. What happens to Leonard is at the core of the novel's certainty as to the importance of money, and its doubts as to whether money is predominantly enabling or destructive.

D. H. Lawrence considered Leonard the best character in *Howards End* (he thought Forster came close to ruining it with 'those *business* people'[19]), but others have criticised the characterisation for a patronising ignorance. It is true that Leonard is largely sketched from the outside, as object rather than experiencing subject, although this might seem appropriate to the use the other characters make of him. Actually, if one accepts the predominance of plot-necessity in the narrative, psychological depth and realism become less substantive issues. What is more important is the positive point that Leonard is relentlessly contextualised, inserted into 'all that was actual and insistent' (ch. 6, p. 47) in his life. The problem is not so much the detail of his life (although the selection can be challenged as tendentious, with its implication of an inevitably 'reduced' existence), as the ambivalent and not completely controlled authorial stance. The narrative voice often frames descriptions of Leonard with a mannered rhetoric, and, although Forster should not be simply equated with his narrator, the device does point to a need to adopt a distancing mechanism in order to cope with an awkward figure.

For Leonard the practical problem of money hinges on the need for work, food and a place to live. His only capital is the claim he has to a particular skill: once that is spent, he is bankrupt. Leonard, at the 'extreme verge of gentility' (p. 43), is permanently at risk, precariously balanced between comparative ease and fear of 'squalor'. When we first meet him he is a clerk with the Prophyrion Fire Insurance Company. On Henry Wilcox's advice he leaves his job, to take a post at Dempster's Bank, at a lower salary. He is already on the way down, and, when staff-cuts make him redundant, he has no further chance of employment (we have already heard that 'situations' are scarce, with hundreds of applicants for the vacant posts).

The clerk, together with the typist, formed an important service-class for Edwardian industrialism and finance; but, partly as a result of Victorian rural depopulation (Leonard Bast is two generations removed from farmers) the cities were crowded with potential labour. Moreover, the clerk was in a curious position with respect to class and the distribution of earned income. Addressed as 'Mr' by his employer – unlike the domestic servant or factory worker – he was at the lower edge of the middle classes, with aspirations of upward social mobility. But his salary was lower than the better paid skilled manual worker.[20] This anomaly of status and salary entailed social and economic pressures, and intensified job-insecurity. Leonard Bast was reasonably content with his post at the Prophyrion, and upset by the aspersions which the Schlegels cast on the company. When he loses the job at Dempster's his only social mobility is downwards, towards charity or destitution. He is now on the edge of the 'abyss'.

The 'abyss' which haunts *Howards End* was a widely used image, as a selection of titles confirms: Masterman's *From the Abyss* (1902); Jack London's *The People of the Abyss* (1903); and *Glimpses into the Abyss* (1906) by Mary Higgs. As these titles indicate, the standpoint of the observer varied. Peter Keating suggests that the prevalent and new use of the term at the turn of the century (which he traces to direct derivation from a short story by H. G. Wells, 'In the Abyss') reflects despair and impotence in the face of worsening social conditions, together with a sense of political threat from mass insurgence of the newly enfranchised populace. Keating stresses the potency of the image: 'The gap between the classes is now "deep" and terrifying, a matter of delicate balance and subtle gradation, of possibly climbing up or clinging on or falling down.'[21]

It is when Leonard Bast comes 'near the abyss' (ch. 26, p. 224) that he articulates the fragility of his position, and the limited social mobility at his disposal. He sees 'clearly' that 'I could do one particular branch of insurance in one particular office well enough to command a salary, but that's all.' He is pessimistic as to the prospect of begging money, because he has seen that 'in the end they fall over the edge. It's no good. It's the whole world pulling. There always will be rich and poor.' This fatalistic 'two nations' speech represents Leonard's high point of realisation, and he speaks from direct experience, as against the Schlegels' idealistic hypotheses. His account of falling 'over the edge' balances but undermines Helen's objective of raising one person from the abyss. Leonard's ruin comes from the attempts of the rich to advise, help and rescue him. Even before money becomes an acute problem for him, he is the victim of both the Schlegel leisured classes and the Wilcox plutocracy, who equally encourage him to strive for upward cultural as well as financial mobility. His climactic awareness includes, implicitly, the Schlegels' encouragement of his cultural aspirations – 'Poetry's nothing' – and the damage caused by their interference.

Leonard's personal debate between money and culture is apparent in both his attendance at the concert (ch. 5) and his reading of Ruskin (ch. 6). The Schlegels also attend the concert, and, when Helen takes Leonard's umbrella by mistake, he suspects her of theft. As the point of view shifts from Margaret to Leonard, we understand why. Leonard suspects the Schlegels because he can survive only by constant suspicion. Lack of money renders him insecure and suspicious, and drives him, by way of compensation, to aspire to an idealised world of culture. Leonard has come to the concert to 'acquire culture' (p. 37), but experiences a conflict between material conditions and cultural aspirations. They do not cohere for him: Monet and Debussy are not part of his grammar, and 'the trouble was that he could not string them together in a sentence'. Leonard aspires to make a sentence of the vocabulary of 'culture', but what is actual and insistent in his life blocks the attempt. While ostensibly listening to the music, he is thinking about his umbrella. Earlier he had worried about spending two shillings on a seat; earlier still, whether he should try to do without a programme. At the centre of his reverie we find that 'the umbrella was the real trouble'. The umbrella has real and multiple significance for Leonard. It is portable property – the only kind of property he can own – and, being portable, it is easily stolen. It is a status-symbol, and useful too: it will keep him dry, and his clothes respectable for the office. Helen is not concerned about umbrellas because she could afford a cab, while Leonard worries over money for public transport (he wonders whether to take a tram from Wickham Place, but decides to save a penny by walking). Helen can't identify her own umbrella, and offers him the pick of the bunch. Her derisive dismissal of her collection – 'I do nothing but steal umbrellas' (p. 38) – ironically signifies her leisured life, and the gulf between Leonard and herself. (This is, however, the first connection between them, by what Virginia Woolf surely recognised as a phallic symbol when she joked about Leonard begetting a child on Helen with his umbrella.)

It is through Leonard, constantly anxious over what he spends and what he owns, that we register the 'actual and insistent' metal of money. For Leonard, money comes not in banknotes or paper investment but in coins, one by one. When, in this same scene, Frieda forgets her reticule, he offers to return it, in an effort to regain his dignity. The bag contains Frieda's address-book, pocket dictionary, map of London – and some money. Leonard 'took the bag – money clinking inside it – and slipped up the gangway with it' (p. 34). The money clinks. The solidity of these coins, which have weight and density, and sound together in their own music, is set – as with Leonard's umbrella – in the cultural matrix of the music. This is a discriminatory currency: the coins, jumbled up with assorted items of information, enable Frieda to move around London among her friends. The bag containing unearned money which clinks, for a short time, in Leonard's hands, is a token of the distinction between Frieda's opportunity, and his financial constraint. Money clinks once more in the novel, when Leonard, filled with remorse over Helen, decides to travel to Howards End. He finds that his money is 'running low again, but enough for a return ticket to Hilton. As it clinked Jacky opened her eyes' (ch. 41, p. 319). There is double irony here: in their conversation, which proves to be a final farewell; and in that return ticket. As it turns out, Leonard didn't need a return: he was going only one way. If he hadn't had enough money for a ticket at all, he might have survived. The processes of Leonard Bast's life and death are constituted of minute choices and chances, and usually involve small sums of money.

I have implied a total imaginative sympathy with Leonard in the narration, but there is a hint of condescension towards him, as a figure wrongly seated in the musical audience. Latent snobbery regarding Leonard's cultural aspirations is arguably also evident in his reading of Ruskin's *The Stones of Venice*. This text is an appropriate choice: the sandbanks attain by degrees a higher level, as Leonard aspires towards culture and upward social mobility. His adaptation of Ruskin to suit his own environment points up the glaring contrasts in architecture and in living conditions: 'My flat is dark as well as stuffy' (ch. 6, p. 47). In fact, Ruskin is a pertinent focus for Leonard's aspirations. We might say that Ruskin, like the Schlegels, operates on Leonard as a humanist cultural equivalent of Wilcox material exploitation: such cultural persuasion places Leonard in a double bind, insisting on the absolute value of 'culture' and urging its acquisition as essential to personal 'improvement', while at the same time withholding the money which is the actual enabling factor. But the difficulty here is that the stance of the text is hard to discern. It may be that Leonard has some perception of the irrelevance of Ruskin to his own life, and that he is justifiably angered by what he reads. But the indirect speech – 'Those were the words for him' – is loosely situated between narrator and character; it may be, after all, that Ruskin is accepted, and Leonard patronised, by the author. This uncertainty is repeated elsewhere, as the narrative voice roams between 'authorial' comment and free indirect speech: 'was there anything to be learnt from this fine sentence? Could he adapt it to the needs of daily life?' This is succinct, but ambiguous: again, we might read in this either that Leonard is obtuse or, alternatively, that Ruskin is materially and seriously irrelevant. Leonard may be a satirised object, a 'half-baked mind', or a sympathetic subject. There is an uneasy ambivalence, too, in the account of his 'conversion', when he is described negatively (that is, by omniscient narration) as having 'no conception' of a 'heritage that may expand gradually' (p. 48). Leonard is not blamed, but the 'heritage' is, by implication, totally endorsed. As elsewhere, the dominant values are smuggled in, to operate at Leonard's expense.

An ambivalent authorial stance – a gap between observed detail and narrative tone – pervades chapter 6, which gives a glimpse into Leonard's home life. The opening is notorious: 'We are not concerned with the very poor. They are unthinkable, and only to be approached by the statistician or the poet. This story deals with gentlefolk, or with those who are obliged to pretend that they are gentlefolk' (p. 43). However, this is not, it seems to me, 'innocent' narration. It is rhetorically foregrounded, using a persona to point to what is potentially problematic: the scope of the novel, the circle which it draws, in Jamesian fashion, round the middle classes, excluding the extremity of the abyss. '. . . gentlefolk' includes not only the characters but also the narrator and reader, the 'We' who constitute the standpoint and focus of the story. There is acute irony here. If 'We' are not 'concerned' we ought to be, and, if the abyss can indeed be *reached* only by statistics or poetry, the issue of how it is to be 'approached' is of continuing concern to the novel. Both 'approached' and 'unthinkable' imply a genteel distaste. This is, surely, not an unthinking elitism, although it is certainly a coping mechanism. Forster adroitly *permits* his novel its delimitation, by simultaneously *admitting* the inadequacy. This first paragraph delimits the novel with subtle irony and measured self-criticism.

Chapter 6 as a whole belongs, almost, to another (and naturalistic) novel, partly because of its exclusive focus on Leonard and Jacky, but more because we seem to be in the fictive mode of Wells or Bennett. What is extraordinary about this chapter is its peculiar combination of detailed verisimilitude – which Forster conceded to be the inspired guess of total ignorance – and suggestiveness as image of modern urban experience. The emotional life of Leonard and Jacky is, by implication, contingent on the conditions in which they live. Contact is minimal, perhaps to preserve the limited privacy. They talk *at* each other, with a 'degraded deafness' (p. 52). Jacky calls vainly for love from the bedroom while Leonard goes on reading in the sitting-room. This reduced relationship will reverberate, not only in the scene of the typist and the house-agent's clerk in *The Waste Land*, but also in the comic patter of *Waiting for Godot* and the pauses and fragments of conversation in *The Caretaker*.

The basement flat is described by 'documentary', clinical observation. The passage is barely more than a list of contents – rooms, furniture, objects – but the spare, taut prose implies a concomitant restriction of experience: 'Opposite the window was the door, and beside the door a bookcase' (p. 45). Each object is named and placed, with the suggestion of living minimally – even only a 'little tea' and 'some dusty crumbs' (p. 46). The itemisation and implied 'squalor' apply too to the makeshift, artificial meal – soup-square dissolved in hot water, tinned tongue, and 'jelly: pineapple' (p. 51) made from another cube. The convenience food contrasts sharply with the extravagant wedding-feast at Oniton (also consumed by Jacky). The spare style may indeed stem from lack of experience, but it renders all the more powerfully Leonard's social and emotional deprivation.

The descriptions of Jacky, by contrast, use a florid rhetoric, with marked 'intrusions'. 'Take my word for it' (p. 46), the narrator assures us of Jacky's smile, and he invites consent by a deft disclaimer: 'It is only you and I who will be fastidious'. We hear the narrator choosing his words – 'of whom it is simplest to say' (p. 48) – in dealing with this awkward figure. The grotesque, Dickensian rendering distinguishes Jacky from the other charac-

ters, but the manner is appropriate to her role. She will blunder –
painfully solid, an embarrassing encumbrance – through the
novel. Jacky is aptly cast as comic caricature with pathetic
overtones.

However, for all its decorative or condescending irony, the
narrative takes Leonard very seriously indeed. He is essential to
the final configuration, and this in turn necessitates sexual
intercourse with Helen Schlegel. The coming together of 'L. &
Helen' (as the working-notes enigmatically put it) is often seen as
the most improbable feature of a frequently improbable fiction:
this brief encounter is arbitrary, implausible and psychologically
unmotivated. Nothing, it is thought, leads up to it, and nothing
away from it. Forster bowed to criticism perhaps a little too
readily, though with a degree of ambivalence. At the time of
publication he was worried that his mother would be shocked by
the illicit sex and the illegitimate child (she was).[22] Later in life he
wrote in his Commonplace Book that the 'non-sexual embraces
irritate'.[23] Between these two extremes, of a highly charged, or
minimal, sexual content, we find the encounter (or 'seduction', as
it is termed by Henry and Charles Wilcox). This sex-act is central
to the novel, with respect both to its position in the story and
thematic significance. It is, however, consummated in parenthesis, between chapters. The sequence goes like this: in chapter
27 Helen and Leonard are alone together at the George Hotel. As
they draw closer, the narrator withdraws discreetly, and what we
have in place of the intercourse which 'follows' is (in chapter 28,
which loops back to show us what Margaret was doing 'during'
chapter 27) Margaret – on the sexual sidelines, as usual –
agonising over her vicarious sexual humiliation by Henry's past
affair with Jacky. This substitution ironically sets the formal
engagement of Margaret and Henry, with its social and moral
considerations, against the casual intercourse of Margaret's sister
with Jacky's husband – an act which is, moreover, the novel's
sexual consummation, leading to the affirmative vision of the
ending.

There are further ironies. For all her moral scruples, Margaret
is unwitting agent of this fertile liaison. In a sense she 'procures'
the provision for the inheritance of Howards End. It was she who
sent the Basts to the hotel, and she later brings letters for Helen
and Leonard. Her crossing of the square (ch. 28) seemingly
coincides with the point in the preceding chapter when Helen

turns from the window, her eyes shining. What Helen saw, presumably, was Margaret, and she expected good news. Margaret's personal delivery of the letters which dash Leonard's hopes may well be the final impetus which throws him into Helen's arms. More than this, though: although sexual intercourse itself takes place between chapters, the foreplay is graphically depicted, in terms of persuasive argument. Chapter 27 enacts the 'seduction'. Helen, dynamic and eloquent in contrast to Leonard's passivity and reticence, energetically attempts to dissuade him of his new realisation of the importance of money. She 'catches' him by implying their shared superiority to the hollow supermen who cannot say 'I', and by somewhat mischievously enquiring into the state of his marriage (having ascertained that Jacky is likely to remain in her room). Helen becomes more pressing and ardent, Leonard more vulnerable. The language is quasi-sexual ('Her excitement grew' – p. 236) and the entire discussion is a thinly disguised seduction, with Helen in the active role. It is Helen who seduces Leonard.

The seduction is, moreover, not an isolated event, but the culmination of Helen's sexual development in the novel, which runs parallel to that of Margaret. This is not to suggest a sustained relationship between Helen and Leonard (and in fact she flees immediately after consummating the desired connection), although there is sufficient evidence of what leads up to their night together. However, their previous connection has largely to be inferred from gaps in the narrative. The most marked is Helen's lengthy absence – which Margaret notes for the reader – when she is sent after Leonard (again by Margaret), who had left their tea-party in a huff. However, although the text provides for their connection, this does not amount to a close intimacy. Helen seizes on Leonard as a cause, and an outlet for her spleen against the Wilcoxes. For Leonard, intercourse with a Miss Schlegel he can call his own is the climax of his cultural aspirations. The motivation is sufficient, but based on plot and theme, rather than psychological. The event is, for example, appropriately placed in the context of Evie's wedding, which also combines money and sex. The intercourse of Helen and Leonard transforms money-guilt into sexual 'gift': Leonard subsequently refuses money, but accepts the transposed sexual guilt.

What leads away from the incident is the disappearance of both characters, to re-emerge at the end – Leonard to die, and Helen to give birth. They and the others converge on Howards End in what reads as a secular Nativity, as Helen, transfigured (in the cameo of her sitting in the porch) becomes the bearer of the saviour: 'And all the time their salvation was lying round them . . . there would after all be a future, with laughter and the voices of children' – ch. 37, p. 296). The son of Helen and Leonard will inherit Howards End, but Leonard dies. Leonard's death, like his intercourse with Helen, is parenthetical: 'They laid Leonard, who was dead, on the gravel' (ch. 41, p. 321). Forster is much given to sudden deaths in his novels, but this one in particular may read as arbitrary and understated, out of proportion to the weight which the narrative attaches to Leonard. The description is, in fact, non-realistic: this is perhaps the most marked shift of mode in the novel. It has the clarity of a completed sign: this is the epiphany of where Leonard Bast stands and falls in the Edwardian power-divide of money and culture. Because fall he does:

> 'Mrs Wilcox,' said Leonard, 'I have done wrong.'
> The man took him by the collar and cried, 'Bring me a stick.' Women were screaming. A stick, very bright, descended. It hurt him, not where it descended, but in the heart. Books fell over him in a shower. Nothing had sense.

The simplicity and economy of the account sharpen the significance of the books, and the sword of the Schlegels, now in Wilcox hands. 'Nothing had sense' dimly recalls Leonard's vain attempt to make the syntax of culture 'tell'. This *tableau vivant* holds the essence of Leonard's position: not only is he ruined by money and culture but, even though the immediate cause of his death is heart-failure, Charles Wilcox's attack exposes Leonard's vulnerability to a latently violent society.

What really matters, though, is that Leonard has finally arrived at Howards End. Even though he dies, he has managed to get inside the house, and, as father to Helen's child, he has successfully invaded the middle-class stronghold fought over by Wilcox and Schlegel. Because, seen the other way round, Leonard is not merely passive victim, but the agent of change in the novel. It is Leonard – and Jacky – who constantly knock on the doors of the rich and intrude into their houses – Wickham Place, Oniton, Howards End. The Basts are disruptive, unintentionally and by default: in them the lower fringe of the middle class, on the edge of the abyss, challenge those with money and property. Jacky shames two Mrs Wilcoxes; Leonard 'ruins' the reputations of Helen Schlegel and Charles Wilcox; in the future, a Bast child will inherit 'England'. Leonard is the point of collision between Wilcox and Schlegel, and a force for connection and disruption. Yet it appears that the narrative uses him to father Helen's child and secure the property for the Schlegels, only to dismiss him – rather as Helen is able, conveniently, to put him out of her mind. It is as if the novel – or indeed Forster – could not permit Leonard to stay inside Howards End, even though he must reach the house. But Leonard dies at Howards End, and his absence is significant in the final configuration. What, then, is the significance of his death? The complexity of the signification, and an authorial uncertainty, are manifest in the ambivalent status awarded to Leonard by his death. Forster uses a coping irony yet again, as the narrator (or Margaret) declares, 'Let squalor be turned into tragedy' (ch. 43, p. 328) to raise and dismiss the issue simultaneously. But the transfiguration of Leonard is not so easily put aside: he is indeed on the edge of tragedy, with some claim to be the hero of the novel.

Several issues arise here. One is the active sympathy with which the novel has engaged in the details of his life, and its concession to him of moral sensitivity. Leonard may be socially and culturally inept, but his instincts and judgements show sense and dignity. He was right to suspect the charitable motives of the Schlegels in inviting him to tea, and even more justified in mistrusting Helen's avowed aim 'To help you, you silly boy!' (ch. 16, p. 139). He is uneasy at being dragged off to Oniton, and protests vehemently at further attempts to adjust his life. He returns the cheque which Helen sends him via Tibby (who remarks that Leonard is a 'monumental person after all' – ch. 30, p. 252). He is, throughout, considerate towards Jacky: in fact he displays a marked – and fatal – tendency towards rescue, which perhaps burlesques the same trait in his social superiors. Yet, even if his moral instincts are mocked by their objects, they remain sure, and directly felt. Finally, in his pilgrimage to Howards End, his sacrificial gesture concentrates the money-guilt of the entire group into his own deep sexual remorse, his 'private sin' (ch. 41, p. 320). In a sense, Leonard is the tragic hero who dies for all the characters in the novel.

What I am suggesting is that, whether or not Forster saw

Leonard as peripheral, the text moves him closer and closer to the centre. This is the case, too, with the positive significance of his death. Leonard is ruined by money, but triumphs over it by death. Death, in the terms of the novel, is a triumph over materialism: both Mrs Wilcox and Helen testify to that. If, looked at one way, *Howards End* turns on the sexual relationships of the Schlegel sisters, looked at in another, it turns on the deaths of Mrs Wilcox and Leonard Bast. Both deaths contribute to the inheritance of the earth, and both see death as triumph. The difference between them is that Mrs Wilcox's death belongs to the natural cycle of decay and renewal, as is implied in her funeral, witnessed by the village community and watched over by the choric figure of the woodcutter. Leonard's death is premature, unnatural and violent: yet it too was 'bound to happen', the inevitable product of a deeply divided society. Both deaths connect with the 'unseen', as Helen suggests: 'Death destroys a man: the idea of Death saves him' (ch. 27, p. 236). Helen does, as we have seen, persuade Leonard of the transcendence of the 'idea of Death' over the mere fact of money. She ruins him doubly (as the novel will prevent him from reaching either wealth or heroic death), and there is a direct link between the seduction and his death journey. For one thing, their conversation is followed by intercourse, and it is to atone for this private sin that he travels to Howards End. Moreover, he travels not only with the negative emotion of remorse, but an active death-wish. He wants to 'get clear of the tangle. So does the suicide yearn' (ch. 41, p. 316). With a sense of 'innate goodness elsewhere' (p. 320), even of joy, he reiterates to himself the 'incredible truth' (p. 321) of the transcendent power of death over squalor, and walks semi-deliberately to his death, impelled by the need to confess, a suicidal temperament and Helen's paradox.

Leonard's death-wish connects him with the figures of Boss Mangan in *Heartbreak House* and Gerald Crich in *Women in Love*. The deaths of all three display a certain 'yearning' (and regression, into a womb which proves destructive). Mangan rushes for 'protection' into the gravel-pit (also described as a cave), which contains dynamite. Gerald walks to his death in a cradle of snow. Leonard has travelled to the consolation of Margaret and Howards End, to be met with violence. For all three figures, moreover, there is a decisive point at which they 'decide' to stay with events, when they might escape. Mangan will determine to leave Heartbreak House, but be prevented by the taunts of the other characters, his infatuation with Hesione Hushabye, and the intervention of the burglar. Gerald Crich will reject Birkin's advice to leave Gudrun, and knowingly embrace the destructive finality of their relationship. During the tea-party at the Schlegels' (ch. 16) Leonard decides to go, asks directly, 'What do you want to have me here for?' and, silently, 'Why should he come again?' (p. 139). The questions were justified, but he did 'come again', to Oniton.

It seems, then, that in each case the text puts the mark of death on these figures. These are the figures which the plot decides to eliminate. (In Shakespearean comedy, we might see this as the group expelling the ambitious outsider, to seal a new social contract.) Certainly the choices are significant: in each case the eliminated figure has focused for us the centrality of economic and industrial power, acting as token of the negative pole of the split society. Mangan and Crich are the bosses, and apparently stronger and more powerful than the clerk with a weak heart: but their strength is equivocal, and they are hollow men emotionally, while Leonard, as we have noted, feels deeply, if mistakenly.

That deep feeling is important. The focus on these characters is such, and the cruelty and violence that attach to their experiences so intense, as to move them to the heart of the respective texts. Even the process of rejection, of 'selecting out', endows them with tragic stature. (As in Shakespearean tragedy the deaths are cathartic, and precede an affirmative coda.) Far from being diminished, the eliminated character becomes *inclusive* symbolic figure for the text, and his death a ritual act, both elegy and warning for a whole society. This inclusiveness disturbs the texture of the narrative and denies it simple, unambiguous closure. One factor here, it seems to me, is precisely that quality of 'object' which has already been noted in Leonard, which distinguishes him from the novel's experiencing subject, the central consciousness of Margaret Schlegel. That quality is also found in the description of Gerald Crich's death in the snow. Leonard's death is rendered from the outside, his consciousness terminated: 'as he approached the house all thought stopped' (ch. 41, p. 321). The object-ive rendering, with its exclusive focus, impressionism and lack of ironic rhetoric, invites total identification with Leonard's actions and, by implication, his experience. I say 'by implication' advisedly: partly because Leonard is essentially passive here, but more because of the non-realistic mode, which permits Leonard, and his death, a symbolic significance.

At this point we can focus on the 'ending' of the novel – from the death of Leonard onwards – with its oscillations of narrative mode, and the suggested alternative endings within the narrative closure. We have already considered the fates of the main characters: Leonard's death, the imprisonment of Charles, the birth of Helen's child, Henry's submission to Margaret and his declining health, Margaret's inheritance. Each of these might have 'ended' differently, as the narrative makes clear (by, for example, the surprise over the arrest of Charles). There are, too, the variations from Forster's working-notes (Charles might have been killed). The chosen endings for each character are nevertheless held together in the mind until the closing scene, to constitute the final configuration. But there is a further complication: the several fates belong to different genres or modes, and do not entirely cohere. So, for example, the reconciliation of Margaret and Henry is comic or satiric realism, while the death of Leonard is symbolic melodrama or even tragedy. Then there is Helen, her child, and the pastoral utopia of the haymaking, clearly symbolic. This does not belong with either the painful realism of the will scene, nor with the symbolic death of Leonard. Indeed, both Helen and her child, and Leonard's death, are distinct and complete: in between is the grey area of Margaret and Henry.

The several fates of the characters, and the separate modes which are called on, render the final configuration problematic and complex, and its normative signification elusive. It seems that Forster goes for an affirmative vision of Helen and her child, contained and muted by the ironic ambience. But how are we to characterise this configuration? We might say, simply, that 'connection' has been made, drawing together Wilcoxes, Schlegels and Bast: England's hope is the integration of its divided classes, cultures and environments. This is certainly normative, but it is only one way of describing the configuration. We might say, less neutrally, that the Schlegels have come into property, taking possession of and inheriting Howards End, containing by a childless marriage, on the one hand the Wilcox plutocracy, and integrating, by an illegitmate child on the other, the lower middle class which reaches in its lineage back to the land. Put yet another way, it reads more insidiously: the text opts for total conservation of Schlegel interests at the expense of both the plutocrat and the clerk. In this perspective, the text appears less to express money-guilt than to enact a liberal wish-fulfilment of total control. In fact, as we step further back from the normative 'statement', the tensions within the 'inclusive' vision multiply, and undermine its affirmation. After all, the final configuration 'also' shows complete female power, with all adult males removed in a symbolic castration. It seems then that we must modify the description of the end-directed narrative of *Howards End*: although the narrative *is* both purposive and normative, it has neither singleness of purpose nor clarity of direction and destination. What it attempts – to define a normative 'England' at its best – resists resolution.

Even the affirmative focus on Helen and the children is barely sustained within the context of the 'ending' as a whole. In the final scene, after the numinous exit of the Wilcoxes, Margaret and Henry remain together in the gloomy interior. Helen rushes in from the sun outside, with Tom and her baby and 'shouts of infectious joy' (ch. 44, p. 340). The novel 'closes' with a buoyantly optimistic declaration. Yet in this final chapter, both in the field and in the house, another note creeps in. That note is a hint of further crisis, even of lurking apocalypse. The subtle, persistent threat is recognised by Helen in the field as the 'red rust' (p. 337) of London, encroaching on the horizon. The city has already been imaged as destruction and loss, and Helen extends the vision: 'London is only part of something else, I'm afraid. Life's going to be melted down, all over the world.' Helen's end-anxiety is countered by Margaret, who interprets the 'melting-pot' hope-fully, as a 'temporary craze' for motion. Her optimism rests on something similar to what we shall find in *Women in Love*, the notion of a pause between two phases or civilisations. *Howards End*, then, envisages, and partly defines, a dimension of crisis beyond that which the narrative has dealt with; but it contains this vision only with some discomfort, and with yet more irony.

Despite Margaret's hopes, even that rapturous final idyll of rushing mother and child is suspect: 'We've seen to the very end, and it'll be such a crop of hay as never!' (p. 340). There is irony both in Helen's optimistic finality ('to the very end') and the colloquial negation of 'such a crop of hay as never', which implies an unrealised utopia. This is more, we suspect, than the end of a novel. The anxiety and threat of a hidden, deeper crisis are felt too in the Wilcoxes repeated goodbyes: these, listed separately, echoing and elegiac, form a mournful chant. Elegy and decline are even more marked in Margaret's unspoken response – 'And again and again fell the word, like the ebb of a dying sea' – which compresses many of the novel's motifs and images. The 'word' *fell*, like Leonard and like the houses. We hear again the imagery of 'Falling towers' (*Waste Land*, 373); and the implications of 'Again and again', a recurring apocalypse, may be inferred from the chapter later in this book on *The Waste Land*. The 'ebb' of the sea takes us back to the opening and closing passages of chapter 19: what was there implicit is here made explicit in 'dying sea'. Margaret's response expresses both her alienation, and the decline of what Henry has stood for. Things fall apart.

This, like her inward response to the revelation of Mrs Wilcox's bequest, is typographically foregrounded by separation from the remainder of the text. Indeed, a glance at the final page of the novel shows its fragmentation: the disjunctions, and the montage of discrete resolutions and disparate modes, are reflected visually in brief paragraphs, rapid shifts, 'lyric' and 'dramatic' passages. These are virtually a juxtaposition of separate closures, and read less like smooth narrative than as non-discursive modernist prose or indeed poetry. The novel thus draws self-consciously and jerkily to an end. The defiantly joyful cry, 'We've seen to the very end', has an irony beyond Helen's consciousness, and operates as a self-reflexive comment on narrative closure, the end of the novel – and on the validity of the vision, what it 'sees'. *Howards End* opened with Helen writing to her sister '*It isn't going to be what we expected.*' The compression of this privileged foresight of a limited hindsight, which conflates past, present and future, encapsulates the complexities of the novel. Helen's remark might well replace the existing epigraph of *Howards End*. It also anticipates the articulation of crisis in *Heartbreak House* and in *Women in Love*.

3 *Heartbreak House*

In *Heartbreak House* the chronic Condition of England becomes acute, and quite possibly terminal. In this extremity the play asks: who can save the country? The quest for national salvation, which underpinned the narrative of *Howards End*, is here explicitly articulated in the inquiry in Act III, 'chaired' by Lady Utterword, into who should govern England, and how. In the course of this discussion all the male figures are considered – and rejected – as candidates for the role of national leader and saviour. The question of who is to save the country gathers in the motifs of the preceding action: we might say that the entire play is an inquiry into the proper organisation of society, in the line of Plato's *Republic* and the writings of Carlyle and Ruskin. But the debate in Act III is, too, a satirical thrust at this leisured after-dinner conversation, pursued while the ship of state is about to 'strike and sink and split',[1] as Captain Shotover vehemently puts it. And discussion of a potential saviour is interrupted and nullified by an actual emergency, in the obliquely rendered bombing-raid which closes the play. Here, then, is the immediate issue – kill or be killed, sink or survive – which disturbs and complicates ethics and political philosophy. In the face of this *deus ex machina* intervention the goal is retracted, from salvation to mere survival. At the final curtain all except Boss Mangan and the burglar are 'safe', even if only temporarily; and Mazzini Dunn can remark with some surprise, 'It is we who have survived' (p. 181).

Salvation – 'Life with a blessing' (Act III, p. 169), in Ellie Dunn's terms – is the urgent and persistent concern of *Heartbreak House*. This is the end and solution, expressed in religious language, towards which the action is directed. The play seeks salvation for the individual as well as society: the connotations of

'salvation' embrace emotional fulfilment and spiritual enlightenment as well as the social millennium. The more general
question which *Heartbreak House* asks is, in effect: What must we do
to be saved? Moreover, the play is concerned to explore exactly
what 'to be saved' *means*. The words 'safe', 'saved' and 'salvation'
recur frequently and in varying contexts, ironically setting the
religious against the secular, as well as discriminating among
various secular salvations. This protracted play on words constitutes an iterative and punning imagery which highlights the
paradoxical nature of *safe*ty, and defines, if only by its absence, the
'salvation' which *Heartbreak House* reaches for.

Several scenarios of salvation are proposed, but they are
demonstrably insufficient or ambivalent. One such is rescue from
poverty by money; but money, and Mangan, are false saviours.
Shotover retorts that 'Riches will damn you ten times deeper.
Riches won't save even your body' (Act II, p. 145); and indeed
the damnation of riches is very evident in the play. In fact,
damnation is the prevalent condition of life in Heartbreak House.
Although the terms 'Damn', 'damned' and 'damnation' recur as
slang expletives, something of their religious force remains:

> MANGAN. Well, I a m damned!
> CAPTAIN SHOTOVER. I thought so. I was, too, for many
> years.   (Act I, p. 89)

The gulf that yawns between Heartbreak House and salvation is
most pointedly indicated by the recurrence of the word 'safe'.
Ariadne Utterword is, we note, a 'safe' woman, and she survives.
Mazzini Dunn worries as to whether 'poor Mangan' will be safe:
Mangan does not survive. Being safe has, however, equivocal
value: the ambivalence is expressed with bitter irony in the
sequence of dialogue which marks the end of danger:

> LADY UTTERWORD. The danger is over, Randall. Go to bed.
> CAPTAIN SHOTOVER. Turn in, all hands. The ship is safe. [*He sits
> down and goes asleep.*]
> ELLIE [*disappointedly*]. Safe!
> HECTOR [*disgustedly*]. Yes, safe. And how damnably dull the
> world has become again suddenly!   (Act III, p. 181)

Safety is disappointing and disgusting. Hector's disgust is partly nostalgia for the thrilling moment, partly regret that the scourge of the heavens wasn't more thorough. Ellie's disappointment, more importantly, indicates that to be 'safe' is not necessarily to be 'Saved': survival may be at the cost of salvation. By contrast, the 'danger' which Shotover looked for in his youth may be positive and regenerative.

We could pursue this topic further, in a scrutiny of the usage of the terms 'danger' and 'dangerous' as they recur in the dialogue. However, the point to take here is that this word-play is neither casual nor merely decorative, because the terms it manipulates have a profound centrality. In *Heartbreak House* the claim of salvation comes up against the hard facts of danger and the need for survival: the 'actual and insistent' which presses in on the leisured conversation of Act III is the First World War.

Heartbreak House was written in 1916–17, and published in 1919 together with *Great Catherine* and 'Playlets of the War'. The Playlets are topical pieces, as their titles indicate, and the subtitles emphasise: *The Inca of Perusalem: An Almost Historical Comedietta*; *O'Flaherty, VC*; *A Recruiting Pamphlet*; *Augustus Does His Bit: A True-to-Life Farce*; and *Annajanska, the Bolshevik Empress: A Revolutionary Pamphlet*. Written between 1913 and 1918, they address contemporary political events and issues satirically but directly. By contrast, perhaps the single most notable feature of *Heartbreak House* is that this, Shaw's major drama of the war-years, refers only intermittently, obliquely or symbolically to its context. Again by contrast, the Preface which was written for the 1919 volume explicitly and almost relentlessly situates the play, giving a definite historical and intellectual formulation of the events which surround and impinge on the action. The Preface is not, however, wilfully misleading, or tangential: it should be read, not as a gloss on the play, but as a final, and distinct, stage of composition – as the completed articulation, or rationalisation, of the themes and concerns of *Heartbreak House*. At the other end of the spectrum is the draft typescript of the play, itself heavily revised and rewritten, and differing substantially from the final, published version. The draft typescript of *Heartbreak House* throws light on many of the problematic areas of this complex and difficult play, and its evidence will be drawn on extensively in this chapter. The typescript illuminates problems, although without completely solving them: the play remains ambiguous and unresolved, holding in tension contradictory impulses, and alternative dramatic progressions and resolutions. What becomes apparent from a scrutiny of the draft is the foundation within the text itself for the widely divergent, even diametrically opposed readings which have been offered by critics – including, notoriously, conflicting interpretations of the ending as either symbolic affirmation, cynical irony or total despair.

One issue which the typescript does, however, help to resolve is the date of composition. The play was written, it seems, between 4 March 1916 and 26 May 1917, when Shaw finished off the stage directions and sent the typescript to his printers. He made further substantial changes in two stages of unpublished rough proofs, the second of which, with the printer's date-stamp of 28 December 1917, is identical to the published play. The play was not revised for publication in 1919: Shaw reserved the wisdom of hindsight and the 'judgement' of history for the Preface, and left the play where it was – at the heart of the war.

The Preface declares Heartbreak House to be 'cultured, leisured Europe before the war' (p. 12). '. . . before the war' is slightly misleading. In *Heartbreak House* we see, certainly, a pre-war society drifting aimlessly in that golden Georgian afternoon (which turns out to be rather less than golden); but just as clearly, in the course of the action, the war catches up with *Heartbreak House*. In effect, Shaw compresses the behaviour, mood and responses of the years before the outbreak of war, and up to the time of writing.[2] *Heartbreak House* belongs to the crucial years of 1916–17: the years of the Somme and Passchendaele, of conscription, of the declaration by Germany of unrestricted submarine warfare; as well as of the Easter uprising, the trial and execution of Roger Casement, and Lloyd George's 'Business Government'. This is the period of what A. J. P. Taylor calls the war of 'deadlock' as opposed to the 'war of movement' of 1914. By the time Shaw came to write *Heartbreak House*, 'The war ceased to have a purpose. It went on for its own sake, as a contest in endurance.'[3]

Shaw did not fight in the war (he was fifty-eight in 1914), but he was by no means inactive.[4] His war began with the controversial article, 'Commonsense about the War', published as a War Supplement to the *New Statesman* of 14 November 1914. Shaw maintained that war could have been avoided by frank dealings on the part of the Foreign Secretary, Sir Edward Grey; that neither England nor Germany could claim moral superiority, since each had built up armaments, issued propaganda and formed secret alliances; and that the issue of the violation of Belgian neutrality was a pretext, since both France and England stood to gain by confining the war to the Franco-German frontier. Shaw's views were devastatingly frank, and even treasonable, in 1914, although, as the war dragged on to the disillusionment of the Somme and after, attitudes caught up with him. But in 1914 he caused an uproar: Asquith said he ought to be shot, and Henry Arthur Jones sallied forth to lead the move to expel him from the Dramatists' Club. Shaw would not compromise his position: nevertheless, despite his sceptical mistrust of patriotic nationalism, he found himself increasingly convinced that Britain must win the war, in order to crush Prussian militarism, and avoid a *delenda est Britannia*. And, as the war wore on, the *enfant terrible* became accepted as a venerable national figure, and useful publicist. Early in 1917, at the invitation of Sir Douglas Haig, Shaw made an official visit to the Front at Flanders. He visited Arras, the Somme, Ypres and Tréziennes, with a brief to record his impressions in three 'war dispatches' for the *Daily Chronicle*. Shaw wrote cheerfully of the pragmatic attitude of the soldier to fighting, and affirmed the aim of achieving peace for all time. At around the same time, in 'Fabianism and the War', he wrote of the 'unspeakable frightfulness of war on the modern scale'.[5] And he had written privately to Arnold Bennett on 9 November 1916, 'one can only wonder whether this control of unprecedented powers of destruction in the hands of little frightened spiteful people does not mean the obliteration of everything that Europe means'.[6] The sentiment is close to that voiced by Hector Hushabye in Act III: 'Think of the powers of destruction that Mangan and his mutual admiration gang wield! It's madness: it's like giving a torpedo to a badly brought up child to play at earthquakes with' (p. 175). At about the time when he wrote to Bennett, Shaw was searching around for an ending to *Heartbreak House*.

The play's closing sequence stems from Shaw's direct experience of a wartime Zeppelin raid. This was the Zeppelin which passed over Hertfordshire on the night of 1 October 1916, and was brought down at Potters Bar. Shaw cycled over to see the wreck, and described the incident at length in a letter to Beatrice and Sidney Webb. A significant feature of Shaw's account is the ambivalent response which he registers in himself, and in other witnesses:

What is hardly credible, but true, is that the sound of the Zepp's engines was so fine, and its voyage through the stars so enchanting, that I positively caught myself hoping next night that there would be another raid. . . . One is so pleased at having seen the show that the destruction of a dozen people or so in hideous terror and torment does not count. 'I didn't half cheer, I tell you' said a damsel at the wreck. Pretty lot of animals we are![7]

The equivalent dramatisation in *Heartbreak House*, which is astonishingly similar in its detail, disperses the excitement, the hope of another raid and the equivocal celebration of destruction among the reactions of the characters of Hesione, Hector, Ellie Dunn and Nurse Guinness. Two aspects of the ambivalence of this episode will be discussed later. One is the splendour and enchantment of the sight and sound of the Zeppelin, which has something of the quality of a divine manifestation in the heavens. The other is the hint, slight in the passage quoted, but reinforced by Shaw's report of the captain of the Zeppelin as a splendid personage, of less than complete conviction of the unremitted villainy of the 'enemy'. As we shall see, the crisis articulated by *Heartbreak House* in the First World War is that of defining, or redefining, the Enemy.

The final scene of *Heartbreak House*, as the 'magnificent' noise thunders overhead, is thus not merely a factual record or a topical allusion. This is the dramatisation of a particular event which has wider reverberations, and which in itself raises problems of how to characterise the war, and therefore also of its meaning. Moreover, the episode has a peculiar status in the play as a whole: it recapitulates, or restates in symbolic representation, what has happened so far, bringing the action historically up to date. It renders obliquely the response of England, and particularly those at home, to wartime events. It even, apparently, symbolically depicts the actual outbreak of war in 1914. We might say that war is declared in *Heartbreak House* by that dull, distant explosion (which echoes the remote gunshot in Sarajevo, juxtaposed by Wells to the game of hockey at Matching's Easy in *Mr Britling Sees It Through*), heard just at the point when Mazzini Dunn, liberal humanist with a sneaking belief in Providence, has reassured everyone that nothing will happen:

MAZZINI. I thought all that once, Captain; but I assure you
    nothing will happen.
A dull distant explosion is heard.
HECTOR [*starting up*]. What was that?
CAPTAIN SHOTOVER. Something happening [*he blows his whistle*].
    Breakers ahead!
The light goes out.   (Act III, p. 177)

(Shaw originally wrote 'The lights go out', unconsciously influ-
enced perhaps by Grey's famous remark 'The lamps are going out
all over Europe.'[8] We shall see the lamps similarly extinguished in
a comparable sequence in *Women in Love*.)

The events of Act III, then, bring the action up to date; but this is
not to say that the war is not registered in earlier stages of the
action. Topical allusions are numerous, particularly to the
weapons of the new technological warfare: submarines, machine
guns, tanks and torpedoes. The 'submarine peril'[9] was felt from
1915 onwards, and with particular horror at the torpedoing of the
civilian ship *Lusitania* in that year. Germany declared unrestricted
submarine warfare from 1 February 1917, and the retaliatory
blockade of ports led to hardship and lasting damage. Shotover's
invention of the ship with the magnetic keel that sucks up
submarines is not totally eccentric: the various anti-submarine
devices introduced to counter the 'peril' included hydrophones,
'Otter gear', depth charges, smoke apparatus, shells and mines.
Submarine warfare is, in any case, an appropriate as well as a
topical reference for *Heartbreak House*, with its dominant symbol of
the ship. Both submarines and Zeppelins embody the unprecedented menace of the unknown and the unforeseen which
characterised this war, and which is felt, beyond the topicality
and specificity of the references, as the ambience of war in
Heartbreak House. Indeed, it seems to me that what *Heartbreak House*
has centrally to offer in rendering the experience of the war is the
sense of threat and menace, focused in the catastrophe from
the skies which contains and eclipses all preceding, separate
anxieties.

Two events really brought the war home to Shaw, as to so
many. One was the advent of aerial warfare (the first Zeppelin
appeared over the coast on 29 December 1914[10]), the other the
introduction in 1916 of compulsory military service. With air
raids this became a civilian war, eliminating the choice of

individual engagement, and reducing the value of personal heroism. Shaw complained that 'Every day one's life was likely to be reduced to absurdity by a bomb dropping through one's study roof.'[11] It is perhaps hard to sympathise deeply with the plight of non-combatant authors; Shaw was, nevertheless, correctly alerted to the absurd world created by what was, potentially at least, total war. What he realised was the destruction not only of normal daily routine but of an expected and predictable framework within which to act. This was the nullification of intellectual endeavour by the hard fact of the bombing-raid, the 'obliteration of everything that Europe means'.

Conscription had little personal relevance for Shaw by virtue of his age. He was not himself a pacifist, nor did he object to conscription in itself; but he deplored the persecution of conscientious objectors, and supported many individual cases. As with the 'conchies', the trial of Roger Casement raised complex questions of freedom of commitment. Shaw was drawn into the argument, and the Casement affair was on his mind when writing *Heartbreak House*.[12] The specific dilemma of Roger Casement's allegiance and activities highlights the more general, but acute, problem of the Enemy 'within'. *Heartbreak House* is intensely committed to defining, or redefining, the Enemy, as well as to finding the Saviour. The play identifies the Enemy within as the international adversary, capitalism, in the representative figure of Boss Mangan the financier. Identification and elimination of the Enemy – selecting out the undesirable – constitute the negative pole of the play's solution. But the problem proves to be complex and finally intractable, and a single identification, as well as a mode of complete elimination, elude the play. The Enemy of capitalism and the Enemy of the national conflict are blurred, in what may read as the dilemma of Shaw's socialism, faced in 1916–17 with the immediate national crisis of the war.

Boss Mangan is killed off by the play (just as Forster, as we have seen, dispatches Leonard Bast, and deals only slightly less harshly with the Wilcoxes; and, as we shall see, as Lawrence executes Gerald Crich, whose affiliations to Mangan are strong). Billy Dunn the burglar dies too; and the play draws an analogy between the two figures of the burglar and Mangan. These are the 'two burglars', or the 'two practical men of business' (Act III, p. 181), as Hector Hushabye and Lady Utterword respectively term them, in what amounts to an epitaph. The idea of business as crime, of the respectable businessman committing legal theft, is central to the play.[13]

The burglar episode in Act II, often dismissed as an exasperating and irrelevant interruption, is in fact structurally and thematically integral. Its function is to release the metaphor of capitalism as theft. When the burglar enters, he bodies forth a cluster of latent ideas about the relationships of the characters, generating a metaphoric language which permeates the texture of the play. After his intrusion, images of stealing, selling and imprisonment steadily inform the action, endorsed by the pointed analogy drawn between him and Mangan. Mangan is curiously resentful of the burglar, feeling that he has displaced – or actually replaced – him: 'The burglar has put my nose out of joint' (Act II, p. 139). His complaint is preceded by Randall Utterword's reverberative comment, 'there is more than one burglar in England' (p. 139).

Billy Dunn and Boss Mangan are, then, the 'two burglars', as Hector calls them, although the analogy is not simple or clichéd. In fact Dunn is not a burglar at all (although he did rob Shotover), but a con-man and ex-pirate. At this point it might seem that the comparison falters, but we find two reversals. First, Mangan is also not what he seems: the captain of industry turns out to be a financier and politician. Secondly, his *modus operandi* is really very like Dunn's – swindling. The two practical men of business are parasites on society, neither of them actually a thief, but both in the business of swindling, and of consuming what they do not produce. They can both be figuratively dubbed 'burglars', and the correspondence between them is sealed by their deaths together in the gravel-pit: a symbolic elimination of capitalism.

The instrument of this elimination is the bomb which drops on Mangan and the burglar: the Enemy within is destroyed by the external Enemy, in a symbolic rendering of the war. The agency of this elimination is, however, complicated by the play in such a way as to render its definition of the Enemy ambiguous and elusive. One complication is to be found in the multiple connotations of the figure of the burglar, which carries associations of invasion as well as of theft. It has in fact been suggested that the descent of the burglar from upstairs prefigures the ending of the play, when the bombs drop: both interrupt and 'invade' the life of the household, from above (and we might compare this prefiguring, in *Women in Love*, with what I shall suggest are two separate

renderings of the war, in 'Water-Party', and the death of Gerald in
'Snowed Up'). If we read the burglar episode in this way, then his
'invasion' of the household, and his intention of depriving the
privileged class of their jewels or their money is a genuinely
subversive attack on the citadel. The attempted 'robbery' links
the burglar both with the capitalist Mangan (the 'internal' but
international Enemy) and with the bomb (the external, national
Enemy). We may then confirm a suggestive identification between, not only Mangan and the burglar, but also the burglar and
the bomb. The motif of burglary suggestively links the internal
'enemies' of the state and those outside; and the Enemy is
embodied in a threat to both life and property, in the thing from
the air, either invader or bomb.

And now we find a further complication. Mangan is killed, it
seems, by the unwitting collaboration of Shotover, with his
dynamite, and the external Enemy, with his bomb. Shotover
remarks of Mangan's exit to the gravel-pit 'My dynamite drew
him there. It is the hand of God' (Act III, p. 179). The 'judgement'
which descends from above may be apparently the Enemy, yet
actually providential. Moreover it is uncertain whether Mangan's
death is to be celebrated (as by Nurse Guinness) or lamented (as by
Mazzini Dunn). In so far as Mangan is the identifiable Enemy
capitalism, which can be isolated and eliminated, his death is a
triumph and a solution, brought about by the combined forces of
Shotover and the Zeppelin, which is also the 'hand of God'. In so
far as Mangan becomes inclusive symbol for the suffering and
decay of a whole society, his death is both a lament for ourselves,
and evidence of our own death-wish.

What I am suggesting is that a clear 'solution' for this war play
becomes problematic as soon as the national crisis is recognised in
Act III, because the play is then torn between history, speculation
and prophecy. The negative solution – away with capitalism – is a
consistent moral judgement but historically a bad prophecy.
Moreover, Mangan's death is dramatically redundant, in that he
is by then already a dead man, obliterated by heartbreak. And the
agency of the bomb, as noted above, adds further provocative but
'unnecessary' dimensions to the action. Shaw wrote to his
Swedish translator Hugo Vallentin in 1917, sending him the first
rough proof of *Heartbreak House*, that it seemed to him 'a fine
opening spoilt by the War'.[14] His unease was justified: not only is
the 'fine opening' of the stable household disturbed by invasion

and danger, but the direction of the action becomes confused and dispersed. In a very real sense the war does 'spoil' *Heartbreak House*, precisely because it raises, pertinently, the question of who the Enemy really is (that is, the 'true meaning' of the war), without providing a conclusive answer.

Threat and anxiety pervade *Heartbreak House*. The play registers the tension and fears of wartime England, and communicates at the same time a Chekhovian mood of dreaming and drifting, and a Carlylean foreboding of nemesis and an inevitable 'smash'. Response to threat is split between the extremes of Mazzini Dunn's complacent self-delusion and Mangan's paranoid, but well founded, 'presentiment'. The threat which overhangs the action is intensified by its very obscurity, and its dispersal between 'Mangan and his mutual admiration gang' and the unseen 'murdering blackguards' (Act III, p. 180) in the air. The focus of fear shifts. It is neither decorum nor coyness that dictates the disguise of the Zeppelin raid in Act III: the uncertainty as to the exact nature of the overriding Enemy is wholly appropriate.

Nevertheless, the fear and anxiety of *Heartbreak House* are rendered peculiarly naked when the play is read, or experienced, in history. The play was not seen on the English stage until October 1921. Had it been produced earlier, there would surely have been no problem for the audience in recognising contemporary allusions: what in retrospect may appear as a curious absence, or minimality, of reference is rather an index of the play's total immersion in its context. The world outside the theatre was only too close, and the membrane enclosing the dramatic fiction only too fragile. This, the interpenetration of play and reality, lies behind what Shaw wrote to his actress friend Lillah McCarthy, explaining his reticence over a wartime production of *Heartbreak House*: 'the raid at the end of it would become a real one every time the moon and the weather gave the Germans their chance'.[15] Even if there were no raid, one might predict audience hysteria before the close of the play.

What is essential to an understanding of *Heartbreak House* is that the war catches up with the play in a particular way, trapping it in unresolved crisis. By his own account, as Lady Gregory records in her diary for 19 November 1916, Shaw had difficulty in finishing the play, it was 'so wild'.[16] What is 'wild' about the play is the various dramatic progressions which vie for centrality, and the alternative resolutions subsumed in the ending which he eventually came to write. Even after he had completed the play Shaw confessed to Lillah McCarthy that he was 'not quite convinced that it is really finished'.[17] And for a revival in 1943, during the Second World War, he 'finished' it by adding a new final line, of which more later.

I am not suggesting that the wildness, complexity or ambiguity of *Heartbreak House* diminish its artistic achievement. On the contrary, I could perhaps sum up these features as a kind of *positive insecurity*. The play, with its final but inconclusive explosions, is an experience precisely of violence and near-despair born of irresolution. It yearns for an ending, but its end-anxiety cannot be satisfied. In the final Act Hector asks, 'How is all this going to end?' (p. 174) Shaw noted to his French translator Auguste Hamon that this line always got a laugh (*Heartbreak House* is a very long play). But this end-awareness is more than a theatrical joke, and the question is deadly serious. How *is* this play to end? It cannot of itself end the war: in that sense, there is in 1916 or 1917 no ending for Shaw to write. In desperation, searching for dramatic closure, he turns to an ending – and an image, albeit bathetic to the point of absurdity, of the End, of Armageddon, *Götterdämmerung*, and the Last Judgement – which he has already experienced: the Zeppelin raid over Potters Bar. But beyond this he, and the play, cannot go.

The problem of closure is demonstrated by alterations within the draft typescript, relating directly to the way in which the play is to end. The movement of the plot has hinged substantially, and conventionally, on whom Ellie Dunn is to marry: in the event, she decides not to marry Boss Mangan, and to contract instead a 'spiritual' marriage with the aged Captain Shotover. Ellie's decision is crucial to the final configuration of *Heartbreak House*; but, as with her radiance at the prospect of another raid, it is equivocal. This spiritual marriage has been variously interpreted as either an affirmative vision – the play's symbolic investment in a future – or as a gesture of surrender. Now one of the most notable changes to the draft typescript is the insertion of the marriage of Ellie to Shotover, at some stage during or even after the typing of the whole of Act III, as an additional page of longhand.[18] It is, in effect, an afterthought; or, to put it more positively, a late inspiration which shows the play working itself through in the author's imagination. And it seems that, once Shaw had thought of it, he shuffled the episodes around in order to highlight the marriage as a preliminary climax to Act III. However, it is possible to read the Act, omitting the inserted section, without noticing very much difference, as there is no subsequent reference to the marriage. Hesione, after all, dismisses it as a cheap trick, and Shotover (who was asleep at the time) at no point confirms what Ellie has said. What this faces us with is that an apparently crucial element of the play's resolution is not fully integrated in the action, or completely *necessary*. Nor, for that matter, is Mangan's death necessary, in the sense that the sole plot-decision *required* by the motivating question 'Should Ellie marry Mangan?' is a negative one. As already stated, Mangan is effectively destroyed, his personality dismantled, before the ending. The upshot is that the difficulties Shaw spoke of in trying to finish his play are amply evidenced by what he wrote and rewrote. *Heartbreak House* holds in tension a number of possible developments, and its 'ending' juxtaposes several resolutions which do not entirely hold together. It must be stressed, nevertheless, that the very anxiety to find the 'right' ending (or indeed to interpret the ending 'correctly') underscores the end-direction of the play, its drive towards a definitive statement.

The society which *Heartbreak House* brings to Judgement is portrayed, like that of *Howards End* and *Women in Love*, as deeply divided. Lady Utterword's division of 'good society' into the 'equestrian classes and the neurotic classes' (Act III, p. 160) burlesques what is nevertheless registered by the play as profoundly problematic. The centre cannot hold: the dominant middle class is radically split, with a divorce absolute between material power, and wisdom or culture.

The familiar framework of a weekend party in a country house allows Shaw to draw into the household a selection of characters representative of a cross-section of contemporary society. The inhabitants of Heartbreak House – Captain Shotover, his daughter Hesione, and her husband, Hector Hushabye – have, variously, a kind of wisdom, moral, political or emotional. Collectively they embody the impassioned but impotent conscience of society: they are implicated, by the connections we see in the play, in the very power-structure which they recognise as corrupt. The arrival at the house of Boss Mangan, and the homecoming of Hesione's sister Ariadne, wife of Sir Hastings Utterword, bring on the scene representatives of power: capitalist and imperialist, economic and political. The introduction of such guests and visitors permits a consideration of who should govern, and how. The split between power and wisdom is not simple, however, and the play is neither a socio-political diagram nor a political allegory. The characters are indeed representative, but each has a multiple signification, and this is further complicated by the symbolic potential of the various groupings.

One effect of multiple signification is the wide historical perspective on domestic and foreign affairs for which the action provides. Shotover, for example, may be seen as the contemporary moral consciousness of England, impotent and decayed; but, historically, the eighty-eight year old sea captain represents England in the period of adventurous expansion following the amendment of the Navigation Laws in 1829, as his description of his youthful career suggests. Mazzini Dunn recalls, in his allusion to his namesake, Giuseppe Mazzini, the nationalistic fervour of the nineteenth-century Italian patriot, as well as voicing the liberal humanism of the immediate pre-war period.

Moreover, apart from its historical inclusiveness, the society of *Heartbreak House* is rendered dramatically. As in *Howards End*, the dramatic narrative is directed towards establishing a descriptive and, to an extent, prescriptive model of society; but the model presented by the play is dynamic, not static. Individual figures gather resonance and significance as they interact, and it is accordingly often more helpful to consider what the characters do, or what the plot does to them, rather than what they represent: to ask, for example, 'Why can't Ellie marry Mangan?' or 'Why should Mangan die?' rather than 'What does Mangan stand for?' To answer such questions is to look closely at how the action works.

The notion of a 'model' of society (or indeed of the universe) is particularly relevant to this acutely self-conscious play. The model which *Heartbreak House* establishes is in part located within the moral and political consciousness of its highly articulate characters. As the characters are more or less self-aware, they comment to a greater or lesser degree on what they do, and on the meaning of events. The dialogue consists substantially, in fact, of the characters working towards a definitive description of themselves and others. As the dramatic action models for us the world of the play, so the characters engage in making sense of things.

Lady Utterword's analysis of 'good society' is one example. The moral anguish of Hector and Shotover over a mechanistic and brutish universe is another. And Ellie Dunn, whose evolving model of her own situation is perhaps the central experience of the play, eventually articulates the 'meaning' of Heartbreak House: 'this silly house, this strangely happy house, this agonising house, this house without foundations' (Act III, p. 171). Boss Mangan is the least self-aware of all; but at the bottom of the scale of articulate utterance, his behaviour can speak for an attitude or an ideology. When in Act III he *'wildly'* (p. 166) tears off his clothes, and dodges an imaginary missile, his actions have a collective significance, as a crazy epiphany of the confessional and self-destructive impulses of Heartbreak House. Indeed, the chief entertainment of the house party is a kind of intellectual strip poker in which the characters undress themselves and each other. 'Our game is to find out the man under the pose' (Act II, p. 151), Hector says. The game is ruthless and relentless.

Boss Mangan, businessman and financier, is the focus of economic power in *Heartbreak House*, and the play's epitome of modern capitalist enterprise. As the intrigues of his career are unravelled Mangan is revealed, in a sequence of reversals, as at once less eminent and more vicious. He is unmasked partly by the probing of the other characters, but also by his compulsion to enhance his standing in Heartbreak House, an alien environment to the man from the City – by giving away his secrets. Mangan's strategy ironically rebounds, as his successive disclosures earn him not greater respect but increased ridicule. The scene is set for the unmasking of Mangan by Ellie's account in Act I of his business relationship with her father. Mangan, she tells Hesione, rescued Mazzini from financial ruin long ago, and is the family's continuing protector and benefactor. However, as Mangan himself reveals in Act II, the relationship is actually one of unscrupulous exploitation: he ruined her father deliberately, as a matter of business. Finally, in Act III, the reality of Mangan's millions is exploded as a sham, merely 'Travelling expenses. And a trifle of commission' (p. 162) for the enterprises he promotes.

Nevertheless, Mangan *is* money, even if he is not, after all, 'disgustingly rich' (Act I, p. 74); and in embodying money Mangan provides a particular model of the 'bloated capitalist' (p. 99), a 'perfect hog of a millionaire' (p. 71). These descriptions connect Mangan with the wealthy plutocracy whose greed, extravagance and narrowness of vision were condemned by *Howards End*; and in several respects he resembles both Charles and Henry Wilcox, as well as Lawrence's Gerald Crich. But the play takes pains to define Mangan, and in him a paradigm of contemporary capitalism, in terms of what he is not. It is important to note that the text discriminates among various aspects of capitalist industry and business, in separating Mangan off from them. So, for example, he does not fit Hector's illusion of the master swindler, in so far as his factories are genuine. There is a further point here: we are concerned not only with what Mangan tells us of his business concerns, but also with the image which other characters have of him. Their impressions broaden the potential picture of capitalism. It is largely, for example, through Hesione Hushabye's misconceptions, her characterisation of 'Boss' Mangan in terms appropriate to the attitudes of, say, Carlyle or Dickens towards industrialism, that the play provides for an extended historical perspective on the development of capitalism. Mangan is certainly not the 'Captain of Industry' envisaged by Carlyle in *Past and Present*, leader and hero of a positive industrialised society. Nor, on the other hand, is he the harsh master manufacturer of *Hard Times* (which Shaw particularly admired). Hesione graphically presents for us a Dickensian slave-driver who 'spends his life making thousands of rough violent workmen bend to his will and sweat for him: a man accustomed to have great masses of iron beaten into shape for him by steam-hammers!' (Act II, p. 116).

It is Mazzini Dunn who points out the inadequacy and inaccuracy of Hesione's 'romantic ideas of business' (p. 116). The word 'romantic' alerts us to the double irony involved here: Mazzini's attempt to defend Mangan operates as an unwitting indictment, as he assures Mrs Hushabye of Mangan's total ignorance and incompetence in dealing with men or machinery. Mangan is, simply, 'wonderful about money' (p. 117), and thinks of nothing else. Hesione's romantic idea rested on a premise of managerial power and industrial expertise; but by his own admission Mangan knows nothing about machinery, and is afraid of the men. There is an implicit contrast here with the 'romantic' Carlylean vision of the Napoleon of industry; but what is even more damning is that the transition from Dickensian factory-owner to rootless financier represents actual decline, not progress. Mangan's sole skill is that of *damaging*; and the only relationship of which he is capable is one of exploitation. The main indictment of capitalism in *Heartbreak House* lies precisely in its distortion of relationships, and in the inner poverty of Mangan. The Boss emerges as a weak and insubstantial figure, who collapses inwards under the pressure of the other characters. The collapse is partly punitive, Mangan brought to judgement; but the play suggests too that capitalism of itself emotionally impoverishes those who profit by the system. It additionally involves, in the view of Shotover and Hector, a dehumanising and brutalising survival of the fittest. Shotover sees 'Mangan and his mutual admiration gang' as the power that drives a mechanistic and animalistic universe, the 'hogs to whom the universe is nothing but a machine for greasing their bristles and filling their snouts' (Act I, p. 100). Hesione echoes this hoggish imagery; but Hector, more moderately and subtly, sees the problem of moral gradations and connections within the community: 'We are members one of another' (p. 101). Hector's vision of intricate interdependency is borne out by what we see of the stance of characters in relation to Mangan, and the various subgroups. Mangan and his mutual admiration gang extend beyond those with direct power, in a broad spectrum ranging from conspiracy or complicity to consent, willing or by default.

The analogy between Mangan and the burglar – capitalism and theft – was considered earlier. It is Ellie Dunn who registers the impact of the metaphor of theft 'released' by the burglar episode (as Hector registers the topic of imprisonment, and gives it emotional and spiritual dimensions). Ellie sees Mangan's dealings with her father as robbery; and theft and commerce now haunt Ellie's imagination and infuse the vocabulary of the play. It is not only the burglar, though, who is implicated with Mangan. We might assume that what Ellie Dunn comes to realise is her father's position as dupe and slave of capitalism, an innocent victim like herself. But, although Dunn has indeed been ruined by Mangan in the past, he is in a sense a willing slave, consenting by default to his own exploitation by continuing as Mangan's manager. He is, after all, remarkably calm and clear-sighted in talking about Mangan to Hesione; and, if what he tells her is correct, then it is Mangan's obsession with money which creates profit. Mazzini is poor, and humble. He realises that what is the matter with him is precisely his poverty; but he is in league with Mangan's wealth and power. He makes Mangan possible. As

Ellie tells us, Mazzini and Mangan 'were boys together' (Act I,
p. 74): their history is interwoven.

There is, too, the curious analogy drawn between Mazzini and
Billy Dunn. This is initially suggested when Shotover 'mistakes'
Ellie for the daughter of the sailor who robbed him. The running
gag of mistaken identity is sustained even when Mazzini appears,
and is only resolved at the entry of Billy Dunn. Even then the
comparison stands: the two Dunns are after all related, and Billy
accuses Mazzini of attempted suicide in shooting at him. Despite
Mazzini's claim to be a 'very different person' (Act II, p. 137), it
seems that the Captain has perceived a profound imaginative
congruence between them. After the burglar episode no more is
made of the resemblance: one sequence is concluded, and the
emphasis passes to the analogy between the burglar and Mangan,
as another sequence begins. Not only does the play hint at a
reciprocal, tacitly agreed relationship between master and slave
in Mangan and Mazzini: it goes further, in the configuration
formed by these two and the burglar.

Of all the characters in *Heartbreak House*, Captain Shotover most
vehemently denounces Mangan, and it would seem that he is
devoid of economic power. Yet Shotover supports his family by
inventing weapons to serve the war-machine: death and destruction show good profits. The £500 which Shotover earned for his
lifeboat is far outweighed by the sums he can command for
destructive inventions. Shotover's 'powers of destruction' extend
to the bundle of dynamite which operates as a symbol of the
impulse towards violence in the play. With his dynamite,
Shotover recalls Shaw's earlier armament-manufacturer, Andrew
Undershaft in *Major Barbara*. Both plays examine the facts of
money and power;[19] and the attributes of Undershaft are as it
were divided between the money of Mangan and the moral energy
of Shotover. Undershaft combined the profit-motive with an
almost mystical belief in the power to kill. Shotover, the would-be
dynamitard, shares his faith, as we shall see later in considering
his political philosophy. To Undershaft, money represented the
positive power to change the world. Unlike Undershaft, the
Captain is not 'Unashamed': as the light fails, at the end of Act I,
and he settles down to his work, he demands, 'Give me deeper
darkness. Money is not made in the light' (p. 105).

Money and government, economic and political power, are
closely related, in the play's examination of contemporary society.

The government from which Shotover is alienated is represented, in home affairs, by Mangan, and abroad, in the Crown Colonies, by Sir Hastings Utterword. Capitalist and imperialist both represent power without moral scruple. Mangan's position as 'dictator of a great public department' (Act III, p. 163), at the direct invitation of the Prime Minister, is ridiculed. Mangan has no political policy, and can cite no 'administrative achievements' (p. 164); but it is clear that he will succeed, if at all, by inflicting harm; and his role in government is condemned.

Hastings Utterword stands consciously for Empire. As governor of one of His Majesty's Crown Colonies he does not set foot in *Heartbreak House*, and indeed is divorced from it by both temperament and position. This absent character is however represented in the play by Ariadne, whose views are completely identified with those of her husband. Ariadne was attracted to Hastings because he resembled the figurehead on her father's ship; and 'wooden yet enterprising' (Act I, p. 63) aptly describes his combination of unimaginative rigidity with energy and efficiency. Ariadne endorses her husband's authoritarian rule: 'Get rid of your ridiculous sham democracy; and give Hastings the necessary powers, and a good supply of bamboo to bring the British native to his senses' (Act III, p. 165). This regime is repressive, and ultimately absurd, as 'the British native' implies. There is nevertheless a certain attraction in the strength and pragmatism of a Hastings Utterword (even Shotover wavers in his opinion), but rule by the stick is not 'God's way', and cannot be allowed to 'save the country' (p. 164). Lady Utterword commands, however, increasing respect; and Shaw altered the typescript to give her a central position in the final Act, stressing her natural authority and cool courage. Ariadne's hammock is also her *'cradle'* (p. 178), towards which Nurse Guinness moves to guard her former charge when the crisis approaches: the cradle, we might say, of Empire.

Actual political power is restricted in *Heartbreak House* to Mangan and the Utterwords. Randall Utterword, the soft-centred 'Foreign Office toff' (Act I, p. 99), embodies an effete and privileged civil service which supports their rule. The other male characters occupy various positions of – largely ineffectual – protest. Mazzini Dunn embodies a complacent, *laissez-faire* tolerance: 'It's amazing how well we get along, all things considered' (Act III, p. 175). But in his youth Mazzini was politically active, joining societies (such as the Fabians and others), making speeches and writing pamphlets. He changed his socialist or revolutionary views because the members of the societies held no economic or managerial power. This is what has led him, apparently, to admire such men as Mangan. He was also disillusioned when the expected 'revolution, or some frightful smash-up' (p. 175) did not materialise, and he has concluded that the 'blunder and muddle' (p. 175) (Forster's pet terms) will simply go on. The unrelenting irony which piles up against Mazzini, as his predictions prove wrong and his opinions misguided, enacts the play's 'judgement' on him. His liberal humanism is part of the fabric of *laissez-faire* capitalism.

Unlike Mazzini Dunn, Hector Hushabye is not optimistic: Hector is close to despair at the state of society, but torn by inner conflict, and given to extravagant gesture and escapist fantasy. In fantasy Hector is more militant than Mazzini, engaging in direct action rather than a battle of words: his alias and *alter ego* Marcus Darnley, aristocrat and rebel, is a militant socialist who 'despises rank, and has been in three revolutions fighting on the barricades' (Act I, p. 82). The protest which Hector makes in *Heartbreak House* is a defiant invitation to the enemy, when he turns on all the lights (Marcus might well have set the house on fire, as Ellie urges). But this death-defying bravado is empty posturing; unable to take decisive action, Hector *reacts* (rather than acts), to the stimulus of emergencies such as the burglar or the bombers. As his name suggests, Hector is the hero *manqué*, the warrior whose sword is sheathed in a swordstick, and flourished in romantic dumbshow. Hector's vision is a late development of the Romantic rebel: the intellectual, isolated from society by superior insight, and hero in his own imagination of a world drama, is the heir of Byron and Shelley. His dream of cosmic defiance is cast in the Shelleyan mould; but this new Prometheus remains firmly bound, by sexual slavery and domesticity. In Hector the play 'selects out' the possibility of salvation by romantic heroism. As his surname 'Hushabye' suggests, the hero has withdrawn to a cradle. But the allusion to the nursery-rhyme also hints at the imminent crash: 'When the bough breaks the cradle will fall, / Down will come baby, cradle, and all.' Hector is not, in fact, lulled to sleep: painfully aware of the useless and dangerous anachronism of Heartbreak House, he recognises (unlike Mazzini Dunn) that 'this cant last' (Act III, p. 175). Hector directs his anger against the heavens, invoking nemesis: 'Fall and crush' (Act II, p. 157). But he can envisage, too, another outcome: one which goes beyond the social or political, and is part of an inevitable historical process: 'I tell you, one of two things must happen. Either out of that darkness some new creation will come to supplant us as we have supplanted the animals, or the heavens will fall in thunder and destroy us' (Act III, p. 159). This is natural selection imbued with a moral imperative, and juxtaposed to the thunderbolt of Zeus, in a kind of fundamentalist evolutionism. But Hector's is a universe without God: Shaw took care in revising the typescript to make him swear 'by thunder', and to remove all reference to a single deity. The alternatives which Hector envisages are equally pessimistic, what Lawrence calls 'purely destructive, not . . . destructive–consummating':[20] there is no future for the species. But Hector's vision, like that of Rupert Birkin, makes an evolutionary necessity of the immediate crisis, places it in a cosmic perspective. Beside this vision we shall place the alternatives envisaged by Birkin for *Women in Love*, as he contemplates the corpse of Gerald Crich. Birkin can accept, and even welcome, the elimination of the species, as the transition to a new phase of existence. Both visions must also, however, be compared with that of Shotover.

Unlike Hector, Shotover would kill, not spare, the enemy. The 'political philosophy' of *Heartbreak House* is expressed largely as a debate between these two characters: Hector with his swordstick, Shotover with his twentieth-century dynamite. The 'debate' is formalised in their discussion, towards the end of Act I, of the respective merits of extermination and compassion. This conversation is the negative pole of the quest for elimination of the Enemy; and the method it proposes of selecting out the undesirable – that of exterminaton – is in a sense enacted at the end of the play. It is balanced, positively, in Act III by the quest for a saviour of the country. At both these points the discussion opens up, to move from the immediate and personal towards the articulation of a political philosophy. (We might add a parallel, in Act II, in the debate between Ellie and Shotover over the claims of materialism versus a concern for spiritual values.) Seen in this way, the movement of the dramatic argument focuses on three debates. Each is central to the respective Act, and generates possible answers for the play as a whole to the problems posed: in the deaths of Mangan and the burglar; the marriage of Ellie and

Shotover; and, negatively, in the rejection of all candidates for the role of national saviour.

Shotover is not explicitly considered as potential saviour; but his claim to the title is implicitly considered in what he says and does. His 'political philosophy', in both its critical and its visionary aspects, is central to *Heartbreak House*. Shotover's denunciation of capitalism and materialism is in the vein of Carlyle and Ruskin. With them he shares a faith in strong leadership, which connects with his career as a sea captain. The ship is the dominant dynamic (and male) symbol for *Heartbreak House*, which overlays, even in the non-realistic stage-set of the house built to resemble a ship, the static (and female) symbol of the house, centre of personal relationships. The ship of state – for this is indeed a metaphor for the organisation of society – needs direction and responsible leadership: navigation. Carlyle used similar imagery; but we can also detect here some influence of Plato's *Republic*. Shotover voices, and the play ratifies, the ideal of the philosopher–ruler; the negation of that ideal, in the status quo of *Heartbreak House*, is implied in Hector's observation that 'Mangan's son may be a Plato' (Act I, p. 101).

Shotover's ship must steer a course away from 'the rocks' (Act III, p. 177) towards 'God's open sea' (p. 178). In 'God's open sea' we shall discover Shotover's positive vision, in which the political merges with the religious. Against the materialism embodied by Mangan, and argued for by Ellie Dunn in their confrontation in Act II, Shotover stands for spiritual values. Ellie decries his ideas as useless and out of date; but she eventually abdicates this position, to embrace his spirituality. To this extent *Heartbreak House* endorses the claims of the soul in a materialistic universe. The 'spiritual' element in Shotover is, however, ambivalent. His aspiration to attain the seventh degree of concentration turns out to be rum; and, in their scene together, Ellie progressively demystifies the Captain. Nevertheless, he gives Ellie the memories of his 'ancient wisdom' (Act II, p. 146). This phrase recalls the title of Annie Besant's treatise on theosophy, *The Ancient Wisdom*; Shaw was acquainted both with this book and with the doctrines of the esoteric and eclectic cult founded by Madame Blavatsky. Shotover has many of the attributes of a 'Mahatma' (Act I, p. 95), and his educative relationship with Ellie is very much that of the Master and the *chela* or disciple. Ellie progresses on the path to mystical enlightenment, beyond hope and despair; in this state she can be compared to the initiate in theosophy as described in *The Ancient Wisdom*, beyond desire and the stimulus to action, and liberated from the binding element in Karma. A mystical interpretation of the union of Ellie and the Captain is certainly possible.

Shotover adds to his mystical aspect a Christian moralistic fervour. He is the prophet–preacher of the play, who announces that 'The judgement has come' and warns that 'Courage will not save you' (Act III, p. 179). Shotover is one of the few characters who (unlike Hector) believes in, and names, God. To an extent, he himself incarnates the 'hand of God' and speaks for 'God's way'; but with a hint as well of magical, even diabolical power. The 'vibrations' registered by Mazzini Dunn, who declares the Captain to be 'so fearfully magnetic' (Act II, p. 115), are echoed, farcically, in the superstitious awe with which he is regarded by Billy Dunn. When the burglar sees Shotover he instantly kneels and, as it were, prays to him in an attitude of confession:

> THE BURGLAR [*falling on his knees before the Captain in abject terror*].
> Oh my Good Lord, what have I done?   (Act II, p. 136)

The effect is repeated when the explosions begin in Act III:

> CAPTAIN SHOTOVER. . . . Stand by, all hands, for judgement.
> THE BURGLAR. Oh my Lordy God!   (Act III, p. 178)

Billy Dunn 'recognises' in Shotover the incarnation of divine retribution; and Dunn is characterised by the sureness of his instincts. By contrast with *Mazzini* Dunn, *Billy* is always proved right; and here he accepts not only the pronouncement of judgement, but also that it is he who is destined for punishment.

Billy Dunn maintains that Shotover possesses magical powers to match his mystical aspirations. Those aspirations, embodied in the mind-ray which will replace the dynamite when the Captain has attained the seventh degree of concentration, reach towards the triumph of mind over matter, the spiritualising of the body. Shotover is the precursor of the Ancients in Shaw's next play, *Back to Methuselah*, who attain longevity by an act of will; and significantly the Captain remarks, 'I refuse to die until I have invented the means' (Act I, p. 100). His psychic ray also anticipates the power of the Ancients over matter, and he may be

compared with them in having a strong evolutionary appetite.
Shotover is the embodiment in *Heartbreak House* of the Life Force,
and spokesman for creative evolution. To an extent, Shotover's
evolutionism is Darwinian. When he urges, of navigation, 'Learn
it and live; or leave it and be damned' (Act III, p. 177), the 'laws of
God' which he propounds are those of adaptation to the
environment. But, in so far as this is a matter of 'choosing freely',
the Captain is closer to Lamarck, or to Bergson, than to Darwin.

If Hector identifies Darwinian natural selection with the wrath
of the heavens, Shotover sees in the Zeppelin the 'hand of God',
blending the Christian Day of Judgement with progressive
creative evolution. His God, like that of Mr Britling, is one
striving to become, and is identified with the workings of the
universe. The point is perhaps obscure in the finished play, with
minimal overt allusion; but the draft typescript shows extensive
rewriting of the entire debate between Hector and Shotover in Act
I. In the earlier stages of composition the issues appear more
clearly: here we find Hector more liberal and tolerant, more aware
than Shotover of the difficulty of distinguishing enemy from ally.
Correspondingly, Shotover speaks up even more fiercely for
extermination. It is of course debatable whether we see, in these
deletions, the fuller and sharper dialogue 'behind' the allusive
texture of the final version, or features which were rejected or
improved upon in rewriting. A comparison is, nevertheless,
illuminating.

We find in the typescript a revealing deletion in one of
Shotover's speeches: 'What then is to be done? Are we to ⟨work
hand in hand with God for raising of our kind to the planes of
heaven, or to⟩ be kept for ever. . . .'[21] What is more easily
discerned here is that, unlike Hector, whose alternatives were
both negative, Shotover sees purpose, and the possibility of
progress; moreover the positive he envisages is the progress of
creative evolution, expressed in religious terms. To work 'hand in
hand with God' *is* creative evolution. Even though the clause was
deleted at an early stage, the final version of the play retains an
echo, or transmutation of it, in the 'hand of God'. And it seems to
me that, even if Shotover's dynamite is 'wasted' by the explosion,
the play endorses and enacts his aims. What happens in the play,
in so far as it is at all conclusive, ratifies the implied 'either' of
Shotover's alternatives. Events show the hand of God, and of
creative evolution, in the co-incidence of the bomb and the

dynamite. What I am getting at is that Shotover's eccentric quest for the seventh degree of concentration, and the bomb that falls in his gravel-pit, are not discrete concepts of retribution. The Zeppelin identifies and locates the 'real' Enemy, and its 'judgement' coincides with Shotover's.

It must, however, be recognised that the triumph envisaged by Shotover is violent, and that his God is a destructive process. Shotover longs for the God-like power over life and death: the mind-ray which will replace the dynamite is the ultimate weapon, total power. Shotover's leanings towards violence, and his propensity for extermination, are also both clearer in deleted passages from the draft. Extermination was expressed as direct physical violence: 'Shall we not wring their necks?'[22] And, when Hector forced on the Captain the ultimate decision of killing his own daughter Ariadne if she proved to be the Enemy, he replied, 'When my dynamite is so perfected I shall ask you to spare a father's feelings and kill her for me.'[23] The revisions tone down Shotover's violence. Nevertheless, the Captain combines compassion with savagery, and remains the focus of violence in what is, after all, an extremely violent play.

The constant undertow of undirected anger in *Heartbreak House* is focused from time to time in direct emotional or psychical assault, as Ellie tortures Mangan by hypnosis, Hesione indulges in cruel flirtation, and Ariadne reduces Randall Utterword to tears. Hector shakes his fist at the heavens in rage and guilt, and Shotover means to 'blow up the human race if it goes too far' (Act I, p. 95). In a sense the suppressed anger and violence 'explode' in a moral catharsis (or incomplete catharsis) at the end of the play. It is as if the destructive energy generated during the action were concentrated in the final explosion, a total theatre which commands the participation of actors and audience in its terror and elation. The explosions, we might note, were extremely important to Shaw: he always insisted that the theatrical effect be as extreme as possible. One of the last notes he wrote for the final dress rehearsal of the first London production in October 1921 was 'Explosion no good'.[24] The explosions of *Heartbreak House* can be compared with similar catastrophes in other of Shaw's plays; and it is tempting to conclude that he liked to play the vengeful deity with his stage thunderbolts. These explosions are Shaw's own weapons against a wicked and heedless nation: the playwright's reformist zeal blows characters and play to pieces. But there is, too, a more sinister tendency latent in this violence, which will lead towards a totalitarian stance. The associated imagery of destructive weapons – guns and dynamite – can be considered alongside Shaw's confessed fascination with the power of killing at a distance which a gun endows,[25] and his desire to wipe out his enemies by the sheer force of moral hatred.

We must conclude, nevertheless, that Shotover's philosophy of total power does not speak for the play as a whole, nor, consciously at least, for Shaw. The Captain is presented with irony, and oscillates between sagacity and senility. His sermon on navigation is stern Carlylean invective, but it is delivered in the same farcically eccentric manner which the Captain adopted in Act I. In the closing scene he is again decentralised, reverting to a character role: his invective is 'nothing but echoes. The last shot was fired years ago' (Act III, p. 176). At the final curtain he is asleep (he has in fact been dozing for most of Act III). Shotover's position in the final configuration is clarified, it seems to me, by contrast with the new ending which Shaw wrote for a production in 1943. Robert Donat, who was playing Shotover, thought that the existing ending was too negative for wartime. At his request Shaw provided an additional line to follow Ellie's 'I hope so', just before Randall's flute solo brought down the curtain. Shotover now declared, 'Well said, child. They will awaken your country's sleeping soul.'[26]

In the 1943 ending Shotover – the 'country's sleeping soul' – wakes up and comes downstage to join Ellie. Here is a Shotover awake, alert and moralising. Shotover is clearly Ellie's mentor, and *Heartbreak House* becomes his sermon. The raid, and indeed the entire action, is a political exemplum viewed by Shotover and Ellie. The precarious poise and irony of the ending as Shaw first wrote it disappear: the Carlylean voice speaks again, to render the play overtly didactic and even jingoistic. The failure (as it seems to me) of this afterthought is that it closes down *Heartbreak House* to an unambiguous and unironic resolution. In his old age, and for a revival staged when England was in the throes of a Second World War, Shaw *reduces* the play, by a moralistic comment on the final scene. The revised ending highlights the inconclusiveness and also the inclusiveness of the original. *Heartbreak House contains* Captain Shotover: it includes, and goes beyond, the exhortation and the vision of the preacher–prophet. It may be that in 1943 Shaw, then himself virtually the same age as Shotover, identified more closely with the Captain. But Shotover is not the Shavian spokesman (no single character is); he is, to an extent, a surrogate in which the play exorcises the dynamitard in Shaw.

The sense of terminal malaise in the play is also conveyed through the futility of its sexual relationships. A desperate and trivialised sexuality seizes Heartbreak House. In this community bound by futility and sterility, we see people interacting sexually, even while talking economics or politics. But the sexuality of Heartbreak House is what Lawrence calls sex in the head, and is in part at least a Bohemian affectation. One of the major points to apprehend is that there is no central, revitalising act of sexual intercourse for the play: indeed, there is no sex-act at all. At the symbolic centre of all the texts we are looking at in this book is a sexual fulfilment which becomes emblematic of social renewal. The parenthetical intercourse of Helen Schlegel and Leonard Bast produced the infant which was to be England's hope; *Women in Love* hinges on two heterosexual relationships, and perhaps a homosexual love as well; and in *The Waste Land* the typist and the clerk make passionless love in a context of casual sex. No sex-act is directly consummated in *Heartbreak House*; yet the entire action could be said to rest on an assumed framework of attempted seduction; and the play enacts a frustrated, or sublimated, sexual drive.

The situation of the weekend house party itself carries sexual innuendoes, with the implied wealth of opportunity for temporary or permanent matings. All the characters – even the burglar and Nurse Guinness – are involved in marital or extra-marital relationships; and our attention is drawn continually to the abundant sexual possibilities. Act II, in particular, is an extended post-prandial flirtation, between Mangan and Ellie, Mangan and Hesione, Hesione and Mazzini, Ellie and Shotover, and – in one of the many triangles of the play – Hector, Ariadne and Randall. Ellie, Hesione and Ariadne are at the apex of these separate but overlapping triangles. Another way of characterising the action of this part of the play would be to invoke the metaphor of comedy as an extended joke, and of both as a delayed orgasm. The orgasmic climax and release of *Heartbreak House* is achieved in the destructive explosions of Act III: these apart, its sexual drive is frustrated. The universal outcome of the aimless 'fascination' (Hesione's word for it, which was consistently added in longhand at a late stage of revision of the typescript) is what Hector puts bluntly to Randall, speaking of his relationship with his sister-in-law Ariadne: 'when pay-day comes round, she bilks you' (Act II, p. 156).

The emergence of the peculiar sexual ambience of *Heartbreak House* can be discerned in the revisions of the typescript. Shaw made a number of apparently discrete changes which nevertheless hang together in a certain way. He altered the ages of both Ariadne and Randall Utterword, to match more closely those of Hesione and Hector, and thus form a quartet of sexually active (or potentially active) characters. Yet he removed references to Ariadne's precocious sexuality, and to Hesione's thoughtful provision of interconnecting rooms for her and Randall. He also removed, in Act II, Mangan's explicit explanation to Ellie of his sexual need to live close to Hesione Hushabye. Additions, on the other hand, include Hector's obviously sexual description of himself as a 'goat' (Act I, p. 98), and the numerous allusions to the sexual attraction of the 'demon women' (p. 102). Overall we find an intensification of potential, and a reduction of actual, sexual activity. What is going on is an increase in net, unrelieved sexual tension, at the same time as an insistence that sexual flirtation is a silly, cruel game.

It is, moreover, this negative sexuality which is the context for the positive bond contracted by Ellie Dunn and Captain Shotover. This connection between extreme old age and youth is the symbolic centre for *Heartbreak House*. Its positive symbolism has analogues and antecedents in plays by Shaw and other dramatists. But this too is sterile and unproductive, a sexless and childless marriage. It is perhaps not entirely evident from the play that, in choosing Shotover, Ellie rejects sex (although Mangan disparagingly remarks of the Captain 'And him a mummy!' (Act III, p. 168). Shaw stressed, in a letter to Lillah McCarthy, that Ellie is 'born to immaculate virginity';[27] and in the little puppet-play *Shakes versus Shav* (1949), which includes an extract from *Heartbreak House*, he designates Ellie 'THE VIRGIN'. Ellie remains *virgo intacta*, and there is no prospect of her producing a child. As she cries to Hesione, 'You have stolen m y babies' (Act II, p. 126). The significance of her childless spiritual marriage to the eighty-eight-year-old Shotover is emphasised by Lady Utterword's reminder, 'The point for a young woman of your age is a baby' (Act III, p. 174). Yes, indeed: this is the underlying 'point' in the marriages which, conventionally and ritualistically, end comedies. But there will be no baby for *Heartbreak House* (and, for that matter, there is no young man of Ellie's age to father one). We might wish to weigh carefully that phrase 'immaculate virginity', with its echo of the Virgin Mary, immaculately conceived. Ellie may be the Virgin Mother but the 'child' that results from her spiritual marriage is her own reborn self, the offspring and fruit of her union with her 'spiritual husband and second father' (p. 168).

The tension of *Heartbreak House* between a heightened sexual temperature and low sexual activity is overlaid by another feature: the sexual and emotional domination exercised by the 'lovely women'. Despite the philandering of Hector and Randall, it is in fact the women in *Heartbreak House* who hunt down their sexual prey. Inversion of traditional roles is familiar from Ibsen and from Shaw's earlier plays, and is connected not only with sexual politics but also with the idea of the Life Force, the biological imperative of creative evolution incarnate in woman the huntress. But in *Heartbreak House* the sexual predator takes on the character of a castrating goddess (we might compare the Syria Dea of 'Moony', in *Women in Love*). These are the 'devil's granddaughters' (p. 165), the 'Vampire women' (Act I, p. 102) whose attraction, like Shotover's magnetism, is weird and almost diabolical. In *Heartbreak House* the women are totally in control, their men reduced to tears, senile dozing, domestic slavery, even death. 'Is there any slavery on earth viler than this slavery of men to women?' (Act II, p. 156) asks Hector of the audience. The slavery of men to women has reverberations beyond the sexual or emotional: sexual dominance is linked to the play's concern for power in society, and, ultimately, operates as a metaphor for political failure. The inquiry in Act III into the possibility of saving the country is concluded and ironically undercut by Hesione Hushabye:

MRS HUSHABYE. Oh, *I* say it matters very little which of you governs the country so long as we govern you.

HECTOR. We? Who is we, pray?

MRS HUSHABYE. The devil's granddaughters, dear. The lovely women.

HECTOR [*raising his hands as before*]. Fall, I say; and deliver us from the lures of Satan!   (p. 165)

Hector's extravagant despair emphasises the serious issue behind Hesione's flippancy: in the society of *Heartbreak House*, inversion of sexual roles is an image and index of power diverted and perverted, both cause and symptom of the malaise in public life. The men of Heartbreak House are, we might say, symbolically emasculated. Hector's sword is sheathed; Shotover must keep his dynamite in the garden, and be careful not to drop it round the house.

The house itself is a complex and controlling symbol, both parallel and contrastive to the symbol of the ship. It takes in female sexuality, marriage, domesticity, and the conservatism of the status quo. Heartbreak House has passed from Captain Shotover to his daughter: Hesione is its presiding spirit, while her father is dispossessed and 'eccentric', withdrawn from the centre to the garden outside, and the gravel-pit. The argument about ownership of the house is a running gag, cued by Mangan's bewilderment as to whom he is to address as host or hostess. Its climax is Hesione's instinctive and vigorous defence of her property, when in Act III Ellie urges Marcus to 'Set fire to the house': 'My house! No' (p. 179). Ellie's disregard for property, or her active hostility, is a concomitant of her 'liberation': she has rejected the sexual, domestic and maternal roles implied by marriage. Mangan, on the other hand, expressed himself in Act II as ready to think of 'settling down': to him also, under the sway of Hesione's seductiveness, buying a house signifies sexual fulfilment and domestic stability. Hector Hushabye, already caught in a web of domesticity, urges Mangan to leave Heartbreak House while he has the chance, and to leave his chains behind him. Hector is married 'up to the hilt' (Act II, p. 142): a household pet, at home all day.

The house is thus focus for this female-dominated society: in part a symbol of domesticity, in part – paradoxically – the embodiment of the male–capitalist system of property and marriage. Here, in a play where men rather than women are subject to the slavery of marriage, Shaw ironically inverts the prison of Nora in Ibsen's *A Doll's House*. The symbol is, indeed, predominantly social and ironic in its usage here; if Shaw were aware of the 'eternal feminine' which might be invoked, he would not, in this play, endorse it. The house accordingly differs fundamentally from Howards End. Forster asserted the eternal, mystical and passive femininity of Howards End, in contrast to the mundane masculine world of telegrams and anger. The house was bequeathed not according to man-made legal systems of primogeniture, but by a mystical transmission based on female affinity. Margaret's claim was, we might recall, emphatically subversive, in rivalry to the orthodox heir, the eldest son.

The suggestion of a submerged matriarchy in *Howards End* also obtains in *Heartbreak House*. I noted earlier that the men of *Heartbreak House* were emasculated: more exactly, they are *infantilised*. The demon women do more than 'fascinate' them into submission: they reduce them to small children. Ellie has Shotover 'on a string like a Pekinese dog' (Act II, p. 149): he dozes and dreams in second childhood. In a comic version of the torture of Mangan, Ariadne treats Randall as a naughty, petulant baby. And Mangan, blubbering and whimpering, is constantly referred to as a child. When in Act II he wakes from his trance he begins to *'cry like a child'* (p. 128). Shortly afterwards, Hesione calls him 'Little Alf' and 'Alfy' (p. 129). More importantly, it comes to her suddenly 'that you are a real person: that you had a mother, like anyone else'. This is not simply a realisation of Mangan's common humanity, as we see from the climax of the child-motif in the play, which is also the climax of Mangan's futile but perceptive attempt at self-assertion: 'Am I a child or a grown man? I wont stand this mothering tyranny' (Act III, p. 167). The 'mothering tyranny' which Mangan rightly detects at the core of *Heartbreak House* ratifies the iterative imagery of children and babies, and crystallises the quality of the male–female relationships of the play. These are indeed vampire women, whose emotional voracity saps male vitality: 'They can make them love; and they can make them cry' (Act II, p. 154). *Heartbreak House* sets this mothering tyranny alongside the political tyranny of a Mangan or a Hastings Utterword: both are an abuse of power. It sets, too, the castration-anxiety which is the obverse of a mothering tyranny against the political impotence of Hector and Shotover.

In the sexual wasteland of *Heartbreak House* the governing emotional experience is one of heartbreak. In 'heartbreak' the crisis is dramatised in personal terms, and concentrated in the central figures of Ellie Dunn and Boss Mangan. These are the characters who suffer, change and, to an extent, choose. The term 'heartbreak' has complex associations, both for this play and for Shaw's work in general. Its synonyms, here and elsewhere, are 'disillusionment' and 'discouragement', signifying, we might infer, a negative experience. But Shavian irony and paradox are at work here, to indicate the falsity and evil of illusions which sustain outmoded and repressive values, and the consequent importance of dis-illusioning people into a genuine engagement with reality. Thus disillusionment is a painful but educative process, a *rite de passage* from romantic and idealistic adolescence to moral and intellectual maturity. It is only equivocally negative: more precisely, it is a transitional state, of neutral potentiality. Heartbreak or disillusionment, potentially a positive enlightenment, may be realised as actual regeneration. Even in *Heartbreak House*, but more obviously in plays such as *Major Barbara*, the phase of completed, positive disillusionment merges with 'conversion'. 'Conversion' is yet another instance of Shaw's secular adaptation of a familiar religious concept: as it suggests, the realisation is not passive, but the key to committed and purposeful activity. This, in essence, is the difference between Ellie and Mangan, both faced by *Heartbreak House* with the discovery of unpleasant facts, and profound emotional distress. For Ellie, heartbreak can be liberating, and she moves on to fresh activity in the world; while Mangan, trapped within the negative phase of disillusionment, dies.

It is clear, then, that these key words are a kind of shorthand for a process which is essentially moral and educative; and it is important to be alert to the full weight of the terms as they occur, either in the dialogue or, frequently, in stage directions. The shorthand indicates the compression and non-naturalistic nature of this rendering of experience. It should not, however, be inferred that 'heartbreak' is devoid of emotional content or resonance. Just as we need to recognise the degree of active cruelty and violence in *Heartbreak House*, so we must register the intense emotional experience of the characters, and the inclusive quality of heartbreak as unifying motif and plot-dynamic. Shaw retains the terms 'disillusionment' and 'conversion', which he has used earlier: the term 'discouragement', not very prominent here, will be developed and modified in *Back to Methuselah*. But for his impassioned rendering of a whole society in a crisis of moral identity and survival, Shaw deliberately adopts the term 'heartbreak', and exploits to the full its implications of emotional, and societal, breakdown. *Heartbreak House* presents us with a cluster of 'heartbroken imbeciles' (Act III, p. 173).

Ellie Dunn is confronted early in Act I with the true identity of her lover Marcus Darnley. It is a critical dramatic moment and worth quoting in full:

> MRS HUSHABYE [*laying Ellie down at the end of the sofa*]. Now, pettikins, he is gone. Theres nobody but me. You can let yourself go. Dont try to control yourself. Have a good cry.
> ELLIE [*raising her head*]. Damn!
> MRS HUSHABYE. Splendid! Oh, what a relief! I thought you were going to be broken-hearted. Never mind me. Damn him again.
> ELLIE. I am not damning him: I am damning myself for being such a fool. [*Rising*] How could I let myself be taken in so? [*She begins prowling to and fro, her bloom gone, looking curiously older and harder.*]   (p. 84)

To criticise this as psychologically unrealistic is to miss the point entirely. The passage introduces the motif of heartbreak: it compresses dramatically the emotional crisis which will motivate Ellie's behaviour for the remainder of the play, and prepares for the inversion of our expectations of what it means to be 'broken-hearted'. Both the cues provided by Hesione, and Ellie's responses, point out alternatives, in order to emphasise the significance of what occurs. Ellie could indeed, as Hesione urges, break down and cry, paving the way to the romantic melodrama which Hesione anticipates. What she does instead, after a crucial pause, is to raise her head and 'Damn', not Hector, as Hesione thinks, but (by a further reversal) herself.

It is in the space between these two speeches that the play 'selects out' the way Ellie is to proceed, and establishes the mode of her heartbreak. In two speeches, and one perambulation, Ellie moves through a profound emotional crisis. It leaves her '*curiously older and harder*'. The word '*curiously*' signals the compression and non-naturalistic character of the action. The point is farcically reinforced by the Wildean close of this scene:

> MRS HUSHABYE. . . . . I think I hear Hector coming back. You don't mind now, do you, dear?
> ELLIE. Not in the least. I am quite cured.   (p. 85)

We are close, here, to symbolic farce. Before this closing speech, however, the nature of Ellie's experience, and its reversal of conventional expectations, have been further articulated:

> ELLIE [*staring at her thoughtfully*]. Theres something odd about this house, Hesione, and even about you. I dont know why I'm talking to you so calmly. I have a horrible fear that my heart is broken, but that heartbreak is not like what I thought it must be.
>
> MRS HUSHABYE [*fondling her*]. It's only life educating you, pettikins.

The key words, as we shall see later, are '*thoughtfully*' and 'calmly'. Ellie registers the oddness of her heartbreak, Mrs Hushabye its educative nature. *Heartbreak House*, like other of Shaw's plays, confronts its *ingénue* with the economic facts of life in the capitalist system, in addition to romantic disillusionment. Sexual and economic enlightenment are linked to the conventional comedic motif of the heroine's marriage. It is, however, crucial to realise that the plot-question 'Whom will Ellie marry?' is a moral imperative of central force, and intimately related to the end-direction of the play, its search for a normative configuration. Ellie's progress from heartbreak to marriage is dramatised in a series of encounters with potential husbands. Each represents a particular set of values or a philosophy, so that in rejecting or selecting them Ellie 'chooses' the final grouping. Her 'choices' are, as it were, necessary ones, determined by the play's quest for a solution. She 'couldnt marry Mr Mangan' (Act III, p. 169), not simply because she does not love him, nor even because of his infatuation with Hesione, but because he is unacceptable to the solution which the play seeks, and which is symbolically signified by her marriage.

The starting-point, in Act I, is Ellie's engagement to Mangan, motivated by gratitude, and a scenario of distress and rescue. She is in love with 'Marcus Darnley', but the naïveté of her love is suggested by Hesione's sceptical attitude to his romantic origins and exploits. Ellie is also devoted to her father. These three attachments, to father, lover and fiancé, are the preconditions of her subsequent development; and they embody what could be described as a romantic idealism. The play demands that, in waking into reality (she is, significantly, dozing over a copy of

Othello, Shakespeare's 'romantic' tragedy, as Act I begins), Ellie rejects such idealism.

This she does, rapidly, after discovering, first, that 'Marcus' is Hector Hushabye, and married to her friend Hesione; and, secondly, that her gratitude is misdirected, as Mangan is her exploiter rather than her benefactor. Ellie reacts from romantic idealism into a pragmatic materialism indicated by her determination to marry Mangan for his money. In yet a further reaction, she is apparently converted from materialism to Shotover's spirituality. The scene with Shotover towards the end of Act II effects a double reversal. First, the Captain detaches Ellie from her obsession with money, and so prepares her to switch her dependency to a fresh object. Secondly, however, her new anchor of security is taken from her. She had substituted Mangan's money for Hector's love, and then, under Shotover's tutelage, replaced his money with the soul. Ellie now arrives at the nadir of her disillusionment, when Shotover's 'spirit' turns out to be rum. She is *'frightfully disillusioned'* (Act II, p. 147). Nevertheless she sticks to her resolve, announcing in Act III the result of her confrontations with Mangan and the Captain in the previous Act: she has chosen Shotover. Finally, she expresses renewed faith in the 'reality' of her father and Shakespeare: we might, in fact, conclude that Ellie's quest has after all been for a father and mentor, rather than a husband.

To characterise Ellie's development in this way is to stress its representative, end-directed quality, and to minimise the emotional content. Nevertheless, Ellie *is* heartbroken. Although the play rejects Hector as potential husband early on, Ellie's emotional distress is felt throughout the play. Her state of shock is manifest in a numb indifference, alternating with occasional outbursts of anger. Ellie's detachment and calm acceptance of Mangan's revelations baffle him; but she has withdrawn emotionally; and during Act II a nervous lethargy overcomes her, punctuated with displays of energy and hard business-sense. By the time of her crucial scene with Shotover, Ellie has undergone a fragmentation of response, and her consciousness focuses on two obsessions. The first, her disappointed love, produces an emotional anaesthesia and listless serenity; the second, a complementary absorption with money, raises her to acute alertness. With Shotover, Ellie succumbs to the weary dreaminess which has been growing on her.

The insistence, in dialogue and stage directions, on Ellie's *'strangely calm'* (Act II, p. 140) and *'serene'* (p. 111) detachment, *'utterly indifferent'* (p. 121) to what happens, has occult and even mystical connotations. She can hypnotise Mangan; and she is, for much of the action, in a trance-like condition. Shaw wrote, for the French translation of the play, that after Mangan wakes from *his* trance she must be increasingly *'rêveuse'*:[28] his direction emphasises the meditative state into which Ellie has passed. We may recall at this point the quasi-mystical nature of her relationship with Shotover; and note that in their scene together they jointly redefine 'heartbreak':

> CAPTAIN SHOTOVER. Heartbreak? Are you one of those who are so sufficient to themselves that they are only happy when they are stripped of everything, even of hope?
> ELLIE [*gripping the hand*]. It seems so; for I feel now as if there was nothing I could not do, because I want nothing.
> CAPTAIN SHOTOVER. Thats the only real strength. Thats genius. Thats better than rum.   (p. 148)

This is the state beyond hope and despair, in which the self is liberated from earthly desire. Ellie's heartbreak is synonymous with her progress towards mystical enlightenment. She is, moreover, a visionary figure, and the suffering and articulating centre of heartbreak in the play. She encompasses the experience as it affects other characters, and can verbalise what in others may be an inarticulate cry. So she describes what is the matter with Mangan, in an en-tranced utterance:

> ELLIE [*in a strangely calm voice, staring into an imaginary distance*]. His heart is breaking: that is all. . . . It is a curious sensation: the sort of pain that goes mercifully beyond our powers of feeling. When your heart is broken, your boats are burned: nothing matters any more. It is the end of happiness and the beginning of peace.   (p. 140)

In a sense, *Heartbreak House* is the vision of Ellie Dunn.[29]

Mangan's heart is broken by the seductive wiles of the siren Hesione Hushabye; but there is good reason for his disintegration (in contrast to Mazzini Dunn, who can resist her charms). Mangan has no core of identity: his 'self' persists only as a carefully maintained fiction. Crucial to the survival of his personality is his 'reputation', against the supportive backcloth of the City where he is made much of, and to which he wishes to return. The turning-point for him is the hypnotic trance which binds him to the chair, a mute and helpless victim, while he is discussed by Ellie and Hesione, and then Hesione and Mazzini. Mangan's self-confidence has rested on an *'entirely imaginary dignity'* (Act I, p. 86): during his trance that confidence is destroyed. He awakens to a consciousness of the opinion others hold of him. In the City he can maintain self-respect, but in Heartbreak House he knows he is a fool. The experience is fatal, as Mangan is left with nothing to replace the illusions which, although false, were necessary to sustain existence. The insecurity and poverty of Mangan's inner life have been mercilessly exposed, partly through his own compulsion to tell the truth. His decision to tell Ellie the story of her father's ruin set in motion a gradual stripping away of the images which were his defence. Mangan is not killed off merely because he is a capitalist: he dies because there was no 'man under the pose'. Quite simply, there is nothing left of him.

But this is not to say that Mangan cannot suffer. His suffering is indeed only too apparent and audible, in the continual choric accompaniment of sniffs, sobs, wails and howls. Shotover describes him as a 'soul in torment' (Act II, p. 129) and the torment is heard in *'something like a yell of despair'*. Hesione will lead him away *'writhing but yielding'* (p. 140), and, appropriately enough, *'emotion chokes him'* (Act III, p. 169): a love death, indeed. Mangan has, after all, a heart to be broken, as Hesione discovers: 'you have a heart, Alfy, a whimpering little heart, but a real one' (Act II, p. 129). Two points may be stressed here: the active cruelty with which his heart is broken; and the reverberation of his suffering in the play as a whole, its significance for *Heartbreak House*.

When, unable to contain himself any longer, Mangan tears off his clothes, he farcically but desperately registers both the pervasive moral heartbreak and the approaching nemesis: 'Weve stripped ourselves morally naked: well, let us strip ourselves physically naked as well, and see how we like it. I tell you I cant bear this' (Act III, p. 166). The unmistakable echo of *King Lear* in this *coup de théâtre* should make us pause. Parallels with Shakespeare's tragedy are noticeable at many points in the play, but we

might expect to find the closest comparison between Lear and
Shotover. Here, the comparison is with Mangan (and perhaps
earlier, too, when in Act II Mangan tried to escape from the house
out onto the heath beyond). This in itself points to the centrality of
Mangan not only as comic butt for *Heartbreak House*, but also as a
potentially tragic figure and sacrificial victim. To say this is not
simply to reassess the character of Mangan, but to admit a degree
of tragic weight and inevitability in the way in which the action
directs him to his end. Mangan dies because he stays in
Heartbreak House: he might have survived, had he fulfilled his
aim of leaving, and going back to the City. He remains in the
house because dramatic fate, and the other characters, trap him
there.

The motif of escape is introduced early on. Almost as soon as he
enters, Mangan feels he 'ought to walk out of this house' (Act I,
p. 89). In Act II he announces, 'I'm going' (p. 130). At this
juncture the other characters gather on stage, each successive
entry intensifying the claustrophobic tension. Taunting and
hounding him, their ridicule and mock assistance paralyse him.
At the climax of the sequence the tension is snapped by a
pistol-shot offstage, and the burglar interrupts to thwart, dramatically, Mangan's chance of escape. During this interlude Mangan
broods over his position in the house; and after the burglar exits
Mangan is also led out, weeping, the victim prepared for sacrifice.

This sequence is closely paralleled in Act III. Mangan's
revelation of his political career is greeted by choruses of howling
scorn. He decides to go back to the City, but is verbally battered
into submission, and into staying:

MRS HUSHABYE. Goodbye, Alf. Think of us sometimes in the city.
    Think of Ellie's youth!
ELLIE. Think of Hesione's eyes and hair!
CAPTAIN SHOTOVER. Think of this garden in which you are not a
    dog barking to keep the truth out!
HECTOR. Think of Lady Utterword's beauty! her good sense!
    her style!
LADY UTTERWORD. Flatterer. Think, Mr Mangan, whether you
    can really do any better for yourself elsewhere: that is the
    essential point, isn't it?
MANGAN [*surrendering*]. All right: all right. I'm done. Have it your
    own way.   (p. 167)

Mangan's desire to placate his tormentors assigns to them a position rather like that of cultured Furies. The highly stylised sequences, marked by extreme energy and tension, are a ritualistic hounding of Mangan which imprison him, fatally, in the house which breaks hearts. And Mangan's imminent demise focuses the inevitability of the nemesis which threatens to overtake the whole community. The tragic pulse of the action is measured in the degradation of its comic butt: Mangan stands, or cringes, at the centre of the sickness, and all the heartbreak is concentrated in him. Mangan's death makes of him a scapegoat for society: he atones, an unwilling and ignoble saviour. The action of *Heartbreak House* culminates in a ritual sacrifice to avert the wrath of the gods. By Mangan's death the inhabitants of Heartbreak House gain a reprieve; but, as Hector grimly reminds them, 'Our turn next' (Act III, p. 180).

The effect of Mangan's fatal heartbreak is similar to the death of Leonard Bast, and even closer to that of Gerald Crich. Each of these characters is an outsider expelled by a consolidating group, and their removal seals the final configuration. It seems, however, that they cannot be dismissed *simply*: they are sufficiently important to the text – which strives to eject them – to operate as a centre of disturbance. Another way of putting this is to say that it is precisely because they are in some sense the Enemy that the text expels them with such force. However, the crisis which each focuses is not resolved by their expulsion, and the catharsis is incomplete. And Mangan, at least, is 'feeble' to the end: his undignified scuffle towards death in the gravel-pit ultimately precludes tragic stature.

Heartbreak is not confined to Ellie Dunn and Mangan. During the play it becomes clear that this is a general malaise, endemic to the house. The disease which afflicts the inhabitants has as a symptom the aimless pursuit of happiness in the face of heartbreak. Visitors are drawn into the web: those who enter the house are variously disconcerted, disillusioned, discouraged and heartbroken. The entry of each is marked by a slight disorientation, a sort of preliminary disillusionment as overture to the main action. Things surprise them, disagreeably. They are either not received, not recognised, or not expected. Ellie is upset 'to find that nobody expects me' (Act I, p. 62). Mangan is thrown off balance, first '*staggered*' (p. 87) and then '*irritated*' (p. 88) by the Captain's blunt criticism, but soon '*weakening*', and protesting but '*feebly*' (p. 89).

Lady Utterword, on the point of weeping, is 'really very much hurt and annoyed and disillusioned' (p. 66). Mazzini Dunn is '*dazed*' (p. 86) by Shotover's description of him as a drunkard.

These comic shocks break the characters in to the strangeness of the house and render them vulnerable to what is to happen later, when the currency of their ideas about themselves will be debased. We find a comic equivalent of Mangan's torment at the hands of Hesione in Randall Utterword, whose heart is broken regularly by Ariadne: 'It is a change from having his head shampooed' (Act III, p. 174). Randall's sobs are comically pathetic, but the very normality of the event in the pattern of his relationship with Ariadne is a horrifying example of mothering tyranny. Randall sees himself as potentially cuckolded by Hector, and has a 'rooted delusion' (Act II, p. 153), that he is Ariadne's husband. He is doubly miserable in his infatuation and jealousy: he shares with Hector the humiliation of the enslaved 'husband', but can claim no conjugal rights in return.

The Utterwords – Ariadne and Randall – and Hushabyes form a sexual quartet of shifting and aimless liaisons, compensating in extra-marital adventures for conjugal boredom. Heartbreak is a matter of habit for Hector and Hesione. They were 'frightfully in love' (Act I, p. 98) but the 'enchanting dream' has now faded. Each turns elsewhere, Hector to philandering, Hesione to match-making and flirtation. Hector's marriage drew him into Heart-break House, where he is now a 'damned soul in hell' (Act II, p. 142): Hesione has used him up and left him an empty *poseur*. He identifies with Randall's humiliation, and despises his own continued sexual bondage. But his heartbreak is itself a pose, and the shallowness of his erotic adventurism is evident. Hesione is also given to self-dramatisation. Yet her gay cynicism, the 'coaxing and kissing' and 'laughing' (Act II, p. 123) appropriate to the amorous hostess of a Bohemian household is a mask, to cover anguish at a cruel and damnable world. For both Hector and Hesione, disillusionment has gone deep.

Ariadne married specifically to escape from the household. On her return she succumbs to disillusion, paradoxically because of her apparent coldness. Her secret is that she 'has never been in love in her life' (Act I, p. 98); and her obsession with this deficiency is a driving force below the surface of her cool sophistication. She interprets Ellie's account of heartbreak as an ironic criticism directed against her, breaks down, and makes a scene. Shotover explains that her very fear that she has no heart to break indicates some capacity of emotion; and in fact Ariadne comes very close to heartbreak as her homecoming strips away defences she has built up during her absence. In Act III we find her *'heart torn'* (p. 171), and she realises that the house 'wants to break my heart too. But it shan't. I have left you and it behind' (p. 172). But she recovers from her relapse, and will rejoin her husband.

However, Ariadne's 'scene' also reveals the secret of Shotover's heartbreak. When she breaks down in Act II Ariadne turns to her 'Papa', who comforts her with grim tenderness, in what amounts to a recognition and reconciliation scene. We discover later that Shotover's wilful non-recognition of his daughter was a way of coping with the rejection implicit in her leaving the house as a young girl: 'Was there no heartbreak in that for your father?' (Act III, p. 172). The Captain's 'old wounds', like those of King Lear, are the scars of filial ingratitude; both feel 'How sharper than a serpent's tooth it is / To have a thankless child.'[30] (In the draft typescript Shotover refers to Ariadne as a 'thankless girl',[31] in what seems to be a verbal echo of *Lear*.) Shotover's disillusionment extends further than this, however. He 'cannot bear men and women', and runs in and out because 'It confuses me to be answered. It discourages me' (Act II, p. 145). Shotover cannot bear what he sees of sex in society, his 'daughters and their men living foolish lives of romance and sentiment and snobbery' (p. 146). His *confusion* and *discouragement* signify a profound heartbreak: we recall that the Elderly Gentleman in *Back to Methuselah*, caught between present irresponsibility and the perception of evolution towards greater maturity for the world, dies of discouragement.

The malaise of heartbreak pervades the action of *Heartbreak House*, to become the enveloping experience of the play. In an article written to explain the play to a bewildered public at the time of the first English production, Shaw described the expansive effect of the motif: 'the heartbreak begins, and gets worse until the house breaks out through the windows, and becomes all England with all England's heart broken'.[32] In naming 'Heartbreak House' in Act III of the play, Ellie proposes a dramatic metaphor for the community, token of a disillusioned society. Her visionary articulation of *heartbreak* voices, too, the symbolic significance of the house, and gives the play its title.[33]

Heartbreak is, then, the prevailing condition of existence in the

play; yet one character remains curiously heart-whole. Mazzini
Dunn confronts Heartbreak House with equanimity: he resists
Hesione's blandishments, and is quite at ease in his pyjamas and
dressing-gown. This resilience does not stem from heartlessness:
as Mazzini explains to Hesione, she cannot reach him because he
has been 'in love really: the sort of love that only happens once'
(Act II, p. 119). This was the marriage which produced the
love-child Ellie, to whom he is devoted. It was, as Hesione wittily
remarked, a 'safety match' (p. 120). Her witticism takes us back
to the imagery of salvation with which we began: Mazzini's
marriage, she implies, guaranteed fidelity because he could be
sexually fired by only one woman. But Mazzini's safety goes
beyond this. He is comfortable in his pyjamas because, in direct
contrast to Mangan, he has an inner security which renders him
invulnerable to Heartbreak House, and impervious to Hesione's
attempts at fascination.

Hesione, the demon enchantress who bewitches men, is a
variant of the siren Kundry in Wagner's *Parsifal*, mentioned in the
Preface to the play. Heartbreak House is itself a 'palace of evil
enchantment' (p. 22) of the kind to which Hesione–Kundry
belongs. Wagner's opera, like the Grail legend which is its source,
is a quest for salvation, in which the blighted land is to be saved by
the holy knight Parsifal. Mazzini Dunn is the Parsifal of *Heartbreak
House*, and yet another saviour *manqué*. In the draft typescript of
Act III there is a crucial sequence of dialogue, deleted in the final
version, which introduces the motif of the blessed fool, names him
as Parsifal, and equates Parsifal with Mazzini Dunn.[34] This
variation from the published play begins after Hector announces,
'We are all fools' (p. 170). Ellie claims that she would marry
Mangan if he were only a fool, and adds that 'Parsifal was a fool'.
The contrast here between Mangan, the 'practical business' man,
and Parsifal, the blessed innocent, is explicit and absolute. Mrs
Hushabye claims that she or Ariadne 'could have put Parsifal in
our pocket in ten minutes'; but her sexual boast is refuted by Ellie:
'Then there would have been no Parsifal. Parsifal is only the name
of the man you could not put in your pocket.' At this point
Mazzini emerges from the house, in his dressing-gown: Hesione
cries (a late, handwritten addition to the typescript), 'Oh! here is
Parsifal: the only man who ever resisted me.' The entire motif was
reworked and developed in the typescript, and retained at least
in part in the first rough proof: it was removed completely only at

the last stage of revision. Its excision suppresses a distinct dimension of salvation, which would have given Mazzini Dunn potential heroic stature. As Ellie said, her father might have done very well, and there might after all have been a saviour for *Heartbreak House*. Vestiges of Parsifal remain, I think, in Mazzini's innocence, his faith in humanity, and his belief in Providence: perhaps, also, in the constant wrongness of his judgements. In another ending, or another mode of salvation, Mazzini–Parsifal might have *learnt* from his mistakes: 'I was quite wrong, after all' (Act III, p. 181). In suppressing this motif, Shaw opted for the Wagner of the *Götterdämmerung* rather than of *Parsifal*, and for Armageddon–apocalypse rather than the healing quest of the Holy Grail. Had he opted for the latter, *Heartbreak House* would connect more clearly with the quest of *The Waste Land*; and we could see in Shotover, the sea-captain with his 'old wounds', the maimed Fisher King of a barren and ailing community.

The heartbreak culminates, and the play draws to a close, in a night of love and death, a *Götterdämmerung* which is also the Judgement. Ariadne opens this final Act with her exclamation, 'What a lovely night! It seems made for us' (p. 158). The 'lovely night' is the night of love familiar from literary tradition, and it will be consummated in the spiritual marriage of Ellie and Shotover, as well as the love death of Mangan. Hesione leads Mangan out to starlight and romance, 'like the night in Tristan and Isolde' (Act II, p. 140). Ellie's marriage, the only union achieved by the play, is, as we have seen, shot through with ironies. On one hand, Ellie displays positive strength, and reinterprets with more mature understanding her former vision. But, whatever the positive signification of this marriage, it shares the sterility of the relationships which surround it; and Ellie's dreaminess is really very like Shotover's encroaching senility, just as it is hard to distinguish between her courage and the sensationalism of Hector and Hesione. The ambiguity is most acute, and most intractable, in the final speech, in which Ellie voices her radiant hope at the prospective return of the Zeppelin. However, something of this difficulty, of determining what is to be understood as affirmative, and what as negative, is found at the beginning of Act III in the speech (which Ellie herself claims not to understand): 'In the night there is peace for the old and hope for the young' (p. 158). 'Peace' may be the Nirvana of the mystic or, for Shotover, the luxuriance of decay. The 'hope' which comes to Ellie is a Nietzschean joy in destruction: her beatific vision is the 'magnificent' Zeppelin.

It is both relevant and important to try to make sense of Ellie's development, her marriage to Shotover, and indeed that difficult final speech. But such an inquiry can, it seems to me, only confirm, both from internal and external evidence, that a single unironic reading of *Heartbreak House* is not possible: nor, indeed, would such a reading do justice to the play. *Heartbreak House* resists simple closure, or a consoling solution: the inconclusive and disturbing effect derives from a diffusion of preoccupations and sympathies. The 'stories' of the group, and of Ellie, are discrete, and preclude a single focus on any one character or subgroup of characters. And Shaw is, it seems, divided in his sympathies: he hesitates to let the bomb drop on anyone except Mangan and the burglar, and the play fails either to affirm or to destroy. Its several modes of rendering and dealing with crisis do not cohere. The result is disequilibrium: the play refuses to resolve; it remains in crisis. There is, nevertheless, a pressure to 'end' the uncertainties. Our attempt, as audience or critics, to close the open texture of *Heartbreak House* is understandable (such dis-closure is uncomfortable); but it is unrealisable within the text, which holds in tension contradictory impulses. In such an attempt, however, our end-anxiety merges with that of the play.

Nevertheless, the action of *Heartbreak House* does reach towards that final tableau: the Captain asleep, Ariadne in her hammock, Mazzini and Hector seated in safety once more, Ellie and Hesione in each other's arms, Randall accompanying them on his flute. Integrated in this configuration even in their absence are Mangan and the burglar, lying dead offstage. If the play succeeds at all, that final grouping must be its entire point; moreover, as I have suggested, it must be grasped as an entirety. The night of love and death enfolds all the characters, gathered in the garden on that fine, moonless night to await the Judgement which descends on all. Ellie's marriage-night is, significantly, 'made in heaven' (p. 169): a heavenly night of Judgement which is, as Ariadne says, 'made for us'. The 'judgement has come' (p. 179), and 'all hands' (p. 178) are to stand by.

With the arrival of Judgement, *Heartbreak House* becomes cosmic, apocalyptic and eschatological, invoking imagery and myth ranging from Armageddon to the thunderbolt of Zeus. The immensity of the cataclysm is undoubted, even though it fades into anticlimax: the tension increases, following Shotover's pronouncement, until *'A terrific explosion shakes the earth'* (p. 180). That explosion could be said to reverberate in a number of modern literary texts, including *The Waste Land*. The 'Falling towers' (*Waste Land*, 373) are here those of the established church: the rectory is 'nothing but a heap of bricks' (p. 177), with which we might compare the 'heap of broken images' in *The Waste Land* (22). The *'terrific explosion'* of *Heartbreak House* is, moreover, not unique for Shaw. Several of his earlier plays 'tested' the characters by placing them in extreme situations; and increasingly, after *Heartbreak House*, catastrophe looms, although usually averted. The Day of Judgement, frequently an implicit motif, is used explicitly in the late play *The Simpleton of the Unexpected Isles*, subtitled 'A Vision of Judgement'. Both Judgements are selective and inconclusive: some characters are eliminated (in *Simpleton* they just vanish), others reprieved. We do not quite know what will happen 'next'. This inconclusiveness is central to the purpose of promoting a continuing process of evaluation: the playwright withdraws from final judgement because he is using the concept as a persuasive device. Shaw's Judgement is moralistic as well as apocalyptic: like Carlyle, he threatens society with Armageddon, but offers a consoling vision of the millennium. However, in *Heartbreak House* that vision is barely discernible.

Unlike *The Simpleton of the Unexpected Isles*, *Heartbreak House* is pervaded by a deep sense of crisis and impending doom. The extravaganza of *Simpleton* is intellectual fantasy; but *Heartbreak House* has its dramatic life not primarily in the intellect but in the imagination, and its meaning is articulated not only in dramatic dialectic but also in mood. The mood of the play, dark, mysterious, savage and poignant, expresses both regret at the passing of an era, and bewilderment in the face of the darkness beyond. Heartbreak House is the diminishing or crumbling centre of civilisation. Outside, unseen, lies the heath. Above is the night sky: below, the 'pit'. In Act III the figures move in and out of the illumination of an artificial moon, the *'circle of light cast by the electric arc'* (p. 158); and behind them lies *'the gloom'*. The burglar disappears *'into the gloom'* (p. 178), and Hesione emerges *'panting from the darkness'*. The dramatic experience is compressed and concentrated into stark contrasts of light and darkness, noise and

silence.[35] The sense of foreboding is acute. Survival in Heartbreak
House is precarious and in doubt: the walls still stand, but the
glass is shattered. Perhaps the most poignant expression of
fragility and near-despair is Hector's statement of blind, futile
and helpless self-destruction: 'We of this house are only moths
flying into the candle' (p. 180).

A little earlier (p. 174), Hector has asked, 'How is all this going
to end?' He asks it, '*impatiently*', for the audience as well as for
himself; and his question has a double reference: 'all this' is both
the play, and the crisis which the play enacts. From this point
until the final curtain we find a punning interweaving of the two
senses of 'ending'. *Heartbreak House* is eschatological, 'so end-of-
the-world', as Lawrence wrote of *Women in Love*. It is also
self-conscious of its own dramatic closure, and thereby of its status
as a theatrical fiction, and a performance. The double awareness
is particularly apt for a play which is so deeply immersed in the
world outside the theatre, and which focuses the function of the
drama as 'image of that horror'.

The 'ending' of *Heartbreak House* consists of several distinct
sequences, bounded by heavily marked punctuation points in the
dialogue or stage business. At each stage, the characters adopt
characteristic and representative positions, as they first discuss
what they expect to happen, then respond to what actually
happens, and finally assess for themselves and us what *has*
happened. The first of these sequences is preoccupied with
answering Hector's question, and takes us as far as the 'answer'
given when '*A dull distant explosion is heard*' (p. 177). Various
predictions are offered: something may happen, or nothing may
happen. Mazzini Dunn believes the latter, and proves wrong.
Shotover warns of a smash, and Hector hopes for one. Lady
Utterword believes that Hastings (not Providence) has everything under control; and she points us in a different direction,
towards the conventional ending of a comedy, in her remark
about the point of Ellie having a baby.

A second sequence runs from the distant explosion as far as the
third and major explosion. This deals not only with the characters' expectations, but with how each reacts to imminent catastrophe. Ariadne and Ellie refuse to take cover in the cellars,
choosing for different reasons to remain 'on deck'. All the
characters, in fact, 'Stand by . . . for judgement' (p. 178), except
for Mangan and the burglar. These two, marked down for

Judgement, are those who run away and hide. Increasingly, as we proceed towards the end of the play, we are ourselves involved in judgement, invited to choose between the alternative responses. There is, for example, the compassion of Mazzini, who expects that Mangan will survive, hopes he is safe, and even sympathises with the 'risk those poor fellows up there are running' (p. 180). The text forces us, it seems to me, to give a verdict on this redefinition of the Enemy as 'those poor fellows': Nurse Guinness retorts instantly, 'Think of them, indeed, the murdering black-guards.'

Similarly, the characters display differing responses to the '*terrific explosion*', and in doing so present alternative assessments of its meaning and significance. Mazzini Dunn, to whom all human pain matters, asks undiscriminatingly, 'Is anyone hurt?' Hector's concern is solely that the bomb hit the right target. And Nurse Guinness challenges our response most sharply, answering Hector's question 'Where did it fall?', '[*in hideous triumph*] Right in the gravel pit: I seen it. Serve un right!' This is punitive and moralistic, but with a '*hideous triumph*' that celebrates primitive revenge. It is set against Mazzini's lament, 'Oh, poor Mangan!' But Guinness's savagery is of a piece with Shotover's attitude; and, while she directed Billy Dunn (who has been revealed as her long-lost husband) to the gravel-pit, Shotover's dynamite drew Mangan there. Both celebrate death, and both are instruments or agents of a harsh law of retribution. We must choose, invidiously, between compassion and revenge.

This takes us to the final sequence, after the Zeppelin. The survivors '*wait in silence and intense expectation*' for a further explosion, but the danger is over. Again, responses vary: the safety is, however, generally unwelcome. And the play closes with the hope of a repeat performance:

> MRS HUSHABYE. But what a glorious experience! I hope theyll come again tomorrow night.
> ELLIE [*radiant at the prospect*]. Oh, I hope so. (p. 181)

These final speeches are the most notoriously 'difficult' of the play: they are a distillation of its teasing ambiguity. Critics have variously read them as a vindication of Ellie's unsentimental and radical courage, or as an indictment of her surrender to sensation-alism. The divergence of readings rests on whether Ellie is much the same as Hesione, or really very different. It may well seem perverse to distinguish between Ellie and Hesione at this point. They have, after all, thrown themselves into each other's arms in wild excitement, and they *'hold each other's hand tight'* (p. 180). The text does not separate them: in the final tableau Ellie is physically closer to Hesione than to Shotover, and both hope for a repeat of the experience which has left them elated. To discriminate between the quality and significance of their respective hopes may well be to strain both the text, and the actors' subtlety.

What we have here is, I think, a very real difficulty. Quite clearly, the text does not here choose between Ellie and Hesione: the verdict, if there is to be one, is left open. On the other hand, the pattern we have noted in the earlier sequences of morally contrasted responses directs the audience towards making a judgement. The difficulty, then, is that of *Heartbreak House* as a whole: its striving for meaning, but its 'failure' to find a final unambiguous configuration. It is not normative, and it does not 'close'. *Heartbreak House* is end-directed in a particular sense: not only is the destination not reached, but it is not fully or clearly articulated. The 'ending' can, and does, contain, and permit, either view of Ellie.

Nevertheless, Ellie's stance *is* finally integrated with that of the play: this is a held radiance, an arrested expectation that life 'must come to a point sometime' (p. 174), and we leave Ellie waiting for that point. The difference between Ellie and her father before the explosion was that, whereas Mazzini expected nothing to happen, Ellie was 'always expecting something'. That, it seems, is her position: one of unfulfilled, but undefeated, expectancy. We might say, after all, that Ellie is indeed expectant, and pregnant with the future of *Heartbreak House*. But this is not to suggest a simple optimism: Ellie's 'hope' accords with the experience articulated by the ending of the play, which is indeed one of *'intense expectation'*. The maintained tension of *Heartbreak House* is impatient for finality, but with the emphasis on waiting, on *'intense expectation'*, and the continuing poise of 'hope'.

This is not, in fact, quite the end of the play. Randall Utterword *'at last succeeds in keeping the home fires burning on his flute'* (p. 181). That final success is ambiguous. Ivor Novello's enormously popular song 'Keep the Home Fires Burning' was written in 1914, when it expressed a patriotic concern for the stable continuity of life at home, to be kept safely for the men returning from the

Front. As the war went on, Zeppelin raids gave it the double meaning which Nurse Guinness points out with grim irony: 'T h e y l l keep the home fires burning for us: them up there' (p. 179). *Heartbreak House* exploits the bitter ambiguity of the song, in dialogue and action. It is Lady Utterword, determined to maintain home and Empire, who instructs Randall to play the tune: her understanding of the title is that of 1914. Hector, on the other hand, feels 'We should be blazing to the skies'; and Ellie, taking him at his word, urges that he set fire to the house. She is fired, *'tense with excitement'* at the prospect of setting light to the household, keeping the home fires burning. Hesione, as was noted earlier, will have no such thing.

The title of the song has a further relevance to the ending of the play: *Heartbreak House* wishes to keep the home fires burning in both the conserving and the destructive senses. And, like the song, the play is waiting, and keeping on. The linguistic feature of the present participle, and the images chosen – *'burning'*, *'keeping'*, 'blazing' and *'falling'* – express the continuous present of the play. This continuous present anticipates the mode of crisis which we shall find in *The Waste Land*. There, as we shall see, crisis persists ('London Bridge is falling down falling down falling down' – 426; 'Burning burning burning burning' – 308), and apocalypse may be repeated. Here, in Hesione's hope that 'theyll come again tomorrow night' (p. 181), we have a final pun on the twin connotations of ending, this time with a glance both at the audience, and at the apocalypse they have witnessed. The play ends but does not end: it can keep on happening, 'tomorrow night'.

There is a postscript to the continuous present of this un-resolved ending. In 1920 Shaw sent to Hugo Vallentin some ink sketches he had drawn of proposed stage settings of each Act of *Heartbreak House*. For Acts i and ii he gave a straightforward ground-plan; but for the final Act he drew what appears to be an unrealisable backcloth, which he entitles 'View of Act iii'.[36] The drawing conflates the action of the first two Acts, as Shaw's scribbled note admits. The panorama as viewed from the house is not, as a matter of fact, the way Act iii is usually played: moreover, that Act definitely takes place at night. This little drawing highlights the iconography of *Heartbreak House*, in its diagramma-tic but emblematic simplicity: there is the flagstaff, Shotover's observatory, the hammock, the church-steeple, and so on. But the drawing exhibits a curious 'simultaneity' of discrete temporal events: the sun is still in the sky, setting over the horizon of the South Downs; but the Zeppelin already approaches. This is a spatial representation of images which in the play are experienced as a linear sequence, in time. In Shaw's sketch duration collapses, directing us once again to the continuous present in which the ending of the play operates. For *Heartbreak House* the Zeppelin is forever approaching, the sun forever about to set. Apocalypse is imminent but withheld, and Judgement suspended.

4 *Women in Love*

'Or perhaps there was no end'

To say that *Women in Love* is a fiction of the Great War is not, after all, so extraordinary. Lawrence saw the book that way, at least by 1920:

> it is a novel which took its final shape in the midst of the period of war, though it does not concern the war itself. I should wish the time to remain unfixed, so that the bitterness of the war may be taken for granted in the characters.[1]

As this suggests, the book has its roots in the pre-war period: it formed part of the mass of material which was split and reformed to produce the two novels *The Rainbow* and *Women in Love*. The major rewriting was done in the spring and summer of 1916; in the latter months of 1916 Lawrence again rewrote the novel and worked on the typescript, which was more or less complete by the end of 1917.[2] Like *Heartbreak House*, then, *Women in Love* is a product of the middle years of the war.

Lawrence's account of the novel's relation to the war context is, I think, deceptively understated. '. . . the bitterness of the war' is rendered by the narrative as a whole, not merely registered by individual characters; and the way in which *Women in Love* takes the war for granted is in its complete insertion in the author's apprehension of the experience. Clearly, Lawrence could not have written in 1916 a 'war novel' about life at the Front (although some of his short stories do deal with active warfare). But what he writes, in *Women in Love*, conducts as it were a dialogue with the war: what interests me here is not solely Lawrence's exposed nerve-ends, but his attempt to comprehend the war, to find a meaning for crisis. This is not to say, simply, that we can read Lawrence's life into the novel, although there is a good deal of mileage in the analogies between, say, flitting to the Tyrol and Lawrence's vision of Rananim realised briefly and abortively in Cornwall; or in the notorious prototypes for the characters of Gerald and Gudrun in his friendship with Middleton Murry and Katherine Mansfield. The actual events can be summarised briefly.[3] Lawrence and Frieda perforce remained in England during the war, having arrived in the country shortly before war was declared. Lawrence's war was not one of combat – successive medical examinations, which he found extremely distressing, failed to compel him to active service owing to his poor health – but it was at least one of movement. He and Frieda moved around a good deal, renting one house after another. Lawrence finished *The Rainbow*, which was seized and suppressed almost immediately after its publication in November 1915. This shock was to be followed by a further public 'prosecution': the Lawrences moved to Cornwall, where they lived for most of 1916 and 1917. They made friends, but local suspicions were aroused by Frieda's German background and by what was considered to be their eccentric life-style. They were reported to the authorities, and expelled from Cornwall under the terms of the Defence of the Realm Act as a potential threat to national security. They returned to London, and from there went on to Berkshire.

Such personal upheavals are not similar in kind or degree to the horror of the Somme or Passchendaele, but they represent a period of crisis for Lawrence (he was also very ill in the winter of 1915–16). What Lawrence made of the war is seen in his writings: in letters, short stories and essays of the time, and, retrospectively, in the heavily autobiographical novel *Kangaroo* (1923).[4] His response was not particularly unusual – an initial welcoming of the war, followed by horror, disgust and anger – but, at its height, the frenzy as we can discern it in letters and in biographical accounts was verging on the pathological. The war rapidly became for Lawrence the obscene madness of an 'unclean world'[5] which, in its 'persistent nothingness', had become hell.[6] In the darkest phase, he felt 'The world is gone, extinguished';[7] and, like others, dreaded that 'The cursed war will go on for ever.'[8] But a close reading of the correspondence of 1917 shows both a diminution of despair, and even the hope of a new world arising out of the old: 'I feel the war will end soon.'[9] As the possibility of the war ending appeared more real, so the intensity of his feeling dissipated virtually to indifference. The major writing of *Women in Love* belongs to the period of frenzied despair, and its completion to the period in which Lawrence resolved the war for himself.

Lawrence decided, eventually, that the war was a going wrong in the self, and salvation was to be sought in personal experience: 'The greater the crisis, the more intense should be his isolated reckoning with his own soul.'[10] But this was not the only way in which he shaped the war, although it is relevant to the obliquity of treatment in *Women in Love*. Lawrence came to see the war as a necessity, but from a broader base than the jingoism of 1914. What we find, in effect, in both Shaw and Lawrence, is an attempt to place the war in a progressive evolutionary framework. In a sense, both are post-Darwinian moralists: evolution is for Lawrence 'the creative mystery', and for Shaw 'Life with a blessing'. Mixed with the evolutionary ethic is a reversion to biblical myths of judgement and apocalypse. Sodom is to be punished, and the novel is 'so end-of-the-world'.[11] In July 1917 Lawrence wrote of the 'death which is the rushing of the Gadarene swine down the slope of extinction. And this is the war in Europe.'[12] However, Lawrence does not rest even with extinction. The question that remains – and it is one of the questions that *Women in Love* is to wrestle with – is whether there will be transition via catastrophe to a new world. At this point the cyclical theory of history for which Lawrence was indebted to Herakleitos comes into play; and it is here, also, that we come up again against the Zeppelin.

Lawrence had experienced in London that remarkable sight of the Zeppelin in the night sky. He was indeed under the same sky as Shaw – a sky of threat and persecution unprecedented in civilian life. Like Shaw, Lawrence wrote more than one account of his experience of a Zeppelin raid (of 7 September 1915). Similarly, one is contemporaneous with the incident, in a letter, the other incorporated in the retrospective narrative of *Kangaroo*. It is worth setting them together:

> Last night when we were coming home the guns broke out, and there was a noise of bombs. Then we saw the Zeppelin above us, just ahead, amid a gleaming of clouds: high up, like a bright golden finger, quite small, among a fragile incandescence of clouds. And underneath it were splashes of fire as the shells fired from earth burst. Then there were flashes near the ground – and the shaking noise. It was like Milton – then there was war

in heaven. But it was not angels. It was that small golden Zeppelin, like a long oval world, high up. It seemed as if the cosmic order were gone, as if there had come a new order, a new heaven above us: and as if the world in anger were trying to revoke it. Then the small, long-ovate luminary, the new world in the heavens, disappeared again. . . . So it seems our cosmos has burst, burst at last, the stars and the moon blown away, the envelope of the sky burst out, and a new cosmos appeared; with a long-ovate, gleaming central luminary, calm and drifting in a glow of light, like a new moon. . . . So it is the end – our world is gone, and we are like dust in the air.

But there must be a new heaven and a new earth, a clearer, eternal moon above, and a clean world below. So it will be.

This description of the Zeppelin occurs in a letter to Lady Ottoline Morrell, dated 9 September 1915.[13] The parallel account in *Kangaroo* is this:

And then Zeppelin raids: the awful noise and the excitement. Somers was never afraid then. One evening he and Harriet walked from Platts Lane to the Spaniards Road, across the Heath: and there, in the sky, like some god vision, a Zeppelin, and the searchlights catching it, so that it gleamed like a manifestation in the heavens, then losing it, so that only the strange drumming came down out of the sky where the searchlights tangled their feelers. There it was again, high, high, high, tiny, pale, as one might imagine the Holy Ghost far, far above. And the crashes of guns, and the awful hoarseness of shells bursting in the city. Then gradually, quiet. And from Parliament Hill, a great red glare below, near St Paul's. Something ablaze in the city. Harriet was horribly afraid. Yet as she looked up at the far-off Zeppelin she said to Somers:

'Think, some of the boys I played with when I was a child are probably in it.'

And he looked up at the far, luminous thing, like a moon. Were there men in it? Just men, with two vulnerable legs and warm mouths. The imagination could not go so far.[14]

Harriet and Somers are thinly disguised versions of Frieda and Lawrence, and the incident described in this 'Nightmare' chapter of *Kangaroo* is clearly that of the earlier letter. Both accounts register the sheer wonder of the experience, and its numinous quality: 'war in heaven', as Lawrence writes in the letter. We may note too the ambivalence of response in both Harriet and Somers: their speculations on the common humanity of the 'Enemy' (Harriet has of course divided national allegiance) recall the explosions of *Heartbreak House*, as well as the letter in which Shaw recorded his witness of the Zeppelin. Even more interesting, though, is the symbolic signification of the 'gleaming central luminary': high, tiny and pale, it is a manifestation in the heavens of the Holy Ghost. The Zeppelin, that is, marks the imminent transition to a new era, the era of the Holy Ghost which according to Joachitism is to follow those of Law and of Love.[15]

What is remarkable, then, is not that both Shaw and Lawrence wrote under a Zeppelin-filled sky, but that both looked up and saw a glorious portent. (Not all authors concurred: H. M. Tomlinson, in a short story entitled 'A Raid Night', dubbed the Zeppelin a 'celestial maggot'.[16] Wells's Mr Britling first sees it as a 'phantom yellowish fountain-pen in the sky',[17] but subsequently registers the horror of the ravaged flesh which its flights produce.) Both experiences are apocalyptic; both record a disturbing admixture of joy in destruction. Shaw's mind throws up associations with Beethoven and the thunderbolts of Zeus. To Lawrence the Zeppelin is Milton, or a new moon, or the Holy Ghost. Both, gazing at the heavens, see the military struggle in a cosmic perspective, and view it, from this perspective, as an evolutionary necessity. The response is, exactly, a coping mechanism, an adaptation to the war environment: Lawrence's vision of the Zeppelin allows him a safety-valve of optimism, posited in the survival of the universe, if not the species, race, nation or individual. It remains to be seen how far this – perhaps his major epiphany of the war – relieves the crisis of *Women in Love*.

How, then, is the war rendered in *Women in Love*? There are, of course, explicit allusions to the problems of national leadership: Gerald leads into his discussion with Birkin 'In the Train' (ch. 5) by citing leaders from the daily newspapers; the topic is pursued by the gathering at 'Breadalby' (ch. 8); and in a sense this overt debate continues intermittently throughout the novel. Crisis operates, too, as a kind of bathing-solution in which the action is suspended: the entire narrative represents life as conflict, where violence and the fear of violent death are endemic, and other people are the Enemy. The frenetic madness of both pleasure and sadism recall the desperate bravado and sexual bohemianism of *Heartbreak House*. But we can, I think, be more specific. *Women in Love* has a kind of narrative idiolect which can be identified in its vocabulary, imagery, and action: the war supplies a language for the novel.

So we find that in 'Water-Party' there is a 'warring on the water' (ch. 14, p. 200); and in the subsequent chapter, 'Sunday Evening', we read, 'they trespassed in the air to fight for it' (ch. 15, p. 217). Gerald, who fought in (presumably) the Boer War, comes to regard relations with his workers as a 'state of war' (ch. 17, p. 253). The 'state of war' spills over into personal relationships too: Gerald and Gudrun engage in what proves literally to be a fight to the death; and the conflict between Birkin and Ursula rings to the sounds of Ursula's 'war-cry': 'Do you really love me?' (ch. 19, p. 283). Two crucial episodes in the courtship of Birkin and Ursula, in 'Moony' and 'Excurse', show a sustained use of the vocabulary of battle. The pertinent passage in 'Moony' is the scene by the pond, as Birkin throws stones into the water to shatter the reflection of the moon. The 'burst of sound' 'exploded' on the the surface; the flashing lights are 'battling' (ch. 19, p. 278); indeed the entire scene is a 'battlefield of broken lights and shadows' in which the 'sharp, regular flashes of sound' (p. 279) are an echo of distant gunfire. The description is worth comparing with Lawrence's accounts of the Zeppelin raid, to catch in it the sights and sound of an air raid. This is not, however, to discount the highly charged sexual imagery of the scene; and the assault on Ursula's female psyche by Birkin's male aggression is, we might concede, primarily sexual. But, as we shall see, sexuality in *Women in Love* is itself primarily an experience or an expression of violence and conflict, and the two 'sets' of imagery overlap or even merge. What we are given here, in 'Moony', is attempted rape, and a battlefield. Virginity is to be captured – 'not even now broken open, not yet violated' (p. 278) – by battle, sharp and explosive; and the attack is ultimately orgasmic, with Birkin satisfied and Ursula dazed, her mind all gone. In 'Excurse', which brings the conflict between Birkin and Ursula to climax and consummation, the war-idiom is pervasive, its vocabulary scattered throughout the scene. They leave 'this memorable battlefield' (ch. 23, p. 350) after a quarrel which has been the 'crisis of war' (p. 344) between them, and what follows is 'peace at last' (p. 349).

In 'Moony' and 'Excurse' the vocabulary of battle is embedded in the narrative. 'Water-Party' provides a further dimension, a dramatic set piece which (rather like the ending of *Heartbreak House*) can be read as a symbolic rendering of August 1914. Old Mr Crich's annual party, held at Shortlands for the people of the neighbourhood, distils the essence of the myth of pre-war England. The social picture which it draws is remarkable both for particularity of detail, and for rich if ominous suggestiveness. We might place it alongside *Howards End* as well as *Heartbreak House*; or, for that matter, Masterman or Dangerfield. The glimpsed social occasion recalls the wedding-reception at Oniton (which also presaged tragedy):

> People were standing about in groups, some women were sitting in the shade of the walnut tree, with cups of tea in their hands, a waiter in evening dress was hurrying round, some girls were simpering with parasols, some young men, who had just come in from rowing, were sitting cross-legged on the grass, coatless, their shirt-sleeves rolled up in manly fashion, their hands resting on their white flannel trousers. (ch. 14, p. 177)

This *tableau vivant*, with its figures observed in groups and at a distance, encapsulates in its social rituals the assurance of continued stability; but there are, to counter that expectation, already hints that Crich, and in him the old order, is dying. Moreover, his children resent the event, and Ursula and Gudrun ridicule the reverence of their parents, for whom such a party still holds meaning. It is in fact a 'false situation' (p. 177) for Ursula, who, with her sister, detaches herself from the festivities. But their retreat is a false pastoral: the boat is frail, and on landing they run into a grove 'like nymphs', 'alone in a little wild world of their own' (p. 184). In their regressive fantasy Ursula and Gudrun are as much a part of the Georgian idyll as the other guests, and will be drawn into what was '*bound* to happen' (p. 200). Because, even on that golden afternoon, time is not arrested: the chapter marks with care the gradual sinking of the 'westering sun' (p. 184), and the rise of the 'high bland moon' (p. 207) under which tragedy will occur. Shortlands, like Breadalby, belongs to the 'accomplished past' (ch. 8, p. 108), and is caught at the moment of crisis.

Both the assumption of a stable order, and the threat and onset of violent change, are concentrated in the specific image of the steam launch, the pleasure-boat which epitomises a leisured and moneyed society served by the waiters, and lazily directed by the lounging captain. The image recalls vividly both Shotover's description of the ship of state, and Plato's *Republic*. More than this, though: the pleasure-boat, as societal microcosm, triggers a counter-image of its own sordid economic base, the underbelly of money. Against the steam launch, a pleasure-valve controlled by the Crich bosses, is set Gudrun's description of the Thames steamer. Here is a suggestion of the mud beneath the glinting surface: the boys ran up to their waists in 'that indescribable Thames mud', and 'darted in the filth when a coin was flung' (ch. 14, p. 180). These, like the miners, are creatures of the underworld of the novel; and the sharp contrast of surface and murky depths bears comparison with the 'abyss' which was so potent a terror for Leonard Bast.

The Thames mud 'contradicts' the Shortlands idyll, yet is inexorably part of the same process. This is by no means an isolated image; and, as the chapter proceeds, tension and internal contradictions become increasingly insistent, as the golden afternoon fades into dusk and night. The launch is illuminated, but surrounded by shadows gathering from the trees; even its lanterns have a menacing quality, lighting the darkness 'luridly' (p. 198). The atmosphere of vague threat has suffused the relationships of Gerald and Gudrun, Ursula and Birkin, as flirtation erupts into bizarre cavorting and overt violence. So, in this 'lovely darkness', the boats collide: 'The launch twanged and hooted, somebody was singing. Then as if the night smashed, suddenly there was a great shout, a confusion of shouting, warring on the water, then the horrid noise of paddles reversed and churned violently' (p. 200). The image is sudden, and acute: it parallels, it seems to me, the 'frightful smash-up' expected by Mazzini Dunn, and the moment in Act III of *Heartbreak House* when the first explosion is heard. Everywhere, the lights are gone, put out at Gerald's order. It is Gerald, of course, who dives into the underworld of water and mud, to the echoes of the punning cry, 'Di–Di–Di–Di–Oh Di . . .' (p. 201). And when he stumbles out again it is with an epiphany of the underworld, the abyss of death: 'There's room under that water there for thousands' (p. 206). The experience literally sets him apart, in a universe 'as cold as hell': 'you wonder how it is so many are alive, why we're up here'. Again, the topography, and the insistence on two discrete worlds, recalls the Victorian and Edwardian abyss of social fission. But in the cold and the mud we may surely comprehend too that other-world of the hell of the trenches. (We might also give a forward glance to *The Waste Land*: 'I had not thought death had undone so many' – 63.) Gerald witnesses alone, but for the community, what outside the novel is a shared experience of death, and alienation from the security of life at home. The episode prefigures his death in the snow: both register crisis, with Gerald as experiencing centre, and arguably render the same event, in alternative modes. In 'Snowed Up' (ch. 30) we reach an inclusive symbolic vision of the death of a civilisation, but in 'Water-Party' the more restricted delineation still permits reference to a specific socio-historical context. It is indeed the social dimension here, and the specificity of the violent interruption of death into the festive occasion, in the drowning of the young couple, which invite a reading of this episode as the 'outbreak of war' in *Women in Love*.

Thus the 'ceremony of innocence is drowned'.[18] But the point here is not merely symbolic description of the war, however vivid. It is rather the meaning ascribed to the event in the rendering of the responses of the various characters. We have already considered Gerald's response. The local people respond with a mingling of solemn grief and childlike excitement: 'Did all enjoy it? Did all enjoy the thrill?' (ch. 14, p. 213). Those (apparently authorial) questions might be referred, outside the novel, to the early response at home to the declaration of war and events at the Front. They also point forward to the next chapter, 'Sunday Evening', in which Ursula reflects on the incident of the drowning. Ursula's reverie constitutes *her* epiphany of death, parallel to that of Gerald; and both characters focus an experience which goes beyond the merely individual. In fact, death in *Women in Love* must be read, constantly, in the context of the war. In that context it is not only, or simplistically, the 'bitterness of war' which emerges: Ursula registers, and works through, what it may mean to choose to die, in the new opportunity for such choice opened up by the call to arms in 1914. Her reverie, which is the major direct response to the smash and the drowning of 'Water-Party', reads as what Shaw called 'War Delirium'.[19] Her welcoming of death, for example:

Let us die, since the great experience is the one that follows now upon all the rest, death, which is the next great crisis. . . . Have we not the courage to go on with our journey, must we cry 'I daren't?' On ahead we will go, into death, and whatever death may mean.   (ch. 15, p. 214)

As the narration in this passage expands from its base in the individual character, it takes on an inclusive, declarative, even declamatory quality. The exhortation to share courageously in the 'great experience' of death is echoed, authorially, in the essays entitled *The Reality of Peace* which Lawrence completed in March 1917:

> Sweet, beautiful death, come to our help. Break in among the herd, make gaps in its insulated completion. Give us a chance, sweet death, to escape from the herd and gather together against it a few living beings. Purify us with death, O death, cleanse from us the rank stench. . . .[20]

Here, death is to 'gather together' the heroic few. Ursula, too, measures the adventure of death by traditional concepts of heroism, and projects into it a desire to be purified: 'Was not the adventure of death infinitely preferable? Was not death infinitely more lovely and noble than such a life? . . . How much cleaner and more dignified to be dead!' (p. 216). '. . . grand and perfect death' is embraced as a 'bath of cleanness' (p. 217); and this quality of sacramental cleansing steers us towards the war poems of Rupert Brooke. And not only his poems: as Paul Fussell notes, in *The Great War and Modern Memory*,[21] Brooke was one of the period's most vigorous exponents of the cult of bathing naked (Middleton Murry recalled, too, Lawrence's pleasure in nude swimming, in 1913). This passion was carried over, in Brooke's poetry, into a 'pastoral-erotic' vision of young men swimming in battle, expressed perhaps most strikingly in the sonnet 'Peace':

> Now, God be thanked Who has matched us with His hour,
>   And caught our youth, and wakened us from sleeping,
> With hand made sure, clear eye, and sharpened power,
>   To turn, as swimmers into cleanness leaping,
> Glad from a world grown old and cold and weary. . . .[22]

That 'gladness' is echoed by Ursula, in her account of what it is that death provides a welcome escape *from*:

The sea they turned into a murderous alley and a soiled road of commerce, disputed like the dirty land of a city every inch of it. The air they claimed too, shared it up, parcelled it out to certain owners, they trespassed in the air to fight for it.   (p. 217)

This is a broader characterisation of the crisis, in its conflation of fighting with the methods, and new territories, of capitalism and imperialism. It ratifies John Goode's description of *Women in Love* as a 'chronicle of a moment in history' and his proposal of Dangerfield's *Strange Death of Liberal England* as the best preparation for reading the novel.[23] The 'moment in history' is, it seems to me, registered in a particular way in 'Water-party' and 'Sunday Evening'. Nevertheless, beyond these individual episodes, it is the proximity and the ambivalence, at all points in the novel, of violence and of violent death, together with the anxiety to make death *mean*, that, even more than the explicit imagery of battle, show how the bitterness of the war is to be 'taken for granted'.

Women in Love, depicting a society in crisis, defines a problem and seeks a solution. Like *Howards End* and *Heartbreak House*, it defines the problem as one of a split in society, expressed by means of one or more dualisms. In this novel, however, the sets of dualisms, or binary oppositions, are so numerous as to be almost a habit of thought: their very pervasiveness articulates crisis *as* radical division.

One of the major dualisms is the familiar dichotomy of country and city. Like Forster, Lawrence uses the country-house tradition, and the novel is realised in settings of country houses, set against contrastive city-scapes, each environment contributing to an overall moral and cultural topography. Unlike *Howards End*, however, this novel finds no normative location within English society, in either city or country. The main characters 'flit' to the destructured environment of the Tyrol: this symbolic landscape ratifies, as it were, the iterative imagery of ice and snow already established by the narrative, and confirms the necessity for the novel to shift away from the confines of social realism in order to achieve resolution.

In the country houses of Breadalby and Shortlands we see the old order. Breadalby is 'unchanged and unchanging' (ch. 8, p. 91), like a framed aquatint of the past. There is an artificial fixity here, the imposition of an obsolescent order. Hermione Roddice, presiding over political discussions, concentrates in herself the willed knowledge which this social order represents, as a kind of violence against the natural and the instinctual. It is notable that when Birkin leaves Breadalby, he goes 'straight across the park, to the open country, to the hills' (ch. 8, p. 119). In this rejection of Breadalby and Hermione – a necessary purgation – Birkin strikes out for nature.[24]

By contrast, the Café de Pompadour is desperately contemporary, but it nevertheless equally embodies stasis and sterility. Halliday and his friends belong to the sphere of the aesthetic, as opposed to the political orientation of Breadalby, but it is an aestheticism tangled with vicious promiscuity and cruel gossip. Moreover the Café is the focal point of the hell of the entire city: Birkin feels himself doomed as he approaches it 'In the Train', the realm of the damned, 'licentious souls' (ch. 6, p. 68); and 'Flitting' (ch. 27) from the constraints of society significantly involves a journey through, and away from, London.

Shortlands is not simply a country house. Whereas Breadalby is of the remote past, and the Café de Pompadour is of the decadent present, this home, situated in the community of Beldover, engages in the world of work – the bosses and their dealings with the colliery workers. Shortlands is at the centre of the novel's analysis of a mechanistic, industrialised society. The analysis is carried through in chapter 17, 'The Industrial Magnate', which traces the growth in power of the Criches, their industrial methods and philosophy, over three generations: in Thomas Crich, his father before him, and his son Gerald. The chronology stretches, it would seem, from the mid nineteenth century to 1914, with Gerald's father holding power in the 1880s, during the industrial unrest, and Gerald assuming control after having fought in (presumably) the Boer War. The meticulous dating clearly invites us to read in this account of the Crich family an epitomisation of the development of capitalist industry, and 'the plausible ethics of productivity' (ch. 5, p. 62). But, despite temptingly specific details such as the allusion to lock-outs, the chapter does not read convincingly as a comprehensive or objective socio-historical document. It is, rather, an expression and 'explanation' of the motivation, attitudes and behaviour of Gerald Crich. Gerald *is* 'The Industrial Magnate' of *Women in Love*. Old Mr Crich's philanthropic humanitarianism had come

up against the incompatibility of charity and profit, and could not
survive the crisis of faith. With his father's death, Gerald inherits
the breakdown of 'the centralising force that had held the whole
together' (ch. 17, p. 248). Gerald combats the fragmentation with
a new regime in which Matter is subjugated by Will: he is the God
of, and in, the Machine (significantly, he pushes his way
inexorably through the anonymous mass of the workers, luxuri-
ously ensconced in his motor car). The workers are 'not important
to him, save as instruments' (p. 260): even more pointed is the
phrase, slipped into the narrative apparently casually, which
equates men and machines, as 'instruments human and metallic'
(p. 257). Gerald operates a fundamentally inhuman system, and
the obsession with Will and Matter tells on his personal life. He is
reduced to a mask, and 'It was as if his centres of feeling were
drying up' (p. 261): Mangan, and the dehumanisation of capitalism, again.

'The Industrial Magnate' is partly an account of Gerald's
career as master of the colliery, and partly an expression of a
materialist and functionalist philosophy. The chapter is clearly
located in Gerald's consciousness, even though the narration
holds him at arm's length, and we should not perhaps expect of it
a balancing description of the attitudes of the colliers, or their
work relations with Gerald. The problem is, however, that a
presentation of Gerald's views necessarily involves his perception
of the colliers, and that given the mode of narration it is not
possible to decide whether or not the orientation coincides with
the authorial voice. We may, then, demur at the attribution to the
workers of the qualities of a willing slave-race, 'satisfied to belong
to the great and wonderful machine, even whilst it destroyed
them' (p. 260). (On the other hand, this single sentence might
suffice to ratify Patrick Parrinder's observation that chapter 17
cannot be fully understood without bearing in mind the
thousands of men who went, willing and acquiescent, to the
trenches.[25]) No direct interaction with the workers is possible in
this character-centred survey: such contact or conflict in a specific
social situation would be another story, and one in which Gerald,
as well as the colliers, would be more individualised. (In fact,
Lawrence did make a subsequent attempt to deal dramatically
with the work relations of Gerald and the colliers in the play *Touch
and Go*, written in March 1918. Hardly more successfully, though:
the dialogue is stilted, and the characters stereotyped. The play is

of interest in relation to the present book only in that it marks one of the 'alternative endings' to *Women in Love*, which 'resurrects' Gerald, to return to Anabel–Gudrun three years on.) In 'The Industrial Magnate', and *Women in Love* as a whole, the colliers function as a class, the creatures of the underworld. It is in this sense only that they form one term of a dualism that is meaningful to the novel; and a fuller articulation of *this* split in the society of *Women in Love* remains unrealised. As in *Howards End* and *Heartbreak House*, the main emphasis is on division within the middle class, and on the survival of that class.

Here, then, is one of the major dualisms – the city and the country – by which the novel maps out contemporary life. But this purposive narrative is concerned to project as well as to analyse, and it proceeds by exploring alternative possibilities. Alternative possibilities are often voiced by the characters, who constantly question the meaning and direction of events. The interrogative mood is pervasive, although the 'alternative' may remain unstated or unspecified. So Ursula meditated, 'Was not the adventure of death infinitely preferable?' (ch. 15, p. 216); Gerald asks, 'If death isn't the point . . . what is?' (ch. 16, p. 229); and Gudrun wonders, when Thomas Crich dies, 'Was there no other way? Must one go through all the horror of this victory over death' (ch. 21, p. 322). Even when rhetorically expressed, these are real questions, and demand answers from the novel. The questions may be ethical – how am I to conduct my life? – philosophical – what is the meaning of this? – or speculative – what is going to happen? The categories may, of course, fuse, as when Gudrun reflects, 'One of them must triumph over the other. Which should it be?' (ch. 29, p. 465). Here the predictive and the normative – both end-directed – merge.

The characters may envisage alternative answers or outcomes, and indeed the possibility of choosing *either* this *or* that course of action. But, increasingly, their questions anxiously enquire after the direction of events, and the answers seems both less certain, and less within their control. For Gerald it becomes a matter of 'Where was he going?' (ch. 24, p. 381). Birkin asks urgently, 'Does it end with just our two selves?' (ch. 26, p. 409). Gudrun wonders, when she is in the mountains, 'what next?' (ch. 30, p. 508); and even, 'Shall I die?' (p. 500). Two points emerge from this movement: one is the impression of a gradual diminution of choice, and onset of inevitability; the other is the framing of the characters' questions, and their actions, within the containing, and determining, narrative.

The diminution of choice – itself an index of crisis – is poignantly expressed in the final alternatives which present themselves to Gerald, as he stumbles up into the snow: 'He was between two ridges in a hollow. So he swerved. Should he climb the other ridge or wander along the hollow? How frail the thread of his being was stretched! He would perhaps climb the ridge' (ch. 30, p. 533). This is choice reduced to the minimum, as Gerald withdraws from life. But earlier he had still been able to contemplate his relationship with Gudrun: 'he must stand by himself. . . . On the other hand, he might give in, and fawn to her. Or, finally, he might kill her. Or he might become just indifferent' (p. 501). These possibilities present themselves to Gerald as a choice of actions; but they also provide for alternative narrative endings. They are part, that is, of the intricate network of plot-expectations, through which the narrative defines its pro-gression by selecting out the 'impossible' or 'unnecessary'. Towards the close of *Women in Love*, the pressure of alternative progressions on the reader is very great: as the characters query what is happening, what might happen, and what they could do, so the narrative *expects* a verdict from the reader on how it is to proceed.

The two main plot-expectations of *Women in Love*, weddings and deaths, are highlighted by two of the chapter-headings which Lawrence added to his novel in 1920: 'Death and Love' (ch. 24) and 'Marriage or Not' (ch. 25). The novel opens with a wedding, witnessed by the Brangwen sisters, who themselves debate whether or not to marry. The expectation of death – 'Shall I die?' – is also announced early on, when we learn of the fatal accident in which Gerald killed his brother. In effect, the plot-argument hinges on a binary opposition, *either* marriage *or* death, and in doing so it opts *either* for comedy *or* for tragedy. But this is more than a question of literary genre: what is at issue is the survival of a civilisation, or even of the species. Paul Delaney suggests that the war gave fresh impetus to Lawrence's penchant for dualisms 'by imposing on the entire European consciousness just such a system of binary oppositions: for or against, friend or enemy, kill or be killed'.[26] Whatever its genesis, the either/or base which underpins *Women in Love* impresses on the novel the urgency of deciding between alternatives, and registers the dimension of the crisis.

That dimension reaches towards the cosmic: *either* evolution *or* elimination. These alternatives are conflated in Birkin's nice paradox of 'progressive devolution' (ch. 16, p. 229), which in turn alerts us to the ambivalent status of the novel's 'binary oppositions', which may not, after all, be mutually exclusive, nor indeed exhaust the alternative possibilities. There is without doubt an apocalyptic and eschatological flavour to the 'or' of 'universal dissolution' (ch. 14, p. 193), which is confirmed by the rejected title 'Dies Irae'. And it may seem, in some instances, that the either/or expresses equally negative possibilities. 'Either the heart will break or cease to care. Best cease to care' (ch. 31, p. 538). But here (Birkin is contemplating Gerald's corpse) the terms are reversed, and the second, the 'or', is in fact the positive of evolutionary adaptation. Moreover, what appears to be a restrictive dualism may be an ellipsis which disguises a hidden third term; that term is an 'either' which may precede or follow apocalypse, and it articulates what we must do to be saved. There may after all be a way out.

So, Ursula thinks, 'Unless something happens . . . I shall die' (ch. 15, p. 214). The 'something' is unspecified, but, with the 'Unless', it provides a safety-valve. She goes on to glance at the unknown alternative: 'And the next step led into the space of death. Did it? – or was there – ?' (p. 215). Ursula breaks off at this point, and the force of the unfinished question, and specifically the 'or', is very great. Ursula can, just, envisage a positive alternative to the 'next step' of death, although she can't name it. And Ursula survives.

It is not surprising perhaps that we find Birkin, at the turning-point of the novel, going further than Ursula in working through an understanding of the oppositions and alternatives involved. In 'Moony' he articulates the 'choice' which he, or the text, must make between life and death, as he contemplates the African statuette. After distinguishing between the two ways of dissolution, the 'Arctic north' and the 'awful African process' (ch. 19, p. 286), he continues, 'Was this then all that remained? Was there left now nothing but to break off from the happy creative being, was the time up? Is our day of creative life finished?' (p. 286). The change of tense or voice in that last question allows it to be floated as the crux on which the rest of the novel turns. The 'answer' is immediate – 'Birkin thought of Gerald' – but open to interpretation: 'Was he a messenger, an omen of the universal dissolution into whiteness or snow?' (p. 287). Birkin may raise the question, but it is for the text to answer it, and significantly at this point his 'strange, strained attention' gives way. Instead, Birkin turns to the 'or', which is the 'remaining way' of freedom. Immediately, 'He thought of Ursula. . . .' What Birkin is debating here is a 'choice' which is central to the novel: between death and survival, dissolution and creative growth, Gerald and Ursula. His choice is limited: comically, in this instance, as he rushes off to propose marriage to Ursula (she refuses him). But the limitation will become tragic, in that Birkin cannot choose for Gerald not to die. Gerald's death 'answers' the question which is left open here. Nevertheless, the reflections of both Ursula and Birkin locate the either/or crisis of the novel within individual consciousness; and Birkin's climactic inner debate, in particular, conflates the crisis of civilisation with the scope and limitations of personal relationships. It is to the novel's propositions regarding sexual relationships that we now turn.

In *Women in Love* the diagnosis of crisis is broad in its cultural and socio-historical exploration. But the crisis is also registered within the self, as it relates to others. Thus crisis is expressed as a failure of sexual relationships, in a small group of characters taken as representative; and the solution to what Lawrence referred to as the 'real problem of today', the 'relationship of men and women',[27] is equally projected as a making new of this vital connection. So the plot-argument of *Women in Love* proceeds in its exploration of alternative possibilities by working through the relationships of the four main figures of Ursula and Gudrun Brangwen, Gerald Crich, and Rupert Birkin. The narrative provides an intricate study in parallel of the developing relationships between the two pairs: Ursula and Birkin, Gudrun and Gerald. This delicate counterpoint is more than decorative: the experience for the reader is cumulative as well as contrastive. It is, then, simply a matter of expediency to separate these as two discrete relationships; and it would, simply, falsify the novel to suggest that one is to be read as purely positive and the other as purely negative. At the outset, as both relationships signal change, a moving on for the characters, both hold potential as solutions to the cultural and personal ills. The Gerald–Gudrun affair is obviously 'doomed' fairly early on; but its failure in no way invalidates it as an aberrant experience for this society. Even towards the end of the book, when Ursula and Birkin are married, and Gerald and Gudrun are to part violently, it would still be a misreading to take the one as good and the other as bad. Ursula and Birkin achieve a good deal of what Birkin, and presumably Lawrence, wanted; but it is emphatically not enough. That consummation, flawed in itself, is irredeemably nullified by the absolute failure to establish a full relationship between Birkin and Gerald. To say this is to see the Birkin–Gerald bond as not simply (as Birkin expresses it) an adjunct to his 'ultimate marriage' with Ursula, but as central to the novel – as, in a sense, the missed destination of the novel's remarkably symmetrical progress towards solution. We begin with the two sisters: their sibling adolescent bond is ready to be broken by the onset of adult sexuality. Their heterosexual relationships are interwoven, at each stage of development, with the less overtly sexual progress of the 'Man to Man' love. To appreciate fully what the novel encompasses, we must travel from the sexual isolation of Gudrun and Ursula, through the forging of new relations with Gerald and Birkin, towards the tragically unconsummated relationship of the two men, which is the climax and catastrophe of *Women in Love*.

The 'ultimate marriage' (ch. 5, p. 64) which Ursula and Birkin contract is the closest the novel comes to a positive solution, and a stake in the future for humanity. Nevertheless the relationship is problematic; indeed it proceeds by debate and contradiction, and cannot be consummated before the radical disjunction of attitudes has been accommodated. The chapters in which the lovers pursue a repeating pattern of quarrel and reconciliation – 'An Island', 'Mino', 'Water-Party', 'Moony', 'Excurse' (chs 11, 13, 14, 19, 23) – allow a clarification, and gradual modification, of the distance between Ursula's need for total emotional absorption, and Birkin's denial of such immersion in favour of the stable equilibrium of two single beings. So Ursula's challenge of Birkin's ideas in 'An Island' forces him to articulate his own position. Increasingly Birkin asserts, more clearly and without compromise, the 'pure balance of two single beings' (ch. 13, p. 164); and increasingly Ursula retreats to an equally uncompromising mocking stance, which serves to place ironically Birkin's ideas. The pattern of their encounters is a battering by Ursula against Birkin's theoretic citadel, which characteristically ends in a weary truce. In the passivity of such weariness they regress into childlike games (as in 'An Island'), or even into a physical embrace. It is at such moments – as at the end of 'Mino', when Birkin accedes to Ursula's plea for a kiss and a declaration of love – that Birkin's rationality is most vulnerable, and Ursula's insistent intimacy wins temporary victories.

Sexuality itself, not merely the kind of sexual relationship, is at issue. In a first draft typescript of his novel, Lawrence made Birkin reject sexual passion with Ursula, envisaging instead a 'new sort of intercourse' which would be 'chastity and innocence of itself'.[28] Although in the final version both Birkin and Lawrence accede to a consummated sexual relationship between these two lovers, we may still detect an anxiety to determine the exact nature and significance of that relationship, and some measure of strain in its expression. Birkin has faced the problem of finding a love which is other than hard physical desire, and beyond the *fleurs du mal*. The 'small lament in the darkness' (ch. 14, p. 210) is, presumably, the call for such a love; but one of the problematic issues of the novel is how far Ursula and Birkin do indeed escape the sexual trap.

The consummation of their relationship is achieved in 'Excurse', and immediately followed and paralleled by that of Gerald and Gudrun in 'Death and Love'. In neither case is the sexual union easy or immediate. Ursula and Birkin quarrel violently before making peace yet again, and Gerald clambers through death to reach Gudrun's bed. But, whereas 'Death and Love' will end with dissatisfaction and foreboding, we can at least say that the close of 'Excurse' expresses emotional and sexual satisfaction, and heralds further positive development. However, even here the movement is from conflict to reconciliation, with flickers of the familiar hostility and opposition from the start. Ursula is as usual ready with 'buts' and contradictions, and moves rapidly from doubt, to anger, to offensive jeering. She finally scores with her denunciation of Birkin's previous relationship with Hermione as 'death-eating' (ch. 23, p. 346): the insult exorcises Hermione for Birkin, and the turning-point is marked by the comic interruption of the passing cyclist. At the crisis Ursula wanders beyond our vision, and the central realisation which seals their union is not hers but Birkin's – of a 'certain stimulant in self-destruction' (p. 348). Moreover, when Ursula returns, it is with the placatory peace-offering of a flower.

This moment of hiatus before actual sexual contact allows for an assessment of where they have got to. 'Yes, she acquiesced – but it was accomplished without her acquiescence' (p. 350). The flabby paradox seems to me an evasion: what has Ursula done but barter her subservience for a verbal declaration of love? It cannot be denied that the lyrical, pastoral idyll of the wedding-procession of this chapter, as the couple drift through the late afternoon, is the novel's naturism at its most delightful, and the subsequent account of their lovemaking a hymn to the mysteries of love. But here, and later in the novel, one cannot be quite sure that the mystification, as well as mysticality, of sex is wholly to be attributed to a necessary decorum. Lawrence is clearly anxious to establish this physical union as different in kind from that of Gerald and Gudrun. For Ursula and Birkin, it seems, the anal emphasis on the dark river of corruption is positively opposed to the womb, the 'bath of life' (ch. 24, p. 389), into which Gerald sinks selfishly and gratefully in his intercourse with Gudrun. Yet, elsewhere, anality is equivocally described. Certainly, in 'Excurse', Lawrence's rhetoric works to validate the lovers' world, self-defined by its imagery of fluidity, richness, darkness, subtlety and silence. But the lack of complete overall consistency suggests, I think, a certain embarrassment at the centre of the novel. This may be partly located in the *assertion* of the positive sexuality of Ursula and Birkin, as opposed to the *dramatisation* of the character of the relationship between Gerald and Gudrun. And this in turn points to the major issue of the stance which the novel, or the author, adopts towards Birkin and Gerald. In order to address this issue we need to move towards a consideration of the relationship of the two men, via a consideration of Gerald and Gudrun.

Unlike Ursula and Birkin, what Gerald and Gudrun share is greater than their differences. Theirs is a 'mutual hellish recognition' (ch. 18, p. 272), grounded in violence, the will to power, and a death wish. Sexual passion is for Gerald and Gudrun an experience and expression of cruelty, even of physical violence (to an extent this is true of all the characters). The stages of their increasing intimacy are marked by blood and wounds – a sublimation and metaphoric representation of sexual intercourse, and registered not as physical harmony but as violation. The sexual motif of blood is first used when Gerald subjugates the mare between his thighs in 'Coal-Dust'. This is a vicarious sexual violation of Gudrun herself: when she sees the 'trickles of blood on the sides of the mare' (ch. 9, p. 124), her response is orgasmic. Gudrun is also sexually aroused by Gerald's wound, and his consequent dependency, in 'Water-Party'. His bandaged arm is a taboo subject of conversation, and acquires phallic connotations in Gudrun's clandestine quiver of excitement when he eventually draws it out of his pocket (Ursula is merely shocked, not excited, by the display). When the couple are alone, later in this chapter, their shared intimacy is one of overt violence, triggered by the dominating and destructive will of each. When Gudrun slaps his face, the description we receive of Gerald's feelings suggests sexual tumescence to the point of orgasm: 'his lungs were so suffused with blood, his heart stretched almost to bursting with a great gush of ungovernable emotion' (ch. 14, p. 191).

The blood violence of their sexuality is clear too in 'Rabbit'. Here, again, a wound is perceived by 'underworld knowledge' (ch. 18, p. 272) as a sexual emblem, and the shared knowledge is of sexual shame: 'They were implicated with each other in abhorrent mysteries.' Moreover, exhibitionism again contributes to the thrill, as Gerald shows his 'hard forearm, white and hard and torn in red gashes'. Gudrun counters his display with her 'deep red score down the silken white flesh'. Gerald registers the wound 'as if he had knowledge of her in the long red rent of her forearm'. They are already intimate in carnal knowledge, without direct physical contact; and it is a violent knowledge. Actual intercourse will be experienced by Gudrun as a 'violent sensation', with the 'terrible frictional violence of death' (ch. 24, p. 388). The final sexual consummation for Gerald and Gudrun, in which they achieve mutual satisfaction (their lovemaking typically satisfies only one partner), is a full realisation of the murderous violence underpinning their desire. When, in 'Snowed Up', Gerald anticipates killing her, he trembles 'in his most violent accesses of passionate approach to her, trembling with so much desire' (ch. 30, p. 503). The desire gradually shapes itself as 'what a perfect voluptuous consummation it would be to strangle her, to strangle every spark of life out of her, till she lay completely inert, soft, relaxed for ever, a soft heap lying dead between his hands, utterly dead' (p. 518). Murder and death are equated with post-orgasmic relaxation and detumescence, for both partners. And, in the event, the attempted strangulation does enact a reciprocal climax: 'The struggling was her reciprocal lustful passion in this embrace, the more violent it became, the greater the frenzy of delight, till the zenith was reached, the crisis, the struggle was overborne, her movement became softer, appeased' (p. 531). The lust for death, and the shared orgasm, are the completed epiphany of what that 'mutual hellish recognition' is.

The sexuality of Gerald and Gudrun is, then, violent and even murderous. As in Ursula's reverie in 'Sunday Evening' (ch. 15), sex is associated with death. This persistent expression in the novel of sex as violence, and orgasm as death, reads as a textual embedding of the 'bitterness of war'. Sex in *Women in Love* is imaged as mystical religiosity for Ursula and Birkin, and as violent death for Gerald and Gudrun. Both sets of imagery are of course traditional – we need refer, for example, only to Donne's *Songs and Sonnets* – but the graphic use of the imagery of blood–violence–killing here differs from the Renaissance conceit of orgasm as a little death, in that it is active rather than, or as well as, passive. Here orgasm, or bringing a partner to orgasm, is equated with the perverse thrill of killing (which Ursula, appropriately, could never bring herself to do). Here we have another vocabulary and another context in which the war is to be taken for granted. By a simple reversal, we may say that what this language articulates is not simply the violence latent in sexuality, but the orgasmic excitement of killing.

It would seem, then, that not only is a society in crisis rendered here specifically in terms of a perverse and sterile sexuality – as in *Heartbreak House* and indeed in *The Waste Land* – but also the rendering is itself a seismograph of its context of actual violence. That is, if as in *Heartbreak House* or *The Waste Land* the sterility of sex is an index of a moribund culture, the violence of sex in this novel is its death-throes, the symbolic or psychic point at which sexual desire, the death-wish and a societal auto-destruct intersect.

'Death and Love' are mingled for Gerald and Gudrun. Their relationship is part of the process of death and dissolution, rooted in the mud (Gerald dives into his own element of water and mud, from which springs the fleshy, festering water plants, in 'Diver' – ch. 4) and ending in the snow. Gerald himself is the figure of death in the novel: to borrow Jan Kott's phrase for Macbeth, he is 'death-infected', and carries death with him.[29] He is the death-bringer to the miners and the colliery: 'As soon as Gerald entered the firm, the convulsion of death ran through the old system' (ch. 17, p. 257). Certainly Gerald bears the mark of death: specifically, he carries the mark of Cain, because he 'accidentally' shot his brother when he was a child. He is closely associated in the novel with the deaths of two more members of his family – his sister and his father – before he himself dies. The drowning in 'Water-Party', as already noted, prefigures the ending of the novel. It functions as a kind of preliminary working, using the metaphor of the drowning and of Gerald's dive into the watery underworld, of his own death later on. Gerald voices his response to the drowning when talking 'Man to Man' to Birkin. The meaning of the event is for him the inevitability of death. And death seems to him central: 'If death isn't the point . . . what is?' (ch. 16, p. 229). For Gerald death *is* the point, and the text will take him there.

It is in the course of this conversation with Birkin that Gerald's imagination leaps from the death of his sister to the imminent natural death of his father: 'It will finish him.' The direction of the narrative is clearly signposted here: focusing on death, we focus on Gerald, with a natural transition to his father. In the chapter 'Death and Love' Gerald crosses two thresholds: the death of his father, and making love to Gudrun. Thomas Crich's death struggle engages more than merely his own life, drawing in Gudrun, Winifred (in whom he has vested his hope of life and salvation) and, most importantly, Gerald. It is at this point that Gerald becomes death-infected, 'convulsed in the clasp of this death of his father's . . . the son was dragged into the embrace of horrifying death along with him' (ch. 21, p. 321). Gerald is afraid of 'some horrible collapse in himself' (ch. 24, p. 362). With the fear comes a death-wish: 'he somehow *wanted* this death, even forced it. It was as if he himself were dealing the death' (p. 363). It is as if, indeed, Gerald becomes identified with the 'fearful space of death' (note again the motif of fear, which is constantly attached to Gerald). And there is a compulsion about it: despite Mrs Crich's weird warning, Gerald stays to the end, and walks out of the room as himself a death-figure, a skull with 'A strange sort of grin' (p. 377). Alone with death, Gerald has heard his father's death-rattle, 'his soul echoing in horror' (p. 376). Death passes from father to son, like the family business.

When, after the funeral, Gerald stumbles blindly towards the churchyard, he arrives at a further epiphany of death: 'This then was the grave' (p. 382). Revulsion at raw mortality, cold and clammy, does not prevent a central recognition – 'Here was one centre then' – nor a decisive rejection – 'No, enough of this.' The incident parallels Birkin's meditation on the African statuette and is, similarly, a turning-point: in both cases, epiphany is followed by a choice of direction. For Birkin, the choice was between Gerald and Ursula, between dissolution and a way of freedom; here, Gerald rejects the notion of going home. Instead, 'There was Gudrun. . . .' Like Birkin, he acts immediately: Birkin sped off to propose marriage, and Gerald makes a forced sexual entry.

Gerald enters the Brangwen household as an intruder. Moreover, far from leaving 'corrosive death' (p. 389) behind, he has brought its clay with him. He is revived, almost reborn, by intercourse with Gudrun; but the regeneration is *taken*, at the expense of Gudrun, who registers, with authorial prescience, that 'They would never be together' (p. 390). Nevertheless, Gudrun feels the allure of death, and is ready to receive him 'filled with his bitter potion of death' (p. 388). It is not only Gerald's urge to dominate that excites her. But to read their relationship simply as 'bad sex' would be to reduce the novel: the narrative, far from rejecting the death-and-love of Gerald and Gudrun, embraces it as the epitome of death-and-society, and as a tragic inevitability. It is, however, also inevitable that these two will part.

Gudrun is attracted, in Gerald, to the 'world of powerful, underworld men' (ch. 9, p. 128), which she also perceives in the lives of the colliers. In 'Coal-Dust' she walks directly from watching Gerald subjugate the mare to the town, which seems to envelop her in 'a labourer's caress'. The association is important to an understanding of the relationship of Gerald and Gudrun; but so, too, is the peculiar nature of Gudrun's emotional life. She has a marked tendency to self-dramatisation and to erotic fantasy. She lives at a distance from her instinctual drives which she can only contact, as it were, by means of a mental scenario. The 'labourer's caress', for example, is enacted, by substitution, when Gerald kisses her under the bridge; and the thrill, for Gudrun, is precisely the analogy between this and the behaviour of the colliers. She acts out the scene, as 'the colliers' sweethearts would, like herself, hang their heads back limp over their shoulder, and look out from the dark archway' (ch. 24, p. 373). This is neither simply socio-sexual slumming nor, less simply, a fatal attraction to the glamorous underworld of the machine. It is a matter of

Gudrun's need to think herself into emotional experience, to gain private satisfaction by role-playing.

The need to shape and control experience is, perhaps, that of the artist. But, more than this, Gudrun exhibits a deeply divided nature, with contradictory impulses which she cannot reconcile. Her visit to Ursula forces on her both the attractions and the 'impossibility' of marriage. She quickly rejects her vision of herself as married home-maker; just as quickly reacts against a drifting rootlessness; then turns once more against cosy domesticity. Gudrun is here in a state of radical alienation from social and sexual roles. When, after this episode, she goes to her room, she feels distanced even from functional objects – the clock and her food. Her conflict spills over into the relationship with Gerald, and particularly in so far as that involves even a limited social or sexual conformity. On the one hand, for example, she likes the idea of going to the Tyrol as Gerald's mistress; yet she burns with silent anger when this is openly accepted. What disturbs her, at root, is being placed in a role which she has not finally chosen for herself. But she too casts Gerald in a role, that of the great man who is to solve the problems of industrialism in the modern world. According to this scenario, she is to be the wife of the politi-cian–industrialist. But this is a 'fictitious transport', and she cannot sustain the script: 'something seemed to snap in her, and a terrible cynicism began to gain upon her. . . . Everything turned to irony' (ch. 29, p. 469).

Increasingly, then, Gudrun's self-image is constrained by the drama which she must share with others, until eventually she 'splits' herself between Gerald and Loerke. The point at which, poised between the two men, she finally transfers her sexual allegiance, is marked by an extended interior monologue. The passage is remarkable not only in that it gathers in the dominant themes of the relationship, but in that its very uncertainty of narrative voice, subtly shifting, serves to draw together Loerke, Gerald and Gudrun herself. It is worth noting of this passage that the transition for Gudrun from Gerald to Loerke is signalled by the latter's echoing of what Gerald asked of Birkin: 'What was it, after all, that a woman wanted?' (ch. 30, p. 507).

The point is that Gerald can no longer give this woman what she wants. Gerald was to her 'the most crucial instance of the existing world' (p. 508) of man; but Gudrun now wants 'little, ultimate *creatures* like Loerke'. Birkin and Ursula provide a gloss on Loerke, the artist of the machine. To Birkin he is a 'little obscene monster of the darkness' and 'a rat in the river of corruption' (ch. 29, p. 481). Ursula is horrified at the cruelty of his art. Significantly, it is precisely the casual and callous violence of Loerke's artistic methods which arouses Gudrun.

The crucial passage of reflection which signals the transition of Gudrun's passion from Gerald to Loerke also marks the difference in their respective fates: 'It should not be *her* death which broke it. She had farther to go, a farther, slow, exquisite experience to reap, unthinkable subtleties of sensation to know, before she was finished' (ch. 30, p. 508). Gudrun moves on with Loerke; Gerald dies. Gerald has to die and Gudrun can't die. The distinction is between death, and the process of dissolution rolling on. Universal dissolution is summed up and prefigured in the single event of Gerald's death, but the process itself continues. It is Gudrun, not Gerald, who is to go down the long path of dissolution with Loerke, the 'wizard rat that swims ahead' (ch. 29, p. 481).

The failure to perfect a 'Man to Man' relationship between Gerald and Birkin is central to the narrative: it nullifies the entire regenerative fabric as Birkin perceives it. The centrality of this third, 'Man to Man' relationship accounts in part for the book's intense preoccupation with Gerald's death. To say this is not merely to point to an undeclared or unrecognised theme of homosexual love. Lawrence's very excision of certain overtly sexual passages, and in particular the removal of the Prologue describing the friendship of Gerald and Birkin before the events of the novel,[30] are indicative of an awareness of the delicacy of his material. However, the effect of the deletion and revisions is rather to underscore the relationship, as one of the major forward movements of the narrative.

The 'problem' of this friendship is enunciated at the close of the second chapter, where we find 'a pause of strange enmity . . . that was very near to love' (ch. 2, p. 37). Here the narration voices what the two men deny below the verbal level, a 'strange, perilous intimacy'. We find, too, a curious negativity of assertion: 'They had not the faintest belief in deep relationship between men and men. . . .' Both the negation and the 'belief' will be picked up at the end of the book, when Birkin declares his *disbelief* that there *cannot* be such relationship. The reversal is ironic but appropriate in that it is in this sphere – of homosexual love – that Birkin has most to learn. Indeed, his climactic realisation, reserved until 'Marriage or Not', comes when he says to Gerald, 'I believe in the *additional* perfect relationship between man and man – additional to marriage' (ch. 25, p. 397).

If it is a long time before Birkin can articulate the necessary adjunct to 'ultimate marriage', nevertheless his friendship with Gerald has meanwhile developed in parallel to the heterosexual relationships. Their physical attraction is registered as they travel together 'In the Train': the high point of this scene comes when Gerald, reversing the roles of questioned and questioner, asks of Birkin, 'Have you ever really loved anybody?' (ch. 5, p. 63). In the pause and incomplete utterances which follow we find a highly charged subtext. This, and the resultant tension, are characteristic of their exchanges. Birkin and Gerald frequently engage in ostensible discussions of their respective relationships with Ursula and Gudrun; but invariably there is a telling emotional tension between the two men, and varying degrees of physical and quasi-sexual contact. What we get, in effect, is a series of disguised bedroom scenes, whose anticipation of a sexual fulfilment is akin to that of the heterosexual relationships. 'Gladiatorial' (ch. 20) represents sublimated sexual intercourse – and arguably the novel's central sexual act – for a union which will not be physically consummated. This unconsummated and doomed union provides the main sustaining tension of the narrative – its unreached destination – and the most potent equation of sex and death in the novel.

It may be objected that Lawrence is merely dealing with the romantic male bonding which was fashionable at the time; but, surely, this of all novels cannot escape the effect of foregrounding by suppression. In a narrative which places so much emphasis on sexuality, we can hardly overlook the force of the contrast between the sexual rhetoric of Ursula and Birkin, and the ecstatic sado-masochism of Gerald and Gudrun (both occasionally overstated to the point of flaccidity), and the extreme tension attaching to simple, direct touch between the two men.

This reading of the Gerald–Birkin relationship as dramatically integral – as the 'positive solution' of a genuine sexual love and friendship – might also be countered by the observation that each scene involving the two men consists substantially of a discussion of the two heterosexual pairings, even though this discussion may

range further, to more generalised issues. Perhaps, then, this is a
choric motif, providing a running commentary on the narrative?
This is to see Gerald–Birkin as essentially subsidiary, with
Gerald as a functional figure on hand to listen to Birkin's oracular
pronouncements. But this rather Jamesian reading is, I think,
invalidated by the dramatic rendering and by the extreme
emotional tension of what seem to me to be central episodes.
Certainly, however, their discussions are vital: it is the intersec-
tion of the discussions with the developing physical and emotional
bond between Gerald and Birkin which is the problematic core of
the novel.

The first of what I have called bedroom scenes occurs at the
weekend party at Breadalby, when Gerald is given an intercom-
municating room with Birkin, and maximises the opportunity for
intimacy. Here, as elsewhere, Gerald takes the initiative, coming
in to sit on Birkin's bed. And Birkin, despite a passive and
childlike innocence, is intensely aware of Gerald's physicality, of
his white legs, 'full, muscular' (ch. 8, p. 107). In this scene Birkin
deflects Gerald's advance, turning his face aside at the other's
gaze. But Gerald continues his attentions in 'Water-Party'; and
his promise to explain to Birkin what the latter means to him –
'more than you know' (ch. 14, p. 211) – is fulfilled in 'Man to
Man'. The title of this chapter itself suggests a significant
confrontation. Again, Gerald comes to Birkin's bedroom and,
Birkin being ill, adopts a protective role. But his gaze is
'penetrating' (ch. 16, p. 231), with 'subtle eyes of knowledge', and
there is between them a 'deep, uneasy feeling' (p. 226). The
deepening intimacy produces what is for Birkin a crucial
epiphany: 'the problem of love and eternal conjunction between
two men' (p. 231). Suddenly, halfway through the novel, and
after realisation of the problems of heterosexual love, Birkin
experiences the 'necessity' to 'love a man purely and fully'. Both
the necessity and the purity underline the positive nature of the
realisation (and this is the point at which Birkin is depicted as
learning most, and therefore of having been hitherto limited and
repressed).

The overt declaration of love is translated – or retracted – into
Birkin's idea of the *Blutbrüderschaft*. Birkin's clear, happy eyes
testify to his purity; and he now makes his first physical advance,
'putting out his hand towards Gerald' (p. 232). The reversal, and
the problem, is Gerald's reticent response. It isn't that Gerald is

unattracted to Birkin: he is 'deeply bondaged in fascinated attraction'. But, whereas Birkin invests the *Blutbrüderschaft* with ritual, mystical and even heroic meaning, Gerald thinks keenly and physically of blood, rubbed into the wound. Each, that is, reacts in character, and at variance with the other: their relationship, only just begun, begins to sour. In the opposition between them Birkin, with authorial sanction, perceives the limitation of Gerald, 'as if fated, doomed, limited . . . a sort of fatal halfness'. The episode ends with a sexually explicit cameo in which Gerald, 'turgid with energy' (p. 235), gazes down at Birkin's exposed throat; and an intense sexuality attaches to Birkin's gesture of reaching his hand out from under the bedclothes to clasp Gerald's arm. Gerald's eyes are filled with 'warm light and with unadmitted love' (p. 236). The word 'unadmitted' is crucial, as Gerald will subsequently deny the love that Birkin asks of him.

The wrestling-match of 'Gladiatorial' is even more sexually explicit, and is the first of the three physical consummations, of the three pairs of lovers: from this point on the relationships develop in tight harness. Here, Birkin is the active partner, penetrating Gerald with a 'physical intelligence' and a 'fine, sublimated energy' (ch. 20, p. 305) as they struggle towards orgasmic crisis: 'At length Gerald lay back inert on the carpet, his breast rising in great slow panting, whilst Birkin kneeled over him, almost unconscious.' Even more significant, though, than the sexuality of the encounter, is their difficulty in returning to conversation, when Birkin has 'withdrawn' after a prolonged post-coital intimacy: 'there were long spaces of silence between their words. The wrestling had some deep meaning to them – an unfinished meaning' (p. 307). The 'spaces of silence' and the 'unfinished meaning' are a gloss on the problematic nature of this exploratory relationship. The dialogue is here marked by tentative, negative, incomplete statements: 'I don't know'; 'I can't tell'; 'I doubt it' (p. 311). These fragmented, exhausted exchanges comprehend and anticipate all the possibilities of relationship now open to the narrative progression, and pick up again the topics which the two men discussed 'In the Train', including Gerald's inability to 'express what it is' that he yearns for.

At this stage in the narrative, authorial disfavour for Gerald is beginning to bite. The most stringent statement of his failure to meet Birkin's demands comes, significantly, in the interstices of their discussion, in 'Marriage or Not', of whether Gerald should marry Gudrun. As usual, the debate is tentative: question begets question, side-stepping the issue, with Gerald repeating insistently, 'what's the alternative [to marriage]' (ch. 25, p. 397). This is to be the most urgent question raised by the narrative, crucial to its search for normative configuration; although its binary opposition is demonstrably false, as Birkin implies in rejecting the exclusivity of *égoisme à deux* in favour of 'additional' 'Man to Man' love. Birkin's declaration of faith here is the testing-point of the novel: *this* is the model which the text is to set against dissolution and apocalypse; and it fails.

In fact the declaration is immediately set against Gerald's limitations. He rejects Birkin's affirmation of the value of marriage: he considers it a doom, even if a social necessity. But, equally, he cannot accept the 'additional' love. The signals here are clear: Birkin's other way' is described, authorially, as a 'bond of pure trust and love' (p. 398), and it is evident that Gerald might have had both. The final paragraph of the chapter goes beyond Gerald's capacity to rationalise or verbalise his responses; but its tacit logical sequencing reveals the attitude of the text to him at this point. I have attempted to make this sequencing explicit by italicising the stated and (inserted within brackets) the implied, links:

> [*Although friendship is not an exclusive alternative to marriage*] *Yet* he could not accept the offer. [*Because*] There was a numbness upon him, a numbness *either* of unborn, absent volition *or* of atrophy. Perhaps it was the absence of volition [= *either*]. *For* he was strangely elated at Rupert's offer. *Yet* he was still more glad to reject it, not to be committed [= *or*].

What is damning here, in the authorial analysis of Gerald's motives, is the implicit expansion of the either/or. Neither alternative is complimentary to Gerald, although the comparative leniency of the 'either' – the 'absence of volition' – is compounded by his elation, which at least grants to him divided impulses. But it is the 'or' – which, as the sequencing suggests, is the genuine motive – which stands as a savage indictment of emotional atrophy. This rejection is a crux: Gerald's refusal to commit himself is a tragic choice.

The issue is not, however, a simple one. When, in 'A Chair', Birkin describes to Ursula his synthesised vision – his positive solution for the novel – he is checked by her objection, 'You've got me. . . . Why should you *need* others?' (ch. 26, p. 409). The problem is a real one, as Birkin's perplexity suggests. Not only are Gerald and Ursula uncomprehending or hostile; but Birkin himself doesn't know the answer either; and the question hangs fire until the closing pages of the book.

The relationship of Gerald and Birkin has, virtually, ended by this point; but we see their friendship working through to its end in three crucial scenes, which throw fresh light on the two figures, and cast into question again the motives and experience of each. The first of these, in 'Continental', is brief and slight; but already the two are growing apart. Gerald's thoughts range to 'what *is* the end?' (ch. 29, p. 481), and there is a change in him. No longer detached, amused and patronising, he seems *heavy* with experience, as he speaks in a 'flat, doomed voice' (p. 482). The second of the three scenes is their farewell, at the end of the same chapter. Gerald is now almost totally withdrawn, speaking 'as if in a trance, verbal and blank' (p. 495). As he struggles to articulate his extremity he condemns the dead-end love of female sexual tyranny: 'you blast yourself', 'you're shrivelled'. When they revert to talking of their own friendship, Birkin says bitterly that he has loved Gerald. But Gerald counters his declaration with his 'Have you . . . or do you think you have?' Despite the disclaimer, 'He was hardly responsible for what he said' (or perhaps all the more because of it), that unanswered question, and Gerald's 'icy scepticism', must echo forever in the void left by his death. The point is that Gerald, here, is more in touch than Birkin with direct, ultimate experience (his weird agonised gestures in the snow speak even more than his words); and his question must jerk us into a new perspective on Birkin.

In the third of the three scenes, Gerald is 'present' as a corpse. Birkin laments his death: 'He had loved him. And yet he felt chiefly disgust at the inert body lying there' (ch. 31, p. 536). That 'yet' is the divided response of love set against the fact of mortality. But this is more to Birkin than an epiphany of Death (though it is that too); in the 'inert' frozen body we see with him the *essential* Gerald. But there is even more: 'He reached and touched the dead face' (p. 537). That touch is the final physical intimacy of their relationship – in the final bedroom scene – and encompasses both consummation and loss. What is at issue here – as Birkin's ambivalent behaviour suggests – is the meaning of Gerald's death: what Birkin, and the novel, are to make of it. There is, it seems to me, a disjuncture here, between the two; and I shall deal first with the response of Birkin.

Gerald's death is the ultimate fact of which Birkin must take cognisance. In retracing Gerald's dying steps he envisages alternative scenarios and endings, only to realise their falsity: there was, literally, no other way for Gerald. Having decided on the *necessity* of Gerald's death, Birkin must next find a *meaning* for it. The meaning which Birkin reads into Gerald's death and, by extrapolation, into the possible death of the species, is an evolutionary process, perceived as progress. Birkin is now way beyond race or national death: he takes on the universe.

Like Captain Shotover in *Heartbreak House*, Birkin reconciles religion with evolutionary theory. The vision of both figures is providential ('God, the creative mystery' ch. 31, p. 538) and progressive ('to work hand in hand with God', *FACHH*, p. 64). Birkin, less anxiously and more passively than Shotover, can contemplate without fear the total eradication of mankind: 'If humanity ran into a cul-de-sac, and expended itself, the timeless creative mystery would bring forth some other being, finer, more wonderful, some new, more lovely race, to carry on the embodiment of creation' (ch. 31, p. 538). 'If' is a key word here. Birkin's model copes with Armageddon, but rests on a conditional. This, basically ethical and exhortatory, position is the hidden 'either' or 'unless' envisaged as much by this text as by *Heartbreak House*.

The two texts show, in fact, a close correspondence. Apart from Shotover's warning about navigation ('unless') there was Hector's declamation, 'I tell you, one of two things must happen. Either out of that darkness some new creation will come to supplant us as we have supplanted the animals, or the heavens will fall in thunder and destroy us' (*Heartbreak House*, Act III, p. 159). With this we can compare Birkin: 'God could do without the ichthyosauri and the mastodon. These monsters failed creatively to develop, so God, the creative mystery, dispensed with them. In the same way the mystery could dispense with man, should he too fail creatively to change and develop' (ch. 31, p. 538). Hector's either/or is 'purely destructive', as Lawrence said of his novel: both alternatives are negative. But his pessimism is contained by the play, which overall endorses Shotover's more positive position. Birkin's position is a fundamentally optimistic model capable of infinite recursion: there is no dimension of crisis which it could not contain. Nevertheless, Birkin too is contained by the text. The narrative steps back, to 'place' his reflections: 'It was very consoling to Birkin to think this'. Birkin's model is, precisely, a consoling myth. Moreover, the text takes him out of his reverie in the mountains, to force on him once again the fact of Gerald's body: 'Dead, dead and cold' (p. 539).

If Birkin's evolutionary optimism is a limited vision, we are still faced with the meaning which the *novel* makes of Gerald's death. The balance between Gerald and Birkin in the narrative is crucial: however vividly and sharply the text points to Gerald's inadequacies, it grants him undoubted stature and imaginative sympathy. The account of his death, in particular, with its concentrated anguish, is a supreme moment in the novel. This description gathers force and intensity by what may seem a perverse feature in this experimental novel (it is closer to the method of the short stories). Gerald is rendered not merely from the outside, but almost entirely as an object. He is hardly credited with thought-processes; the changes he undergoes are largely passional and inarticulate; and the strongest impressions we have of him are visual and tactile.

So, in this last passage, Gerald is treated without authorial distance. There is no gap for irony in the narration: we cannot but consent to the short descriptive sentences which fuse observation and experience ('It was as cold as sleep' – ch. 30, p. 533). This might, arguably, be simply the culmination of the portrayal of Gerald's limitation (he has been called *'borné'* – p. 509). But the episode combines a luminous simplicity with very great emotional power. It may be that Gerald, in his absurd and solitary world, reaches beyond *Women in Love* with an existential appeal. Within the text, it is precisely the simple, lucid embedding of Gerald's experience *in* the landscape which is so suggestive. In his mindless actions Gerald moves through a landscape which incorporates iterative imagery already established by the text: ice and snow, valley and mountains, darkness and the small bright moon, the hollow and the ridge, the navel of the world. Gerald's actions here are perfectly fused with the snowy landscape. There is total identification between his stumbling steps and the metaphoric language of crisis established by the novel. That snowfield has been generated by the iterative imagery of the earlier narrative.

The snowy wasteland is not simply a drastically reduced social setting, but a landscape of the mind, whose topography signifies only in relation to the dream vision of the symbolic action. In 'Continental' the characters have passed into a 'different world' (ch. 29, p. 448), a 'waste of snow, like a dream' (p. 449). The landscape has a heavy, solid feel to it, with its masses of snow and walls of rock; yet it is apprehended variously by the characters, in discrete metaphors. To Gudrun, this is a vision of heaven: we see her peeping through the window at the 'radiant spikes of blossom in the heavenly upper world' (p. 452). To Ursula, the very air is 'purposive' and indeed 'malevolent' (p. 458). Being 'Snowed Up' is expressive of the cul-de-sac, the blind valley, which Gerald comes to, and where Gudrun, significantly, has found her place. This is a cradle, where Gerald falls asleep: when he is found, it is in the foetal position, in a hollow basin of snow.

The account of Gerald's death operates as a sympathetic centre, as an epiphany. Gerald, like Gudrun, has found his place. But what *is* this place? Do we have here, for example, the death of a hero? It was Gudrun's reveries which saw Gerald as parliamentary leader and industrial saviour. Her 'fictitious transport' was false, but she perceived the area of falsity; and her perception did not preclude Gerald from the status of hero. Gudrun saw him as the epitome of heroism and imperialism in the old world: 'my young hero' (p. 471). She blames not Gerald, but the collapse of the system: 'the game isn't worth even you. You are a fine thing really, why should you be used on such a poor show?' Gudrun's despairing cynicism derives from a heroic vision of Gerald, faced with the bankruptcy of the world in which the 'hero' must act.

A heroic rendering of Gerald is not restricted to Gudrun's vision. Birkin introduced him to the company at the Café Pompadour as 'a soldier, and an explorer, and a Napoleon of industry' (ch. 6, p. 70). Gerald's career has encompassed the traditional paths of the ruling class. He embodies Empire as well as industrial society: he speaks 'imperiously', he contemplates going down the 'old imperial road' (ch. 30, p. 517). And there is the quotation from *Hamlet*, which here bespeaks the crisis of empire: 'Imperial Caesar dead, and turn'd to clay / Would stop a hole to keep the wind away' (ch. 31, p. 539).[31] Gudrun reflects that the old order is all 'old hat' (ch. 29, p. 471); and, in so far as Gerald is the hero of Empire, his heroism is doomed. When

Gudrun suggests with despair in her voice that they drink to Britannia, it is Gerald who willingly fills the glasses.

There are further heroic intimations in the rendering of Gerald. He is seen, again in the first instance by Gudrun, as a tragic hero. She sees herself as Cleopatra, presumably to Gerald's Antony. Like Shakespeare's Cleopatra, Gudrun has immortal longings in her: in the extended death throes of their love-affair, she constantly gazes out of the window at the landscape, 'transcendent' (ch. 29, p. 472) and 'immortally beautiful' (p. 452). But we do not need to rely on Gudrun for the suggestion in Gerald of a classical and tragic hero. Near the end of the book Gerald is 'agonistes' (p. 491), in a 'real agony' (ch. 30, p. 498). The hint of Samson here, and specifically of Milton's *Samson Agonistes*, is reinforced by repeated references to blindness. When Gerald talked to Birkin, everything was 'horribly blind' (ch. 29, p. 481); after Birkin has gone, he exerts his will 'blindly' (ch. 30, p. 496); Gudrun resents his 'blind force of passion' (p. 508); and the desire to kill her comes in a 'blinding flash' (p. 520). In his last conversation with Birkin, Gerald confessed that sexual love 'leaves you sightless' (ch. 29, p. 495). The analogy with Samson suggests failure and impotence, a bondage to female dominance, as well as heroic suffering. More importantly, perhaps, the trapped hero pulls down the entire fabric around him.[32]

Gerald is a hopeless case. That is why he goes to his death in the snow. Seen simply, the villain of industrial society is eliminated, as in *Heartbreak House*. But that elimination, although clearly a function of the ethical drive of the narrative towards a normative configuration (like Mangan, Gerald is sacrificed for society), is by no means as simply punitive or 'consoling' as either an analysis of Gerald's *Wille zur Macht*, or his inability to return Birkin's love, might suggest. We are dealing, in Gerald's death, with the climax of the fiction, as the process of dissolution and decay finally concentrates in that one figure, dying alone in the snow. This is not, of course, the end of the novel; but what comes after, as epilogue or coda, cannot (as we shall see) deprive it of a peculiar power. Despite the closing emphasis of the narrative on survival, Gerald's frozen corpse still strikes us, as it does all the characters, as momentous, as putting actually into insignificance all subsequent and antecedent events.

To put it minimally, the final configuration does not, and could not, exclude Gerald. His *inclusion* is precisely what matters, to

Birkin. At the same time, his death is the book's absolute loss, its finality. We return, then, to the meaning of Gerald's death, to how it signifies for the text. And we go on, to the question of what ending, or what End, this purposive and apocalyptic narrative has led us to. Is Gerald expelled by the narrative, selected out from the ratified group? Or has he become an inclusive figure, whose death encompasses all else in the novel? Does *Women in Love*, by killing off Gerald, contain and go beyond him, as its negative solution? Or does Gerald, as it were, refuse to be expelled: does he rather 'contain' the novel, as not merely its negative pole, but also its overarching necessity?

These questions direct us towards the ending. The text supplies what are, in effect, two endings. One – the death of Gerald – symbolically encapsulates the fate of a civilisation. The other, a realistic coda, after the cataclysm, places the 'barren tragedy' in the context of life continuing for the other characters. But both endings – 'Snowed Up' and 'Exeunt' – refer everything back to Gerald, as the core of the novel's experience. The close of the novel both accommodates Gerald's death, and is defeated by it. John Goode has pointed to the centrality of Gerald's death, as 'an apocalyptic image of the end of the social world which he dominates and by which he is created'.[33] This puts it succinctly; however, Goode goes on to conclude that *Women in Love* is 'a novel about a world which has already gone'.[34] There is, certainly, an elegiac flavour to *Women in Love*; but is this, even so, merely a threnody for 'things gone dead'? To suggest that the process is completed, the world already ended, seems to me to close down the complexity of the progressions and the closure of the narrative.

This complexity, as in the other texts we have considered, is a matter of multiple endings and of problematic closure. It is not simply, as I suggested above, that we find two successive endings. The last two chapters, 'Snowed Up' and 'Exeunt', each suggest or incorporate alternative endings: set together, their interrelationship is complicated; and 'Exeunt' leads, as we shall see, to a disturbed dis-closure. Moreover, even this need not have been the end, as Lawrence's rejected drafts, his revisions, and the later play *Touch and Go* indicate. However, we do not need to go beyond the end of the book as we have it, to discover in these last two chapters, for all their tensions and irresolution – indeed, because of these aspects – a peculiar appropriateness. These chapters draw into themselves one of the major dualisms of the narrative: the sustained 'debate' between finality and continuance. The End, and ending, are actually and explicitly an issue for *Women in Love*, and persistently foregrounded by the narrative. It is not enough to say that *Women in Love* depicts the death of a society, nor even that it predicts this death. The death is conditional, and the terms of the condition only partially defined: hence the text is more profoundly expressive of crisis than a simple reference to the historical moment might suggest. *Women in Love* is specifically not a novel about a world which has already gone: it is a novel 'about' the anxiety of the imminent disappearance of its world. The text itself, that is, exhibits acute end-anxiety.

Lawrence's rejected titles, 'Dies Irae' and 'Latter Days', would have been appropriate enough: the characters of his novel experience keenly the apocalyptic sense of an ending. Birkin introduces the motif 'In the Train', when he confesses to feeling 'such a despair, so hopeless, as if it were the end of the world' (ch. 5, p. 67). But the end of the world is ambiguous for the text, which is concerned to explore its significance: what does the End mean? and does it matter? Birkin sees the attractions of a 'clean, lovely, humanless world' (ch. 11, p. 142), and welcomes 'the end of the world, and grass' (p. 144). The End may, after all, be the era of transition, according to the cyclical theory which Lawrence adopts from Herakleitos. As Birkin muses, 'And so our world-cycle passes. There is now to come the new day' (ch. 16, p. 225). Against Birkin's muted optimism, and against the relationship forged with Ursula, which may also be a decadent flowering, the text sets the satiric vision of Gudrun and Loerke. They envisage 'the destruction of the world by a ridiculous catastrophe of man's invention' (ch. 30, p. 510). Despite the negativity of their relationship, Gudrun and Loerke must also be taken into account, with their vision of catastrophe as a matter for ridicule. Although Birkin works through the meaning of the End more tenaciously and cogently than the others, his rationalisation and speculation are similarly a measure of crisis. Birkin, too, may be part of things gone or going dead.

The End and ending are emphasised by the ruminations of the characters: they are obsessed with direction, finality and death. Earlier in this chapter we considered the questions they ask, and the alternative possibilities they see. In her reverie on death Ursula said, 'Then let it end', but rejected death in favour of the 'next step' (ch. 15, p. 215). However, the next step is hardly ever certain. As we proceed, the characters peer more anxiously into the future, to 'decide' the direction and outcome of events. One set of possibilities, relating to love, was discussed by Gerald and Birkin:

> 'The possibilities of love exhaust themselves.'
> 'Do they? And then what?'
> 'Then you die', said Gerald.
> 'So you ought', said Birkin.   (ch. 20, p. 301)

The question 'And then what?' can move freely between simple narrative curiosity and the sense of an ending. But, as the succeeding exchange shows, what Gerald and Birkin are here concerned with is the accurate prediction, and the ethical and fictive confirmation, of an ending. And the problem, for the narrative as for the characters, is that the ending is uncertain and its meaning ambivalent.

We read, with reference to Gerald's desire for Gudrun, that 'the finality of the end was dreaded as deeply as it was desired' (ch. 24, p. 375). This is the kernel of end-anxiety, the divided impulse towards finality which pervades the narrative in every aspect of its progression. It affects individual survival, personal relationships, the fate of the nation, and the End of the World. However, even the dividedness of this impulse is not the full complexity. It is Gudrun who voices the alternative: 'Or perhaps there was no end' (ch. 30, p. 525). It is this, dreaded, alternative which provides the dimension of crisis for *Women in Love*. In Professor Kermode's terms, this is a yet more terrifying 'disconfirmation' than the End itself: it is the *endlessness* of the modern apocalypse. Gudrun dubs it 'endless unrelief' (p. 524).

This fundamental dualism of *Women in Love*, the tension between ending and endlessness, finality and continuance, is expressed in a subtle and insistent language. The narrative establishes, by repetition, modification and association, a vocabulary of finality analogous to the vocabulary of war which we discerned earlier. Again we find repetition of sets or clusters of lexical items; and, in this case, the sets define for us the oppositions involved. In a single sustained passage of interior monologue we can find *ending* expressed as 'round and completed', 'closed round', 'close', 'completeness' and a 'last effort'.

In the same passage, *not to end* is 'open', 'disclosure', 'unfolding' 'incomplete', 'unfinished' (ch. 30, p. 501). As these examples suggest, evaluative connotations attach to the terms used to 'define' the dualism: moreover, the implied positive or negative shifts, according to character and context in the narrative (the sample chosen was one of Gerald's 'soliloquies'). The language of finality is not given or fixed: in its language of ending, *Women in Love* may be seen struggling towards definition and judgement.

The impulse towards finality culminates in the ending of the relationship between Gerald and Gudrun. Gerald himself embodies the impulse towards finality, unable to tolerate an inconclusive affair: 'I believe it is over. But it isn't finished. . . . There must be a conclusion, there must be finality' (ch. 30, p. 519). Gudrun, too, longs for closure. She expresses it as 'perfect enfolded sleep' (p. 524), using three highly charged lexical items of the language of finality. But Gudrun can envisage a (limited) number of alternative progressions: 'There is only repetition possible, or the going apart of the two protagonists, or the subjugating of the one will to the other, or death' (p. 508). In effect, the narrative works through each of the possibilities, to arrive at the 'conclusion' of Gerald's death.

The force of Gerald's walk to his death derives substantially from his insistence, even in this extremity, of actively moving towards an ending: 'He was weak, but he did not want to rest, he wanted to go on and on, to the end. Never again to stay, till he came to the end' (p. 531). The agony of his last walk is a blind struggle, without purpose or direction, towards finality: 'He only wanted to go on, to go on whilst he could, to move, to keep going, that was all, to keep going, until it was finished' (p. 532). In Gerald's death we find distilled the tension between going on and finishing, between continuance and finality. His urge to 'move, to keep going, that was all' reads as the life of a Didi or a Gogo, as *Endgame*. Here, as in *Heartbreak House*, we are on the threshold of the Absurd.

Women in Love sets the sense that 'There must be a finality, a conclusion' against the dread that 'perhaps there was no end'. Its language of the End and of ending translates easily enough into the issue of narrative closure; and the text itself provides what is in effect a dis-closure or non-solution, a closure which confirms endlessness. Before we turn, finally, to that closure, we can look first at the endings which Lawrence entertained, and rejected.

What we have to take account of here is both the revisions which Lawrence made to the concluding chapters in the draft typescripts of the novel, and his decision not to use the 'epilogue' which appears as 'Chapter XIII' in his handwritten notebooks.[35] In the first of the two complete typescripts Ursula does not appear at all. The emphasis falls entirely on an emotional close-up of Birkin's misery, as he weeps over Gerald's body. Gerald's death spells the failure of Birkin's vision of complete happiness. Nevertheless, we see the text reaching towards a qualification of Birkin's total immersion in grief. This typescript contains at least one stage of revision, in handwritten alterations and additions. Even before revision, the typescript suggests a 'Perhaps', which strives to discern some positive in Gerald's death: his 'very failure is a fulfilment', with its own integrity. The handwritten revisions move from the tentative 'Perhaps' to a stronger 'But', and shift the emphasis from Gerald to Birkin. Bereavement and loss are transcended by Birkin's recognition of other possibilities: 'we needn't all be like that'. And Birkin comes through his grief with a final note of courage and affirmation: 'I am not afraid or ashamed to die and be dead.'[36] Even here, though, we should note what will carry forward as a persistent tension of closure in *Women in Love*: the articulation by means of negation of what would otherwise read straightforwardly as positive assertion. The syntax retracts and undercuts apparent affirmation. Moreover, the final word is, after all, 'dead': Birkin's courage is the triumph of death.

In revising the ending of this first typescript Lawrence moved outwards from a myopic focus on Birkin's grief, and made the significant addition of Ursula. The text draws back, as it were, to place Birkin and Gerald in a broader perspective, and one which further emphasises not only the wider implications of Gerald's death, but also the problematic areas of tension hinted at in the earlier version. This later, second typescript also contains internal revisions, including a number of handwritten pages added at the end. The additions and substitutions, which render this ending virtually identical to the published version, comprise Birkin's pilgrimage to the site of Gerald's death, and the two conversations with Ursula, over the body, and back at the Mill. In this revised second typescript we are close to the final stage of resolving the fiction; but even here there are important variations from the final version. Ursula's last speech tells Birkin that he could not have his 'Man to Man' relationship because 'it's wrong, impossible'.[37] The subsequent replacement of 'wrong' by 'false' represents a slight, but crucial, shift from the ethical to the theoretical. In the final version Ursula contradicts, rather than criticises in moral terms, Birkin's model of complete happiness.

Before considering the implications, and the tensions, of the published version, we might glance at the extra or alternative ending contained in Lawrence's exercise-book. This ending is the incomplete fragment of a 'Chapter XIII' which survives as the final page of the last of the ten exercise-books which Lawrence used to write his novel.[38] On 31 October 1916 Lawrence wrote to Pinker, his literary agent, that the novel was finished, 'all but the last chapter, which, being a sort of epilogue, I want to write later'.[39] It seems unlikely, from a scrutiny of the second typescript, that this 'last chapter' could be 'Exeunt'. The chapter-heading in itself suggests that this deleted passage (it is crossed out in the exercise-book) was written earlier than the second typescript, which already further subdivides the chapters. It is more probable that the 'epilogue' which Lawrence referred to is the uncompleted 'Chapter XIII'. The status of this fragment remains problematic: however, it may represent an intermediate stage of composition. If this were the case, the sequence would be more or less directly replaced by the scene between Birkin and Ursula.

In this unfinished and discarded 'Chapter XIII' a year has elapsed. Ursula, in Italy, receives a letter from Gudrun, who is in Frankfurt. The letter announces that Gudrun has had a son by Gerald, now six months old, and named Ferdinand Gerald Crich. She has left Loerke, with whom she lived for some months 'as a friend'.[40] The chapter breaks off at the foot of the page, with the incomplete sentence 'Now I am staying';[41] but its alternative progressions and resolutions nevertheless invite comment. Throughout, the narrative of *Women in Love* places a premium on children, or rather on childlessness (in the first chapter Gudrun expressed her distaste at the prospect of having a baby). The birth of Gudrun's child here signifies continuity and regeneration, an opting for life. And the name chosen for this child, whose fair hair 'is like the sun shining on the sea',[42] recalls the character of Ferdinand in *The Tempest*, and the revivifying 'sea change' of the play. This ending would not be a 'barren tragedy': the birth of a son to Gudrun and Gerald would herald a new age, albeit one of dissolution. Even though this could not be an unequivocal affirmation, it would retract the finality both of Gudrun's rejection of Gerald, and of his death. In abandoning this possibility (which invites comparison with the Bast–Schlegel child as a meretricious 'solution'), the novel settles for sterility.

Remnants of the unfinished chapter may be seen in the statement that Gudrun has gone to Dresden, but sent 'no particulars of herself' (ch. 31, p. 541). This information does not, of course, totally preclude her pregnancy (indeed, it recalls Helen Schlegel's disappearance to the continent and her long months of silence). However, the final version does keep Gudrun absent, even though she is 'included' in the configuration by virtue of the mention of her absence. Lawrence's progressive reworkings push Gudrun to the perimeter of the final configuration. From a close-up on Birkin's grief over Gerald's body, we move outwards, to focus on Birkin and Ursula. These two figures finally confront for us the implications of Gerald's death for their own 'ultimate marriage'.

What is most pertinent is, after all, the 'selected' closure; but it is worth noting, again, that even this was not Lawrence's final thought on the matter. The ambivalence of *Women in Love*, its reluctance to let Gerald go, is reflected in his resurrection in the play *Touch and Go*. Here Gerald is exhumed, 'split' into the Norwegian who dies in the ice, and the Englishman who comes home to marry Anabel (Gudrun). Birkin becomes Oliver Turton, and Ursula is dispensed with. The play is primarily concerned to articulate the struggle between labour and capital; but in the process it provides yet another alternative configuration, in which Gerald the industrialist returns from the dead to confront the workers. The problem of Gerald Crich would not, it seems, go away.

'Exeunt' is a post-mortem on Gerald's death. It is a closure which was 'bound to happen' (ch. 30, p. 533), even if Birkin 'didn't want it to be like this' (ch. 31, p. 539); but its tensions resist easy resolution. This final chapter provides an 'Exeunt' for all the main *dramatis personae*, by successive scenes in which all the characters are accounted for. The ending nevertheless calls into question the accommodation or resolution of crisis. We have seen already that Birkin's consoling myth is brought up hard against the fact of Gerald's frozen corpse. What also happens is that the structure of his relationship with Ursula remains permanently damaged by that loss, or rather suspended in a peculiar incompleteness. The pertinent scenes here are the final two: first, when Ursula joins Birkin in contemplating Gerald's body; and, secondly, when they are back in England together, with Gerald now buried. In these two scenes we see the immediacy of bereavement, and its aftermath.

When Birkin returns to look at Gerald, Ursula follows him into the room. These three are to form, as we shall see, an eternal triangle. In this scene we find the first of a series of questions and answers which force into sharp focus the opposition of Ursula and Birkin. This sequence refers us back to Gerald's 'tragic choice' at the end of 'Marriage or Not': ' "He should have loved me", he said. "I offered him" ' (p. 539). Ursula's succeeding question – 'What difference would it have made?' – seeks to thrust Gerald out of the configuration; but Birkin's answer – 'It would! ... It would' – denies her attempt. It is crucial to note, here and subsequently, the centrality, and yet the problematic status, of these questions and answers. Ursula's question can receive no adequate or definitive answer. They are dealing in speculation, and Birkin is reduced to repetitive and empty (because unverifiable) assertion. The force of the questions and contradictions is that they *matter*, and that the 'answers' resolve nothing.

At this juncture Birkin significantly 'forgot her and turned to Gerald'. With the triangle still physically in evidence, he can still 'choose' between Gerald and Ursula. The configuration at this point is rendered visually: 'Ursula stood aside watching the living man stare at the frozen face of the dead man' (p. 540). Ursula eventually draws Birkin back to focus on herself, and they are reconciled by the thought that their love can survive death: 'We shan't have any need to despair, in death.' This is the positive meaning which Birkin and Ursula extract from Gerald's death; but there follows immediately a problematic objection: ' "But need you despair over Gerald?" she said. "Yes", he answered' (p. 541). Again, the question is critical, and the answer absolute and yet empty. Note the continuance implicit in 'need you despair' and in Birkin's unqualified 'Yes'. There is no way in which that need, and that despair, can be resolved. The scene closes here: Birkin is fixed in despair, with no potential for change. He and Ursula must go on living, and the only 'potential' for their lives is that endowed by the narrative. Ursula reminds Birkin, 'You've got me' (p. 540); but he hasn't, and will never have had, Gerald. The effect of this permanent impossibility is to lock

Gerald into their relationship. It is also to leave them where we have so often seen them, in fixed opposition.

The final scene removes Ursula and Birkin physically from Gerald, who has now been buried in England. But his part in their relationship cannot be buried: as before, their conversation intimately and critically involves him. Again, Ursula questions Birkin, radically objecting to his theoretical position, and perpetuating jealousy of her dead 'rival':

> 'Did you need Gerald?' she asked one evening.
> 'Yes', he said.
> 'Aren't I enough for you?' she asked.
> 'No', he said.   (p. 541)

Question and answer here are stylised, bleak and absolute. Birkin replies with a simple 'Yes' to the first question, and 'No' to the second. Ursula is not enough, because Gerald is dead. The three are frozen into a 'pretty little sample of the eternal triangle' (p. 536); and Birkin confirms its persisting incompleteness: 'But to make it complete, really happy, I wanted eternal union with a man too' (p. 541). The implication of the past tense of 'wanted' is that, with Gerald's death, the failure is permanent.

The final sequence sets against each other the two conflicting models: Ursula's, of exclusive heterosexual pairing; Birkin's, of complementary relationships:

> 'I don't believe it', she said. 'It's an obstinacy, a theory, a perversity.'
> 'Well – ' he said.
> 'You can't have two kinds of love. Why should you!'
> 'It seems as if I can't', he said. 'Yet I wanted it.'
> 'You can't have it, because it's false, impossible', she said.
> 'I don't believe that', he answered.   (p. 541)

These last speeches refuse us a consoling, self-contained closure, leaving the narrative in unresolved crisis, and Ursula and Birkin in eternal contradiction. Ursula denies the validity of Birkin's 'theory', as 'false, impossible'. Birkin's contradictory reply is the novel's last word; and that last word is simply a maintained assertion of faith. Moreover, it is assertion expressed as denial, as negation. The language of this closing dialogue, marked by sharp contradiction, undercuts the potential affirmation of the forever-lost relationship which might have been. The narrative stops here, with Ursula and Birkin trapped in incompatible theories which can, by definition, never be proved or resolved, since Gerald – who is the sole test case for the experiment – is dead. And so the novel ends.

The novel has questioned the dimensions of crisis. It has posited an End, and a new beginning, without confirming either. Where it leaves us is precisely where the end of the world frightened Birkin: 'while it hangs imminent and doesn't fall' (ch. 5, p. 67). By virtue of this closing conversation Ursula and Birkin cannot be released from the death of Gerald: it is all referred back to him. But neither can we find a consoling myth of the End in Gerald's death. Humanity, as Ursula rather malevolently commented earlier, persists.

Women in Love is a fiction of permanent and persisting crisis. Its exploitation of the grammar of narrative sequence aligns it to *Howards End* and *Heartbreak House*, and leads us on to the narrative-by-transformation of *The Waste Land*. Responses to *Women in Love* which fret over the authorial sanction on Birkin, or the 'unsatisfactory' rendering of the love of Ursula and Birkin, or the lurid attractiveness of Gerald and Gudrun, or sympathy for the death of Gerald, are not wholly a textual misreading. As a whole, the interest of this text resides substantially in its decentred narrative, in the problematic areas of disjuncture. The novel retracts both its centre and its destination: the centre of sympathy shifts from the ultimate marriage of Birkin and Ursula to the relationship between Gerald and Birkin; and the death of Gerald operates not as liberation by narrative closure, but as a permanent constraint. As was stated earlier in this chapter, the balance which the narrative maintains between Birkin and Gerald, and the authorial stance in relation to these characters, are crucial. There is, in effect, an imbalance; and the authorial stance is uncertain. Imbalance and uncertainty characterise the crisis of *Women in Love*.

5　*The Waste Land*

'with the arid plain behind me'

The overt challenge which *The Waste Land* issues to its readers is that of density and discontinuity. The dense network of historical, literary and mythical allusion is an attempt to depict modern European society and consciousness in the fullness and complexity of its cultural tradition. This allusive method demands that the poem be decoded by a reader constantly alert to subtle counterpoint between text and referent. The historical perspective it provides is both sophisticated and ironic, discriminating critically between past and present, more often than not to the disadvantage of the latter. It is this value-orientation, rather than the density of allusion itself, which raises hackles.

The discontinuity of the poem relates to its organisation, often described as non-discursive and spatial, as opposed to the smooth continuous linearity of a realistic fiction or narrative poem. What Eliot sent to his friend Ezra Pound in late 1921 was in effect a bundle of separate poems. Even after the two poets had collaborated to revise the material, what went forward as *The Waste Land* (together with some fragments, dating from as early as 1911) was at most a series or sequence without apparent connectives. The structuring by juxtaposition, whether seen as genuinely spatial or as a surface 'fragmentation' of underlying continuity, is perhaps *The Waste Land*'s most notable and notorious feature. But both allusiveness and non-discursive juxtaposition distinguish the poem as definitively Modernist – and invite charges of wilful obscurantism and elitism.

Certainly *The Waste Land* has a biography of its own, in the furore which greeted its publication in 1922, and in the weight of exegesis and intensity of critical engagement which have since then attended it. Early reviews, anxious to be positive, made a virtue of non-linearity. The judgement of I. A. Richards (which can now be seen in the perspectives of imagism and his own *Practical Criticism*) was sonorous and influential:

> the items are united by the accord, contrast, and interaction of their emotional effects, not by an intellectual scheme that analysis must work out. The value lies in the unified response which this interaction creates in the right reader. The only intellectual activity required takes place in the realisation of the separate items.[1]

Richards to an extent belied his own strictures. He wrote of the 'compression' of the poem, its vertical layering by allusion, but declared that what was thus compressed was an epic. He countered the despised 'symbolical' approach by an assertion of naturalism – a characteristic of narrative mode, whether in fiction or drama. In fact Richards put his finger on the narrative content of the poem in a derogatory reference to 'squeezing out a doctrine'. The progression, if there is one, rests on spiritual metamorphosis, or a movement towards faith.

Leavis, in *New Bearings in English Poetry* (1932), discerned this element in the 'seeming disjointedness'.[2] He recognised in the framework of myth a potential for narrative progression, although he denied its resolution:

> It exhibits no progression:
>
> > I sat upon the shore
> > Fishing, with the arid plain behind me
>
> – the thunder brings no rain to revive the Waste Land, and the poem ends where it began.[3]

That last phrase is unfortunate – it is hard to see how it could be true of any piece of imaginative writing – but Leavis rightly focused here on the textual crux with respect to progression and closure, and the passage he quotes has preoccupied many critics.

> I sat upon the shore
> Fishing, with the arid plain behind me
> (423–4)

It is not surprising that these lines should so force themselves on our attention. For one thing, they draw on the symbolic landscape, the physical and mental topography, which the poem has by this stage vividly established. There is the shore, the plain, and the stretch of water. And in this wasteland setting we return to what has gradually but insistently emerged as the main voice within the poem, the consciousness which merges elements of Ferdinand Prince of Naples, the one-eyed merchant, the drowned Phoenician sailor and others, and whose failures of perception, knowledge, speech and sexuality connect otherwise discrete experience in the various parts of the poem. This 'I' has been observer and agent, usually silent and passive even when most engaged in the action. Here he is 'Fishing' and again musing, as in line 191. His stance represents the culminating, ambiguous experience of *The Waste Land*, and sets the scope and nature of the text's closure. The Fisher sat 'upon the shore / Fishing, with the arid plain behind' him. His disposition in the topography – his insertion in this landscape – depends on prepositions of place: 'upon' the shore, 'with' the plain 'behind' him. The spatial perspective seems simple enough until we realise that the 'with', placed as it is next to 'Fishing', works slightly against the distancing effect of 'behind'. More precisely, it hints at a temporal mode: the 'events' of fishing and the arid landscape are simultaneous. The ambiguity of the spatial and the temporal extends to 'behind'. In which dimension is the arid plain *behind* the Fisher? The configuration is not certain: he may have passed through or beyond an experience which is now behind him (in the past), or alternatively he may be situated still within the landscape and the experience it denotes, 'with' the arid plain juxtaposed.

The salient point here, which clarifies but does not resolve the ambiguity, is that (as Jessie Weston noted in *From Ritual to Romance* (1920), the book which gave Eliot his title and many of the poem's recurrent motifs) the wasteland is not only spiritual as well as physical, but also temporal as well as spatial. The wasteland has its base in vegetation myths which are seasonal and cyclic, and its landscape delineates duration, an experience in time, a state of being poised between death and renewal. Eliot exploits the metaphoric complexity of this landscape and its legends. The poem increasingly operates by a paradoxical conflation of stasis and progression, the 'fixed confusion' which we find in the early draft 'So through the evening' (preserved in the facsimile and transcript edited by Valerie Eliot[4]), which contributed to the final version of part v, and whose closing line includes this striking collocation.[5] '. . . fixed confusion' forces together contradictory notions of permanence and of temporary, disturbed aberration. It appropriately describes the mode of the poem.

What we are dealing with is a double confusion, of space–time, and past–present. 'I sat . . . / Fishing', where the line-division serves to emphasise the present participle, complicates what is otherwise a statement in the past tense. (The effect is similar to the combined impact of 'with' and 'behind'.) However, the predicate 'sat' is itself ambiguously indicative of a single specific event, or habitual action. (In the longhand draft the forms 'sit'–'sat' are superimposed, but the present tense was apparently Eliot's first thought.) The temporal mode uncertainly modulates from past ('sat') to continuous present ('Fishing'), and on to either the future or a declared intention. 'Shall I at least set my lands in order?' (425) implies the possibility of future events determined by human choice and action, in a prevailing climate of passivity and stasis. The exploitation of tense-shift to produce such temporal uncertainty is a controlling device of the poem. 'What the Thunder Said' is concerned to *situate* in time and space, its connectives 'After', 'now', 'Here', 'this', confronting us with immediacy and a concatenation of events. In linguistic terms, the text plays on and between the proximate and the non-proximate. The present participle, with its alternative verbal and adjectival connotations, enables this manipulation of the time-axis; and the net effect is to suspend the poem in a continuous present.

The Waste Land declares the centrality of its present participles in the opening lines:

> April is the cruellest month, breeding
> Lilacs out of the dead land, mixing
> Memory and desire, stirring
> Dull roots with spring rain.
> Winter kept us warm, covering
> Earth in forgetful snow, feeding
> A little life with dried tubers.

The lyric shape of this opening is sharply etched by the strategies of intense nominalisation; of ending each line with a present participle; and by the counterpoint of line-division, as the caesura after the penultimate word emphasises the participle and urges the eye on to the first (noun) item of the next line. The verse sets up a tension or hiatus – between the old year and the new, dormancy and growth – or between completed and ongoing action. The nouns here form two groups or clusters ('April . . . month . . . spring . . . Winter'; 'Lilacs . . . roots . . . rain . . . earth . . . snow . . . tubers') contained by the axes of 'Winter' – 'spring' and 'dead land' – 'little life'. These noun phrases vie with each other, and also generate tension internally, by such contrastive collocations as 'little life' and 'Dull roots'.

Apart from the noun-series, the notable lexical items are the participles 'breeding', 'mixing', 'stirring', 'covering', 'feeding'. These also fall into two groups, one concerned with spring, the other with winter. Those of the winter group are, surprisingly, caring – concerned with shelter and nourishment – while those associated with spring – 'breeding', 'mixing', 'stirring' – equivocally suggest both generation and disruption, sedition, disorder. The verb-content of these opening lines rests almost entirely on the participles (further intensifying the nominalisation of the passage), and the usage varies. So we find April 'breeding': we might take this either as being equivalent to 'which breeds' – a generic epithet – or as more specifically tied to a particular April, or even as 'because it breeds', linking the 'cruellest month' with its life-force. '. . . stirring' is a little different, I think, in that, although still ostensibly governed by 'April', it can also read as predicated on 'Dull roots'. The use of participle as generic epithet has implications for themes of recurrence and continuity. This is not a simple present tense, but continuing, and set in the context of the seasons.

The tension of the first four lines is further complicated by the introduction of the past tense in 'Winter kept us warm'. This contrasts with 'Summer surprised us' by rhetorical parallel, and alerts us to a progress through the seasons as well as shifting further back from the 'present tense' of the opening. Eventually the proximacy of the poem will settle in the 'brown fog of a winter dawn' (61), poised between winter and spring, dormancy and sprouting. The tension and ambivalence are most concentrated in 'mixing / Memory and desire', or even more in 'feeding / A little life with dried tubers', where a grudging concession of nourishment and growth is retracted into the minimal 'a little life'. Again, the present participle acts as the centre, the focus of the ambivalence.

Not all present participles are equally rich and complex, but some few are crucial. At the opening of part v we read,

> He who was living is now dead
> We who were living are now dying
>
> (328–9)

Here, in lines which distil the paradox of death and life, the subtle shift from past to present is obvious, and the careful rhetorical balancing emphasises the substitutions. 'He' (both Christ, whose agony and crucifixion inform this opening, and Phlebas, the Phoenician, recently subjected to 'Death by Water') is replaced by 'We', a new focus of consciousness for this part of the poem. Also, though, the device of replacement here articulates the transition from death to life, both adjectivally and by auxiliaries of modal verbs of state. This replacement discriminates between being dead and being dying (which is the condition of life in the wasteland). The crucial repetition is 'now': these lines set the immediate present of the final section of the poem. The time-scale of the journey at the start of 'What the Thunder Said' is very close to the implied now–then of 'I sat . . . / Fishing'.

The most significant present participles have a tendency to isolate themselves from their immediate context, and so become free to associate with others of similar weight. Two such are 'throbbing waiting' in 'The Fire Sermon' (217), both of which are reiterated. '. . . throbbing between two lives' (218) suggests a poise between (and ultimately a collapse of) death and life, as well as male and female. '. . . waiting' is, again, the condition of life in the wasteland (and a hint of *Waiting for Godot*): continuance without finality. Both suggest an urgent sense of expectation, and the urgency of experience continues in the sequence (detached from context) 'throbbing'–'waiting'–'Burning':

> To Carthage then I came
>
> Burning burning burning burning
> O Lord Thou pluckest me out
> O Lord Thou pluckest
>
> burning
>
> (307–11)

The repetitions of 'burning', both within the line, and as a single selected item to close 'The Fire Sermon', suggest a continuous present which is purgatorial if not actually infernal. We have moved from the neutrality of 'waiting' to active anguish. The repetitions also oscillate between transitive and intransitive usage: 'To Carthage then I came / Burning' is attributive, alluding to Augustine's fires of lust. But the introduction of the Buddha's Fire Sermon, and a further quotation from St Augustine's *Confessions*, suggest the cleansing (transitive usage) fires of punitive rehabilitation. (These twin aspects might further be related to, respectively – intransitive usage – Dante's *Inferno*, called on so often as analogue of Eliot's Unreal City; and – transitive usage – the Fire of London, as described in Dryden's *Annus Mirabilis*, another poem lurking behind *The Waste Land*, which celebrates the happy sequence of events from the Restoration of 1660 to the Great Fire of London in 1666, taking in both a naval defeat of the Dutch and a fortuitous fumigation of the Plague.[6])

What is arguably the turning-point of 'What the Thunder Said', and of the whole poem, turns on yet another use of present participle: 'Then a damp gust / Bringing rain' (393–4). *Does* it rain in part v of *The Waste Land*? Critics other than Leavis have pondered this question, whose importance rests on the undoubted affirmative significance which attaches to rain as token of fertility and healing resolution. Readings of *The Waste Land* include the specifically Christian (in which the redemptive baptismal waters flow as denouement) as well as the intransigently nihilistic. Some critics read Eliot's later poems 'back' into *The Waste Land*, to see there evidence of the germinal faith which blossomed into active belief with his conversion to Anglicanism in 1927 and the committed religiosity of such works as *Ash Wednesday*. The divergence of these readings is an index not, I think, of special pleading, but of the teasing openness of the text at this point.

Key lexical items here relate to water and wind. The 'gust' is that wind (both desert wind, associated with the dryness of the wasteland, and the renewing breath of the Spirit) which has blown fitfully across the 'brown land' (175). '. . . damp' suggests a potential for rain, and 'Then' marks a specific moment for the event. The crux, again, is the present participle, and again emphasised by the line-division. '. . . bringing' is only equivocally an event in the past: its equivalent might be 'which brought', or rather 'which would bring', or even merely 'of the type which brings'. It may then be generic or specific. The succeeding lines only reinforce the textual dilemma: the scene immediately shifts by a sudden transition, without punctuation and with the typographic marking of a space (that is, by a foregrounded discontinuity, which reads 'naturalistically' as the gap between the flash of lightning and the sound of thunder) to the jungle:

> Ganga was sunken, and the limp leaves
> Waited for rain, while the black clouds
> Gathered far distant, over Himavant.
>
> (395-7)

Despite the sustained past tense, and the transposed but familiar landscape of river, trees and mountain, there is no certainty here, but a suspended expectation. Those clouds – and the mountain – are still 'far distant'. The proximate resolution has tantalisingly retreated.

What might appear as merely rhetorical or linguistic reveals, then, a profound thematic relevance. The confounding of tenses, the quasi-adjectival use of the present participle with or without modal verbs, register anxiety over death and rebirth, stasis and change. The triumph of the present participle as verb-form within the poem denies to it certain completion. *The Waste Land* finally exists and persists in the continuous present, which is the dimension of crisis and apocalypse: 'London Bridge is falling down falling down falling down' (426).

The foregoing account of present participles as 'lexical items' suggests that *The Waste Land* has, or even exists as, a self-contained idiolect. The poem does indeed establish and develop a vocabulary, whose idiosyncratic items substantially coincide with the features of its wasteland-scape. The richness of the characteristic features – the 'arid plain', the 'brown land' – is not merely or even, I think, mainly due to the weight of implied allusion to vocabularies external to the poem, found in Grail material or biblical narrative. Within the poem are concentrated a number of characteristic items which gather into contrastive sets or clusters, those of dryness (the *desert*) and water (the *river*). Other features of vocabulary and landscape, whether nominal ('wind', 'bones') or adjectival ('empty', 'brown') engage in associative relations with these two main sets. The lexis is not of course as thin or simplistic as this might suggest. Sets or clusters intersect and overlap, so that even the *desert* (which includes 'sand', 'rock', 'dry', 'sterile') connects with seasonal-vegetation items ('tree', 'leaf', 'grass', 'spring', 'winter', 'summer') and contrasts with the *river* ('rain', 'shower', 'spring', 'pool', 'wet', 'lake', '*Meer*', 'sea'). There are, too, interestingly independent subsets or image-clusters such as the repeated 'rat'–'rattle'–'bones'. It would overcomplicate matters at this point to examine the distinct but related set of *city*, except perhaps to note that with its major component item 'tower' (which is linked with 'mountain') this represents a transposition from the natural landscape to the man-made environment.

The two main sets might themselves be restated as 'absence' and 'presence', or as the poles of the negative and the positive. Individual items operate by delicate interrelations on a negative/positive orientation. As we have seen, 'arid plain' is a synonym for waste land: 'arid' calls on all associated epithets of dryness, and 'plain' similarly 'contains' all references to the flat, empty desert. This negative noun phrase has a fullness which goes beyond the repetitions and connotations of its components: the phrase actively connotes the absence of its opposite, the river, in a dynamic opposition. What I mean here is that each lexical item contains or suggests its own opposite, to generate a tension which constantly exposes the reader to the wasteland experience of loss, absence and negation. So, in the poem, selection of any given item implies by non-articulation a dynamic, felt absence. Whenever we encounter 'dry', we attach to this, with considerable emotional force, the absence of water. What I have termed 'dynamic opposition' is a device of extreme compression, which underscores the anxiety of 'waiting' for 'rain'. This kind of compression, or double denotation, is expanded in 'dry sterile thunder without rain' (342) and made explicit in 'Here is no water but only rock' (331).

In this lexical topography the collocation of nouns and adjectives is particularly significant. Epithets are frequently used to point up the experiential dimension of the poem, and humanise its landscape ('empty chapel', 'Dull roots', 'last fingers of leaf / Clutch'). What happens also is that recurring epithets fundamental to the basic *desert–river* sets are successively placed with different nouns, with the effect of a continual modification of the overall configuration. The list which follows merely notes the shifting collocations of the basic epithets 'dead', 'dry', 'empty' (and its converse, 'full').

Dead (dying, died, death):	'The Burial of the Dead'; 'dead land' (2); 'dead tree' (23); 'dead sound' (68); 'neither / Living nor dead' (39); 'dead men' (116); 'nearly died' (160); 'my father's death' (192); 'lowest of the dead' (246); 'Death by Water'; 'a fortnight dead' (312); 'now dead' (328); 'now dying' (329); 'Dead mountain mouth' (339).
Dry (dried, drying):	'dried tubers' (7); 'dry stone' (24); 'dry garret' (194); 'drying combinations' (225); 'Sweat is dry' (337); 'dry sterile thunder' (342); 'dry grass' (354); 'Dry bones' (390).
Empty / full:	'empty cisterns' (384); 'empty chapel' (388); 'empty rooms' (409); 'arms full' (38); 'pocket full of currants' (210).

This selection shows nothing of the subtlety of successive intermediate replacements such as 'dead land'–'brown fog'–'brown land', and it focuses on only a few items. But even here we see that a given epithet may cohere with a congruent or a disparate noun, and that the collocations demonstrate that the physical and the spiritual are coextensive.

It may be more helpful here to trace the changing collocations of a single recurring epithet. 'Broken' first appears in 'A heap of broken images' (22), and later in 'The river's tent is broken' (173), 'broken fingernails of dirty hands' (303), 'seals broken' (408) and 'a broken Coriolanus' (416). In the course of this delicate semantic modulation the 'broken images' link with the unbelief of the 'broken Coriolanus' – a secularism and absence of heroic leadership which breed anxiety and despair. The 'river's tent' pictorially links the trees hanging over the Thames with the 'stony rubbish' (20) which cannot adequately root a living tree. But what is broken here, as in 'broken fingernails of dirty hands' is sexual purity (compare the draft of line 103, altered by Pound, which explicitly associates dirt with lust[7]). A hint of sexual violation recurs in 'seals broken', but this moves more obviously into the area of death, and so brings us back to the dead and broken Coriolanus. This again, and indeed all the instances noted, relate to a further cluster, that of *fragments* ('I can connect/Nothing with nothing'). 'Broken' itself is linked with 'Falling' – an important association. Despite the gap of tense between present and past participles, the two have in common the notion of irreversibility, and hint at collapse and apocalypse.

What I have proposed is a subtle syntactic interconnection of lexical items, which produces a language capable of delineating the landscape of anxiety. Most of the foregoing analysis has dealt with the desert, but the central environment of *The Waste Land*, its focus and standpoint, is London, the City. This text too draws on the literary tradition of pastoral, with its contrastive and normative environments. The endless plains (which constitute the 'country' of the poem) sharpen the picture of urban claustrophobia, and the dryness of sand and rock work against the Thames flowing through London. The pastoral here is desert – no contrastive idyll, but rather an extension of the aridity of the city. Contrast functions largely as metaphoric congruence: the desert is coextensive with the city. Each environment has complicating features. Mountains loom in the desert, 'mountains of rock without water' (334), from which the traveller looks longingly to the 'city over the mountains' (371), which might be identified with the ideal contained within the city itself: the Eternal (as opposed to Temporal) City,[8] the new Jerusalem, the City of God. Yet it is in 'this decayed hole among the mountains' (385), with its suggestion of the Grail quest, that hope of regeneration springs. Contrasts turn back on themselves.

Eliot's city, London, depicts modern society as the urban wasteland of Europe in the aftermath of the Great War. His view is densely interwoven with literary and historical allusion – direct or implied – to Spenser's 'Prothalamion', Dryden's *Annus Mirabilis*, Pope's *The Rape of the Lock* (and also perhaps James Thomson's *City of Dreadful Night* and Conrad's *Heart of Darkness*).[9] These, together with the reference to Elizabeth 1 and Leicester, take us from the sixteenth to the twentieth centuries. Eliot's use of an historical literary framework needs close attention, although we need not read it as a simplistically pessimistic or morally tendentious contrast between an heroic past and an unheroic present. The ironic perspective is often complex; some of the poems mentioned above satirise or castigate a vicious and corrupt society, and the use of literary convention in each case is pertinent. These are in the main public and even epic works designed to please a patron as well as to celebrate London as focus of political power. By contrast, the fiscal orientation of Eliot's city suggests a society held together by financial transactions. It is evident, too, that the Golden Age of romantic love celebrated by Spenser has given way, in 'A Game of Chess' and 'The Fire Sermon', to sterile lust. In both cases, then, the contrast seems to work against the present. But on the other hand (and quite apart from the sexual satire of Pope) Elizabeth's flirtation with Leicester is undercut by the fragile and meretricious decoration of their 'gilded shell' (282), and, after all, the Virgin Queen's barren spinsterhood posed a problem of succession and a threat to political stability. And Spenser's bridal poem, in which the Earl of Worcester's daughters appear as swans of chastity, is an uncritical if expedient use of pastoral convention. Literary mediation may disguise and flatter historical truth (although Eliot viewed literature as an invaluable repository of history and tradition).

Even when the allusions extend to cities other than London, the process calls for careful consideration. The perspective *is* undoubtedly epic (we can detect Homer, perhaps Virgil, certainly Dante); and cities are presented in epic as centres of power and culture. But the cities in *The Waste Land* signify empires in ruins, evidence of a destroyed or fallen civilisation. We come up to date with Vienna, centre of the Austro-Hungarian empire of the Hapsburgs, and we have frequently confronted the fate of Carthage. Despite the detail of ironic movement between past and present, it does appear that overall the city registers historical change and decline. Even a simple number-count suggests a tendency towards failure and collapse. Given this perspective we may agree that Eliot views London as on the way down. Moral degeneration is an index of imminent socio-political catastrophe. And yet, in 1921, both war and revolution had already happened. The poem, it seems, is historical record as well as moral warning. It may be remarked, finally, that the historical moments focused by the poem are often those of civilisations engulfed by war. This may be the most pertinent mode of contrast – with the stability, apparent or actual, of London in the time of Spenser, Dryden or Pope.

For all the historical awareness, however, the poetic vitality of Eliot's city lies in the immediacy of its engagement with contemporary conditions:

> Unreal City,
> Under the brown fog of a winter dawn,
> A crowd flowed over London Bridge, so many,
> I had not thought death had undone so many.
>
> (60–3)

The picture has its literary backcloth, in allusions to Baudelaire's 'fourmillante cité' and Dante's *Inferno*; but here is an insistent actuality of everyday life, as the work-force of the South London suburbs converges on banks and offices at the appointed hour. The 'crowd' is the new service class of clerks and typists, the office workers, and their bosses. In *Howards End* we found the clerk at the lower edge of the middle class, characterised by job-insecurity, petty snobbery and an urge for upward social mobility (although Leonard Bast, moving from job to job, descended rapidly towards the abyss). *Heartbreak House* showed the hollow man, the modern financier. Mangan's *'careworn, mistrustful expression'* and *'entirely imaginary dignity'* reflected a career of competitive insecurity: his *'dull complexion'* and *'commonplace'* features registered the small change, in terms of individuality and emotional life, which the City had dealt him.[10]

The office workers who serve the City of *The Waste Land*, in the lines just quoted, are oppressed by anonymity and routine. A faceless and nameless crowd, bored and submissive, their passivity is 'automatic' (see line 255). '. . . each man' is 'fixed' (65) in a system which flows on uniformly, precluding the possibility of personal assertion. Even bodily features ('eyes', 'feet') and expressive action ('sighs' – 64) are detached from individual identity. This mode of disconnected existence reappears when later 'the eyes and back / Turn upward from the desk' (215–16). There is no distinction between items of human anatomy and pieces of office furniture: the 'human engine' has become reified, wholly functional.

We should not miss, though, the wry humour of the fateful hour of nine approaching, with a 'dead sound on the final stroke' (68). Eliot confirms this as 'A phenomenon which I have often noticed', and the witty assurance of his poetic account testifies to direct experience. He had worked for Lloyd's Bank since 1917, until in the autumn of 1921 nervous exhaustion allowed him to escape to Margate and Lausanne, where he wrote *The Waste Land*. This scene from 'The Burial of the Dead' – a further witty allusion for those 'buried' in dull office routine – shows a measure of ironic sympathy for City life, but the tone and effect range widely in the poem's various sections. In 'Unreal City' (60) the voice and standpoint are those of the modulating central consciousness of *The Waste Land*. In the pub scene of 'A Game of Chess' many voices are juxtaposed to produce a comic and colloquial set piece, strikingly dissimilar to both its preceding scene, in the first section of part II, and to other examples of London life.

In Eliot's early design for the poem this scene would have been complemented by two other 'loose' narratives and dramatic monologues. The first section of the poem (originally entitled 'He Do the Police in Different Voices: Part I'[11]) was to have been an autobiographical account of youthful debauch at 'Tom's place', deriving from Eliot's Harvard days. A major portion of 'Death by Water', unwillingly excised at Pound's insistence, was a sailor's tale of shipwreck off the New England coast.[12] The removal of these two pieces leaves the pub scene as the sole section not heavily reliant on literary and mythical allusion. (Although both of the deleted narratives had literary analogues in, respectively, the Nighttown episode of Joyce's *Ulysses*, and the death of Ulysses as described by Dante and Tennyson, with perhaps a sideglance at 'The Rime of the Ancient Mariner'.) The publican's repeated cry of 'HURRY UP PLEASE IT'S TIME' does, however, carry echoes of the themes of *carpe diem* and *tempus fugit*, and anticipates the use of Marvell's 'To His Coy Mistress' in part III. The closing lines allude to *Hamlet*, interweaving Ophelia's mad farewell with the 'Goonights' of the pub clientele. The literary overlay is, however, minimal, and of less interest than the returning soldier Albert who is 'coming back' (142) to life, like a vegetation-god, from a war winter which lasted four years.

The literariness, thin or otherwise, of the scene is precisely not the point. What *is* remarkable is the rich historicity and resonant contemporary idiom, together with the connections made with the recurring themes of (as Eliot puts it in 'Sweeney Agonistes')

'Birth, and copulation, and death'. The scene is set in, or refers to, 1919, after the Armistice, the year of being 'demobbed' (139). This term – a colloquialism for 'demobilisation' – was coined in that year, to describe the common experience, for those who had survived the war, of discharge from the Army (the colloquial term was supplied by Pound[13]). The passage is filled with slangy idiom: 'mince my words' (140), 'a bit smart' (142), 'what you done' (143), 'have them all out', 'get a nice set' (145), 'wants a good time' (148), 'You ought to be ashamed' (156), 'bring it off' (159), 'never been the same' (161). The speech recorded in the woman's story slots together clichés in a vigorous interchange: verbal usage is minimal, largely confined to 'said', 'make', 'get', 'is', 'can't', 'want' and similar forms. (In fact the Cockney dialect was alien to Eliot, and his wife Vivien helped him out with two lines.) But, even if we may suspect the poet to be slightly distanced from his subject, he has nevertheless put his finger on the social pulse of the immediate post-war period. The hasty, careless (or carefree) slang is apt. It accentuates the urge for gratification, and particularly sexual release, after the long duration of the war. Lil's Albert has been in the army four years, and 'wants a good time' (148). But the ending of hostilities gives rise to problems as well as opportunity, and not merely in the reunion of husband and wife after a protracted separation, but in their individual problems of readjustment. Albert's war experiences are not recorded, but in 'coming back' he has certain expectations of civilian life. He and Lil may have had 'a good time' before he went away, but during his absence Lil had been faced with raising five children ('nearly died of young George'), has resorted to a damaging abortion, and is now prematurely aged, 'antique' (a direct echo of the rich woman's 'antique mantel' – 97) at thirty-one. She now has to return to a sexual role of wife, as well as mother, and the prospect is not favourable, given the contrast with the speaker. This woman is clearly a sexual rival – she, Lil and Albert have already met together – and unlike Lil she seems to have relished the emancipation in work and sex which the war gave to women (although the date of Lil's abortion, and the putative father, are not specified). In fact the repeated 'HURRY UP PLEASE IT'S TIME' carries several implications. In part the injunction to enjoy oneself (PLEASE IT'S TIME) registers the licence of post-war indulgence. But this is *closing* time, and the urgency is one of limited opportunity: the threat of mortality is felt too. The Brave New

World of 1919 holds both pleasures and terrors: the poem's pub scene, with its colloquialism, holds promise both of fulfilment and of emptiness. A desperate sexuality is maintained in the face of sterility – Lil's abortion – and promiscuity. Lil needs 'a nice set' of false teeth to regain her sexual status: the teeth need not signify artificiality (although Eliot's fastidiousness may be in evidence here), but they must be a token of decay, as well as of a giving relationship between husband and wife. This is a cynical gaiety, and the mad melancholy of Ophelia meshes with the prevailing mood.

The scene between the typist and the house agent's clerk in part III provides a close-up on the personal relationships of the city population. This episode, by contrast with the pub scene, is emphatically written according to literary conventions, those of satire and mock epic. In this case it is the literary stance that makes for controversy. The entire episode combines sympathetic observation with a physical and moral distaste, and is at the same time extremely witty and more than a little sad. It is for example worth noting that these figures, whose relationship is central to the poem, are not named: they are designated by the occupational group to which they belong. The implication is that they are modern types, whose lives typically lack individuality and excitement; or it may be (more sadly) that their self-images are entirely tied to function.

The episode is introduced by the domestic setting:

> The typist home at teatime, clears her breakfast, lights
> Her stove, and lays out food in tins.
> Out of the window perilously spread
> Her drying combinations touched by the sun's last rays,
> On the divan are piled (at night her bed)
> Stockings, slippers, camisoles, and stays.
>
> (222–7)

The meticulous itemisation and spare detail indicate a confined space and makeshift living-arrangements. The emphasis is on functionalism ('food in tins', washing spread on the window-ledge, the convertible divan), routine (this is implied as a typical pattern for her day) and lack of leisure (the breakfast dishes left uncleared). However, the satiric stance, and archly 'sublime' phrases are not of a piece with the naturalistic detail. A glance at the draft version arouses suspicions that Eliot sees in the circumstances of the typist's daily life not only a lack of civilisation but also a moral shabbiness demonstrated in physical dirt and squalor.[14] It seems that Eliot implies a causal connection between the typist's domestic and her sexual habits, and sees the latter as in effect vicious. The neutrality of her bored indifference disguises a poetic stance of moral condemnation, particularly in the association of dirt with lust.

This is a delicate and precarious area. It is I think of less value to pursue or castigate Eliot's distaste, social or moral, than to draw attention to the parallel with Forster's portrayal of Leonard Bast's flat, and his life with his common-law wife Jacky, in chapter 6 of *Howards End*. The similarities are remarkable: both accounts cast an 'objective' eye over rooms, furniture, personal effects, and food. The impression in both cases is of a quality of life reduced in proportion to the quantity – or lack – of wealth. Both Eliot and Forster infer an equation between material conditions and emotional deprivation: the inference may be to the point, but we feel that, for both authors, responsibility by and large devolves on the individual character. The inferiority is somehow a moral failure.

As it happens, both Eliot and Forster have been criticised in just these pieces of their writing for a patronising and dismissive attitude. The charges hold, I think, and all the more for the relevance of the selected focus to a full discussion of the conditions of modern urban life. If the lives of all clerks and typists are necessarily squalid (and if we accept the images as those of squalor), this needs to be said. Yet as we saw in *Howards End*, there is an *embarrassed* quality in the writing which betrays the text as awkwardly situated in its chosen convention. Forster lunged from slight unease in dealing with Leonard to appalling vulgarity in his portrait of Jacky, and oscillated between extraordinary (in view of his confessed total ignorance) sympathy and conventional disdain on a par with that of the Schlegels. But he did perceive and express with sensitivity the relation between Leonard's unsatisfactory domestic life – Jacky calling vainly for love from the bedroom, as Leonard goes on reading Ruskin – and his social and cultural aspirations, even if he didn't go so far as to question the values aspired to. Eliot, on the other hand, seems to perceive no mitigating factors: the sexual encounter is at best loveless and passionless, and at worst casual and callous lust. His account of the seduction, before Pound exercised a moderating influence, went to further excesses in order to demonstrate moral degeneracy, as the young man delayed to urinate and spit on the staircase.[15]

Even in the finished poem, the scene has its nastiness. If the typist is treated with some delicacy and concern, there is no such tolerance for the 'young man carbuncular':

> A small house agent's clerk, with one bold stare,
> One of the low on whom assurance sits
> As a silk hat on a Bradford millionaire.
>
> (232–4)

There is no mistaking the punning condescension here. The verse of the succeeding lines operates between the 'consciousness' of the clerk and authorial sarcasm. Eliot's multi-layered rhetoric plays on the young man's professional ambition and gaucherie, transferred to the sexual arena. We 'hear' the idiom of business style, which distances emotion by its stilted cliches ('Endeavours to engage her in caresses' – 237). This differs from the authorial voice of 'still are unreproved, if undesired' (238), and the overlaid imagery of a siege. The poet reserves to himself superiority (and there is some evidence in the poem to suggest a discrimination between sexual experience in terms of class difference, if for example we compare this scene with the firmly middle-class encounter, sublimated and unconsummated, of the first section of 'A Game of Chess').

The sexual intercourse in the clerk–typist episode is devoid not only of passion but of communication of any kind (they say nothing to each other). The young man chooses his 'propitious' (235) moment not when she is sexually aroused, but when she is 'bored' and 'tired' (236), and will accept his advances by default. Their embrace is reduced by the linguistic device of pronominalisation, referring to sex as 'that' or 'it', and by the unindividualised, disembodied effect of 'Exploring hands' (240). Indeed their intercourse is described mainly in abstractions which refer obliquely to their bodies and responses ('His vanity', 'no response', 'indifference' – 241–2), and at the climax Tiresias coyly intervenes to paraphrase in parenthesis whatever orgasm is achieved as 'all / Enacted' (243–4). Significantly, we do not know whether they have made love before this occasion, or whether the act is likely to be repeated. When her lover has gone the typist normalises her life again by trivial ritual. She is 'Hardly aware' (250), 'alone' (254), and again her body fragments into brain, hair, hand, and 'automatic' action (255). The satirist and moralist in the poet still set female 'folly' (after Goldsmith – 253) against male vanity as an assessment of casual sex; but in this acutely observed coda to the scene the more neutral observer of modern relationships transfers the epithet 'automatic' from the gramophone to the woman's hand, to conflate the reduction of emotional meaning in the event, and its palliative, smoothing effect.

What confronts us, then, in *The Waste Land* and *Howards End*, is a parallel phenomenon, in which two writers recognise an area of concern in their society – problems of emotional and sexual relationships in an emergent group – and admit its centrality, while failing to render it adequately in their writing. We must, I think, concede their percipience in selecting the incidents at all, and even more in placing them at the core of the novel and the poem. We might conclude that here is literature faced with a particular crisis of its own. Faced with the crisis, both writers retreat, coping with embarrassment by devices of rhetorical distancing. Forster resorts to an archly ironic narrative voice, and Eliot adopts the twin strategies of a containing poetic convention, and a containing consciousness. The consciousness is that of Tiresias, and the poetic convention is the Augustan mock epic. The Augustan framework of this episode owes more perhaps to the stanza and verse-line of Dryden's *Annus Mirabilis* than to the couplets of Pope, although the spacing of the lines on the page disguises the original quatrains, and the analogy with Restoration London is virtually submerged. Part III was to have opened with an extended parody of Pope's *Rape of the Lock*, in which 'Fresca' embodied a modern and cruder version of Belinda at her morning toilet. The opening was eventually deleted, but echoes of Pope remain in both 'The Fire Sermon' and the setting of 'A Game of Chess'.

The focus on sexuality of *Heartbreak House* and *Women in Love* is repeated in *The Waste Land* to suggest, similarly, futility and fragmentation in relationships as an index of the total fabric of modern life. Any awkwardness in the episode of the typist and the clerk should not prevent us from realising that this is the poem's centrepiece in more than one sense. This is in fact the main act of intercourse, and the central dramatic event. It occurs halfway through the middle section of the poem, and perhaps appositely presents an exemplum of lust for 'The Fire Sermon'. Looking at it another way, though, and recalling the framework of the mock heroic, we find that the clerk and typist are hero and heroine of Eliot's compressed modern epic. There are obvious comparisons to be drawn with Leonard Bast. The latter analogy should in particular alert us to the centrality and significance of this seduction. As in *Howards End*, where the 'connection' demanded by the novel was made in Leonard's intercourse with Helen Schlegel, so in the barren *Waste Land* the 'fertilising' sex-act is provided by the typist and clerk. The quest of the poem for spiritual renewal is expressed as a movement from death and burial towards rebirth. Sex, in its function of procreation, is the middle term of this progression: it not only roots *The Waste Land* in vegetation myth and fertility cult, but also links the poem with the other texts considered in this book, projecting a positive sexual 'solution' to the problems of the narrative and of society.

The *Waste Land* inserts its central act of intercourse, its emblematic marriage, in a wide perspective of sexual relationships in literature and myth, as well as contemporary life. The perspective reaches back to the opening of 'A Game of Chess', with its allusions to the doomed (and questionably heroic) love of Cleopatra (in Shakespeare's tragedy); the legend of Philomel raped by Tereus (in the *Metamorphoses* of Ovid); the Duchess of Malfi (in Webster); and the title, which refers to a play by Middleton in which a game of chess was used to mask a seduction. Figures of women as temptresses, abused queens and violated nymphs haunt the poem. In the scenes of contemporary life the 'nymphs are departed': not only has a pastoral romance disappeared, but summer is over and lovers no longer dally on the banks of the Thames. These are the girlfriends of the 'loitering heirs of city directors' (180), their seductions joyless and gratuitous. Their unindividualised voices are heard in the songs of the three Thames maidens, which reveal the experience as one of numb acquiescence. They are detached from 'the event', from their own bodies: 'I raised my knees / Supine' (294–5), 'my heart / Under my feet' (296–7). In their resignation there is no anger: 'I made no comment. What should I resent?' (299). An earlier attempt at this section filled in the social context, to reveal the 'humble people' of the lower middle class, concerned with respectability, their fathers small businessmen in the city.[16] The pathos of their plight disarms the moral condemnation implied in the title 'The Fire Sermon'.

The song of the Thames maidens is a lament for the loss of innocence and the emptiness of experience. 'The Fire Sermon' modulates between lament or elegy and wedding-song. Spenser's 'Prothalamion' used the pastoral mode to celebrate the marriage of the two daughters of the Earl of Worcester, and was also set on the Thames, flowing into the heart of London. In Spenser's poem the 'nymphs' (Greek word for 'bride') are 'the lovely Daughters of the Flood'. His repeated refrain is echoed by Eliot:

> Against the Brydale day, which is not long:
> Sweet _Themmes_ runne softly, till I end my song.

Lament is heard also in 'By the waters of Leman I sat down and wept' (182), recalling Psalm 137, which bewails captivity in Babylon. Marvell's 'To His Coy Mistress' is a seduction-poem, but one which feels the pressure of time and mortality: following the lines adapted here, 'yonder all before us lie / Deserts of vast eternity' (Marvell too envisages the temporal as spatial). The 'White bodies naked on the low damp ground' (193) also yoke sex with death, in an image suggestive of corpses copulating.

The sexual life of the city is, then, sung in elegy and wedding-song. The music goes 'unheard', or at least unheeded. '. . . unheard' (175) refers explicitly to the wind, but it recalls Keats's 'Ode on a Grecian Urn' ('Heard melodies are sweet, but those unheard / Are sweeter'), which freezes into the permanence of art a moment of sexual ecstasy and pursuit, setting this against change and decay. Eliot's 'Cold Pastoral' echoes also the sonnet to Leigh Hunt: 'Glory and loveliness have passed away; / No crowd of nymphs', in both its sentiment and its syntax. There is little glory and less loveliness in Sweeney and Mrs Porter, or the homosexual proposition of Mr Eugenides of an illicit weekend at the Hotel Metropole, or even the hermaphrodite voyeurism of Tiresias. Modern sex, it seems, offers little reassurance of humanity.

The scene which opens 'A Game of Chess' also deals with a sexual relationship, unexpressed and unconsummated. The sexual connotations of the title (which refers to Ferdinand and Miranda in _The Tempest_, as well as to Middleton's _Women Beware_

Women) are extended in the implication of 'And we shall play a game of chess' (137). Sexual repression is felt both in the details of the setting, which contain imagery of violence and passion, and in the emotional force of 'savagely still' (110). The allusion to *The Duchess of Malfi* ('her hair / spread out in fiery points') also suggests menace and violence: after the Duchess's domestic and sexual harmony with the husband she married in secret, her brother forces his way into their bedroom to destroy the union.[17]

But what the woman wants here is not so much a physical as a mental or verbal embrace. She demands communication: 'Speak to me. Why do you never speak. Speak' (112). The edgy, one-sided conversation (she is answered silently, if at all, by her companion) suggests alienation: 'I never know what you are thinking. Think' (114). In fact her jagged, nervous sensitivity picks up the listener's own anxieties, and his experience is analogous to that of the hyacinth garden in part I. (In draft the analogy was explicit.[18]) The return from the hyacinth garden brought impotence and failure:

> I could not
> Speak, and my eyes failed, I was neither
> Living nor dead, and I knew nothing,
> Looking into the heart of light, the silence.
>
> (38–41)

The carrying over of material from part I to part II is a reprise of sexual failure, and the failure of perception, cognition and communication:

> 'Do
> 'You know nothing? Do you see nothing? Do you remember
> 'Nothing?'
>
> (121–3)

The woman's insistent questioning pushes the issue still further, in 'Are you alive, or not? Is there nothing in your head?' (126). Here the text ironically manipulates a logical exclusive disjunction, to express the paradox of alienated existence. 'Are you alive, or not?' expects the resolution of the disjunction in the real world (she assumes that he *must* be *either* alive *or* not, and cannot be both). However the question recalls 'neither! / Living nor dead',

and the listener feels that he is neither, or both. Moreover the
'nothing' in his head is very like the profound experience of 'knew
nothing' and its juxtaposed equivalent 'Looking into the heart of
light, the silence'.

We are dealing here with the very nature and communicability
of experience, a crisis of the human condition. The haunting pun
which inverts Conrad's *Heart of Darkness* distils the crisis and
paradox. *Heart of Darkness* presses in on *The Waste Land* at several
points. Eliot was extremely reluctant to replace the epigraph he
extracted from Marlow's description of Kurtz's dying vision:

> Did he live his life again in every detail of desire, temptation,
> and surrender during that supreme moment of complete
> knowledge? He cried in a whisper at some image, at some vision
> – he cried out twice, a cry that was no more than a breath –
> 'The horror! The horror!'[19]

Eliot rightly maintained to Pound that the quotation was
'somewhat elucidative'.[20] Conrad's narrator, Marlow, can only
guess at the meaning of Kurtz's words, and cannot share his
experience. The interrogative mood captures that anxiety. *The
Waste Land* also reaches after the 'supreme moment of complete
knowledge' and its communication to another human being.
Marlow is deeply preoccupied with the problem and interrupts
his account of Kurtz to express his anxiety to those listening to
him, who are at yet a further remove from the vision itself: 'He was
just a word for me. I did not see the man in the name any more
than you do. Do you see him? Do you see the story? Do you see
anything?'[21] We have, surely, a straight echo of Marlow's
desperate, searching questions in lines 121–3 of *The Waste Land*,
and a similar concern for the isolation of the individual. The
membrane which prevents the shared experience of private
worlds brings to mind the idealist philosophy of F. H. Bradley,[22]
whose *Appearance and Reality* Eliot quotes in the note to the lines
which include the telling phrase 'each in his prison' (413).
Marlow's conclusion was 'It is impossible. We live, as we dream –
alone.'[23]

This scene takes us beyond the motif of sexual repression to the
limitation of all experience. It is confirmed by the incidence of
concessive and restrictive terminology elsewhere: 'you know
only / A heap of broken images' (21–2), 'I have heard the

key / Turn in the door once and turn once only' (411). Other lines negate or minimalise human possibilities: 'You cannot say, or guess' (21), 'Here one can neither stand nor lie nor sit' (340). It is then significant that we can identify this 'listener' with the central voice of the poem: he registers the extreme reduction of cognition and emotion, to a condition of lonely anxiety, insecurity and guilt. This is the human wasteland of the desert and the city.[24]

If *The Waste Land* consisted merely of juxtaposed scenes of life in the 'Unreal City' it might well be seen as a static configuration; but there is throughout the poem a strongly felt urge for onward movement and change. The reader 'travels' progressively eastwards with the Speaker down specific City streets on a journey which leads downriver to Margate Sands. The Thames is a unifying image here, as in journeys of past ages. And other cities imply other journeys: Marie went south in winter; Albert is coming back from the army; Mr Eugenides has come to London; Augustine went to Carthage; the disciples travelled the road to Emmaus.

It is in part v, 'What the Thunder Said', that the journey becomes explicit as the poem's basic thematic unit of narrative progression, towards a destination which is posited as escape from the wasteland, or as spiritual or moral metamorphosis. Between the plains, the mountains and the city beyond winds the 'sandy road' (332) which is the focus of the journey. Eliot noted the use of the 'journey to Emmaus' and 'approach to the Chapel Perilous' in this part of the poem. His bland but tendentious gloss (I shall return later to the 'present decay of Eastern Europe') pinpoints the nature of the 'destination' in each case: transfiguration. He also points very precisely to the stage he is dealing with – not arrival, but the 'journey', the 'approach'.

The disciples of Jesus on the road to Emmaus were to find, after a period of spiritual despair, the fulfilment of the pledge of redemption and of eternal life in the resurrected and transfigured Christ. The 'now' of the opening of part v of *The Waste Land* is a hiatus of suspended uncertainty, 'After' the agony in the garden of Gethsemane, the crucifixion and burial, but before the resurrection is manifest. The 'third who walks always beside' the travellers in the poem (359) is a complex allusion, but with direct relevance to the experience of the road to Emmaus. The unaccounted-for presence provides a spirit for the desert land-scape, which is now impregnated with the possibility of life after death.

The journey through the wasteland – an essential ingredient of all related myth – implies change and movement, a modifying experience rather than a static condition. In primitive material this is both an infertile region and a transitional period of infertility; to be 'in' the wasteland carries both anxiety, and hope of change. In the Grail legends, this means the hoped-for cure of the sick or maimed ruler, the Fisher King, and the restoration of his barren lands and people to fertility and health. The return of fertility rests on the journey of the Quester, as he is sometimes known, to the Chapel Perilous, where he must undergo trials. Many versions of the Grail have a Christian overlay, in the landscape (including the Chapel) as well as the totemic items of Lance and Cup, and it is not always practicable to separate Christian from non-Christian elements. But Eliot's use of Jessie Weston's book gave him access to the full range of motifs, and in the poem this is supplemented by later literary renderings. So the knight's approach to the chapel is suggested in line 202, in the quotation from Verlaine's 'Parsifal', where the children are already singing (in anticipation of a solution): '*Et O ces voix d'enfants, chantant dans la coupole!*' In the portrayal of the 'empty chapel' (385–9) the landscape suggests barrenness and decay, in the 'decayed hole' with its 'tumbled graves', 'only the wind's home'.

Here too then the quest is unfulfilled, the destination unreached. But both journeys, and the myths to which they attach, are quests for salvation, and in each case the saviour must suffer unto death for the health of the community. The focus on trial or even death, and the transition to renewed life, link the Christian narrative and the Grail legend, and indeed the material relating to other fertility cults and vegetation myths which Eliot found in both Weston and Frazer. The poem is filled with smatterings of non- and pre-Christian myths which make sense of the cycle of the seasons, decay and growth. The 'hyacinths' (and, perhaps, by association, the 'Lilacs' and the 'violet hour') allude for example to the Spartan god Hyakinthos, equivalent of Adonis and Tammuz in other regions. Frazer related how effigies of Isis and Osiris were buried to symbolise the death of the corn-god and so make rebirth possible (we might compare the corpse planted in the garden in part I of *The Waste Land*). Images of a dead god might alternatively be cast into the water and taken out again (we might compare the fate of Phlebas the Phoenician in part IV).

The point here, then, is the emphasis on death and burial as *rites de passage*, on the journey towards rebirth. Death and burial are prerequisites for life itself. This seeming paradox, so extensively articulated in primitive myth, is a central preoccupation of *The Waste Land*. Part I, 'The Burial of the Dead', takes its title from the liturgy of the Anglican Book of Common Prayer. (The first text in this burial service is Christ's words to Martha before raising Lazarus from the dead. Eliot used these words to begin one of the fragments which accompanied the draft of the poem ('I am the ressurection and the Life' – St John 11:25).[25] The liturgical title is appropriate to part I, which is substantially concerned with rites of burial. Burial here has wide-ranging connotations: both physical burial, funeral rites for the dead, and psychical or emotional burial of experience in the unconscious, to be exhumed by memory. Memory is another recurring preoccupation, in this section and later parts of the poem (Marie's reminiscences, the hyacinth garden 'a year ago', Stetson at Mylae, the corpse in the garden).

The account of the 'Unreal City' which closes part I reads in one sense as a description of the death-in-life of the office workers, the walking dead of London Bridge. This is however a complex image, and the pun is informed by an allusion to the dead who inhabit Dante's *Inferno*; the dead people of Eliot's poem are also, by extension (as we find a few lines later) the dead of the battle of Mylae, and the corpse which Stetson buried in his garden. There is too, I think, a haunting presence of the recent dead of the 1914–18 war ('I had not thought death had undone so many'). Such multiple reference is not unusual in *The Waste Land*: it asks that the reader hold together in his mind the united ranks of the dead in literature (Dante), ancient history (the Punic War) and the recent past (the Great War, and perhaps Eliot's friend Jules Verdenal, who died at Gallipoli[26]), as well as those 'survivors' who now haunt the offices and banks of the City.

The final encounter with Stetson distils the paradox of death-in-life in this part of the poem. This vivid cameo isolates three figures – the 'Speaker', Stetson, the corpse – and three incidents – comradeship at Mylae, the burial of the corpse in the garden, and the present meeting in which the 'Speaker' and

Stetson emerge from the crowd. Despite the historical distancing of the allusion to the Punic War, the First World War again impinges on the poetry. (At several points in *The Waste Land* – not simply in the pub scene of part II – events of 1914–18 impinge on the poem. Obliquity of reference makes it hard to argue the case, but I shall introduce examples at suitable points in the discussion.[27]) Not only have we been prepared for this by the historically situated memories of Marie (Larisch[28]) relating to the Austrian imperial family, but the corpse was planted only 'last year'. It is not entirely clear whether the Speaker and Stetson are part of the crowd, and it is also equivocal whether they (and the crowd) are alive or dead. 'I had not thought' (63) might be equivalent to either 'I did not think till then that' or 'I would not have thought that death could have'; and 'death had undone' is ambiguously either a completed fact, in which case this is a vision of the dead, or a metaphor for the hell inhabited by the City workers. We have then a conversation whose metaphoric multiple reference conflates the living and the dead. We can again envisage the massed ranks of those who died in 1914–18, and the post-war survivors such as Stetson and his fellow combatant. Stetson and the Speaker are among those, like Lil's Albert, who came back from the Great War.

But who *is* Stetson? If the corpse is totally unidentified, then Stetson exists in the poem only as addressee, and what the Speaker says to him is at least as revelatory of himself as of his friend. His speech here is marked by a vigorous directness which cuts through the subdued lassitude of the silent crowd, as indeed it also foregrounds the two figures. Their encounter suggests reunion after comradeship in an unspecified past ('at Mylae') and at least one more recent meeting ('last year'?). These two events merge in an impression that their shared experience is one of war, death and even murder:

> 'That corpse you planted last year in your garden,
> 'Has it begun to sprout? Will it bloom this year?
> 'Or has the sudden frost disturbed its bed?
>
> (71–3)

The tone is eager and curious, but the memory is violent, and overall these lines show a witty and dexterous manipulation of the motif of burial and the paradox of death. The key substitutions are 'corpse' (for 'seed') and 'planted' (for 'buried'). 'That corpse you planted' tightly harnesses funeral rites and the cycle of the seasons. Burial and planting must precede growth. Again, as in 'There I saw one I knew' (69), the event is in the present tense of the poem: the corpse planted 'Last year' may bloom 'this year'. We are poised between winter and spring. The Speaker's words – 'sprout', 'bloom' – suggest new growth, but hope of renewal is attenuated by the anxiety of a 'sudden frost'. This little exchange is a parody of commuter small talk on the hobby of gardening, with a hint at the supposed English murderer's inclination to bury his victim close to home. But grotesque farce takes a more alarming turn when the Speaker addresses the reader, identifying him by implication with Stetson: 'You! hypocrite lecteur! – mon semblable, – mon frère!' (76). The reader is now 'You who were with me in the ships at Mylae!' (70), and is connected not only with the Speaker by likeness ('mon semblable') and kinship ('mon frère'), but also by common interest (both Stetson and the Speaker are concerned to keep the corpse buried in order that it can sprout), complicity (what happened to 'That corpse'), even conspiracy (to prevent the Dog[29] or a frost from disturbing it). At this point the poem reaches out to the 'hypocrite lecteur', as the Speaker cries to Stetson, in common guilt and anxiety.

It is clear, even from 'The Burial of the Dead', that death is by no means an unambiguous negative finality in the poem. In part III, the rhetorical balancing of lines 191–2 establishes a congruence of 'wreck' and 'death', but this already draws on previous references to Ferdinand, rescued from the waves in *The Tempest*, and prepares us for the positive possibilities of a 'sea-change' in part IV, 'Death by Water'. It is essential to recognise the intimate connection of death and rebirth in *The Waste Land*. The thematic and structural progression of the poem is precisely a movement through and beyond death, towards regeneration. What both fills out and blurs the picture is the ambivalence of death – as physical death, or death in the spirit – and the status in the poem of regeneration or, as we may more helpfully term it at this point, salvation. As we have seen, the poem's mythical and religious backdrop is vast and eclectic; and salvation is posited, even promised, in the suggested scheme. But its status is in fact that of a designated destination, an affirmative closure which the poem denies.

The Grail motif is a case in point. Eliot makes extensive use of the Grail material, even updating it by quoting Verlaine. However, overall the allusion works to inform the poem by providing for progression, while at the same time drawing back from a commitment to a resolution of that progression. Eliot's 'Quester' (whom I have called the Speaker) is an elusive and equivocal figure which merges with others in the poem: the drowned Phoenician Sailor, the one-eyed merchant, Mr Eugenides, and Ferdinand Prince of Naples. More significantly, the Speaker, who, as Quester, takes on the Grail task, assumes an oblique association with the Fisher King himself. The main voice of the poem, the Speaker, has been identified early on with Ferdinand; there is a hint both of Ferdinand and of Christ in the dead figure who is the focus of the first section of part v; and this figure modulates yet again in the final section with the return to the 'I', the first person singular. The voice is now that of the Fisher.

There is, it seems, no saviour for *The Waste Land*. This denial can be compared to the treatment of salvation and the Grail in *Heartbreak House*. Shaw, we remember, asking in Act III who might 'save the country', originally – in the early draft – considered Mazzini Dunn as candidate for saviour on the Parsifal model of the blessed fool. Allusion to Parsifal was cancelled in the final version of the play, although Mazzini Dunn is still considered, and rejected, as potential saviour. *Heartbreak House*, too, finally retracts this mode of salvation.

Both the discrimination and the association of the various Grail figures in *The Waste Land* are suggested in part I by the Tarot pack. Eliot's note warns against taking the Tarot cards too seriously, but his very admission of an arbitrary manipulation of the Tarot figures indicates that they do have a function in the poem. Certainly the Tarot pack and Madame Sosostris, who deals it, are structurally useful. Madame Sosostris, consulted by the Speaker, shows him 'your card, the drowned Phoenician sailor' (47); and her warnings and revelations anticipate 'Death by Water' and provide for the associations of the various figures (Eliot's notes are not really necessary). She is a privileged seer, like Tiresias or the Sibyl, the 'wisest woman in Europe' (45). But Madame Sosostris, 'famous clairvoyante' (43) embodies a vulgarised and trivialised prophetic tradition. All popular forms of the occult had seen a resurgence of interest since the latter part of the nineteenth century. This clairvoyante also dabbles in astrology, and deals with the idle superstition of such clients as 'dear Mrs Equitone' (57). She burlesques the prophet, and her privileged vision is severely restricted: 'I am forbidden to see. I do not find' (54). In her hands the 'wicked pack of cards' (46) represents a drastic reduction in the mythic weight of the Tarot. Nevertheless this reduction, as with all use of the Grail motif, is significant: her failure to find the Hanged Man, whom Eliot overtly links with the Hanged God of Frazer, points to the absence of a redemptive figure in the poem.[30]

The two main journeys of part v, the road to Emmaus and the approach to the Grail chapel, both point to salvation, solution and resolution. *The Waste Land* invokes a narrative progression, with the expectation of closure in the form of an affirmative ending. This is the inescapable effect of incorporating in the fabric of the poem thematic motifs which suggest narrative sequence, such as the journey or quest, or a change of state (seduction, metamorphosis, resurrection). However, the narrative base operates, in the sphere of potentiality, as the expectation of an ending. As Eliot's gloss on the 'road to Emmaus, the approach to the Chapel Perilous' tacitly indicates, we travel in the poem, but do not arrive. Destruction and regeneration, death and rebirth, are held in tension by a strongly marked movement *towards* rebirth and regeneration (or however the 'solution' is characterised) but *not beyond* death and destruction.

This reading of *The Waste Land* proposes an implied or overt narrative base which permits only limited progression, and an ending whose 'closure' works as dis-closure. It may well seem that such a reading aligns itself with the familiar fallacy of filling in the gaps in the story. The point at issue is a kind of *Ur-Waste Land* lurking behind the poem, to be discovered by a deft in-filling of rejected draft material, the sources of allusions, and unarticulated links in a sequence which will reveal itself as continuous and discursive. The draft material, and the allusions, do not materially impinge on this issue; although, as it happens, the process of revision, which is by no means one of straight cutting, has much to say about the way the poem took shape; and there is much to be gained by an appreciation of the significance of the allusions. But one might accept these and still baulk at the notion of *The Waste Land* as actual or potential narrative, because in a particular sense the notion of progression does indeed focus on 'gaps' in the texture of the poem. The 'gaps' are in fact a mode of articulation: the 'silences' are transitions, shifts or modulations which provide for the poetic (as well as thematic) movement. Progression is then a tension or counterpoint between continuity and discontinuity, conjunction and disjunction, silence and articulation. We have already seen this process in operation at a critical juncture:

> Then a damp gust
> Bringing rain
>
> Ganga was sunken. . . .
>   (393–5)

Suspended fulfilment of expectation is signalled here by typographical as well as lexical features. The typographical spacing is a visual representation of a pause, which itself signifies a transition, a shift of focus. That disjunction, a transposed repetition to a scenario of the continued promise of rain, withholds resolution.

It is by such devices, including the manipulation of tense to foreground the continuous present, that the poem structures its expectations. There is a further device to be noted: *The Waste Land* makes rhetorical use of the language of logical argument, and specifically of the terms of propositional logic. It does so in such a way as to emphasise the concern of the poem with fulfilment and deprivation. We find a poetic version, complex and compressed, of an uncompleted logical proposition. The method is most apparent in the passage in part v beginning, 'Here is no water but only rock' (331–58), which expresses with great force the emotional restriction and negation of the wasteland:

> Here is no water but only rock
> Rock and no water and the sandy road
> The road winding above among the mountains
> Which are mountains of rock without water
> If there were water we should stop and drink
> Amongst the rock one cannot stop or think
> Sweat is dry and feet are in the sand
> If there were only water amongst the rock
> Dead mountain mouth of carious teeth that cannot spit
> Here one can neither stand nor lie nor sit
> There is not even silence in the mountains

But dry sterile thunder without rain
There is not even solitude in the mountains
But red sullen faces sneer and snarl
From doors of mudcracked houses
                              If there were water
And no rock
If there were rock
And also water
And water
A spring
A pool among the rock
If there were the sound of water only
Not the cicada
And dry grass singing
But sound of water over a rock
Where the hermit-thrush sings in the pine trees
Drip drop drip drop drop drop drop
But there is no water

   The passage divides internally. In the first part (331–45), the
restricted experience is expressed by the repeated concessives
'but' and 'only', and the extreme denial 'not even'. The minimality of life appears in the absence of 'silence' and 'solitude', and the
negation and reduction of choice of action: 'Here one can neither
stand nor lie nor sit' (340). The articulation of this minimal,
reduced existence rests on a quasi-logical structuring which uses
the implicative function 'If A then B.' This appears most clearly in
'If there were water we should stop and drink'. According to the
narrative expectation of the entire poem, 'water' constitutes the
precondition of refreshment, in dynamic opposition to the dryness
of the wasteland. Absence of water denies the possibility not only
of refreshment ('we should . . . drink') but also of termination ('we
should stop'). That to 'stop' is a desired consequence of the
presence of water is emphasised by the next line: 'Amongst the
rock one cannot stop or think'. The desired change in *The Waste
Land* is also the terminus, the destination (it is worth noting that
this section draws heavily on the narrative of the journey of the
Israelites across the desert towards a promised land). Here, as in
Women in Love, we find acute end-anxiety; as in that novel, the
anxiety focuses on a longed-for finality.
   The cumulative impact of this first part derives from emphatic

reiteration of the lack of water, by means of various equivalents: 'only rock', 'sandy road', 'mountains of rock without water'. What is dominant, then, is the negated proposition, which will be explicitly stated in the second part of the passage, 'But there is no water'. The consequences, in human terms, of the lack or negation are also further articulated, as in 'Sweat is dry and feet are in the sand'. In the shaping of the passage as a whole, what we are dealing with is an expression of the implications for human experience of the material conditions of the wasteland. 'If' these material conditions obtain, 'then' life is necessarily reduced.

The second part of the passage, lines 346–58, is a distillation of the preceding monologue. It recapitulates the event in a condensed form, foregrounding with even greater clarity the selected lexical items, components of the landscape. The movement of the passage is shaped by the sequence 'If there were water . . . If there were rock / And also water . . . If there were the sound of water only . . . But there is no water.' Within this framework the argument is successively modified, as if seeking with desperation to establish minimal requirements for a consequence to complete the proposition. So we find alternative 'suggestions': 'water / And no rock'; 'rock / And also water'; 'the sound of water'; 'Not the cicada / And dry grass singing'. Among the alternatives, one in particular stands out. The 'pool among the rock' suggests not only a temporary (and/or spatial) alleviation, but the coexistence, or even the profoundly conterminous nature, of water and rock. If, as we saw earlier, each lexical item of the wasteland-scape actively connotes its opposite, then in some sense 'water' and 'rock' may indeed be congruent. At this point we depart from logic, to a poetic or mystical apprehension of the immanence, in the deprivation of the wasteland, of plenitude.

Nevertheless, there is no mistaking the pressing sense of deprivation here. And there is, further, no relief: the passage closes with 'But there is no water'. This bleak negation of the antecedent proposition ('But, not-A') precludes any consequence in the world of the poem, and carries with it a full sense of the hopelessness of deprivation. The implication ('Therefore, not-B') is left unstated; but its force is felt in the shift to the next section of the poem (without punctuation, but with an emphatic space). At the culmination of this passage, then, the text clinches the cruel deprivation by articulating the (negated) antecedent – 'But there is no water' – and withholding the consequence. This 'silence' signifies in just the way I have proposed for the overall narrative mode of the poem. Moreover, the articulation of deprivation is so strong, the repetitions and substitutions so emphatic, as to confirm the actual condition obtaining in the world of the poem as one of negation. Overall, the use of a shaping 'if–then' is rhetorical rather than logical, and the passage is not susceptible to thorough and rigorous logical analysis; but, as in the analogous manipulation of exclusive disjunction in 'neither / Living nor dead' (39–40) and 'Are you alive, or not?' (126), it is a rhetoric which employs logical forms and terminology to reinforce strenuously its statement of the conditions of the wasteland.

The primary deprivation of extreme thirst is expressed in this passage as auditory hallucination. The hallucinatory quality shifts and intensifies, first with the presence of the invisible third person on the 'road to Emmaus', and then, with a transition signalled by 'Unreal' (376), to the surreal nightmare of lines 377–84. This, the most hallucinatory sequence of the poem, redeploys, by dream mechanisms of condensation and displacement, the vocabulary previously established. *The Waste Land* as a whole, with its symbolic landscape and fable, might well be placed in the tradition of the dream vision. Throughout, the selection and disposition of features of landscape have been both vivid and specific – the kind of naturalistic detail or hyper-realism of effect which easily modulates into the symbolic or the surreal. However, although, by contrast with the other texts we have looked at, *The Waste Land* makes pervasive use of the symbolic mode to which the others shift to achieve closure, yet we can detect within the poem a movement from the predominance of realistic contemporary detail in the early sections, to the uninterrupted visionary landscape of 'What the Thunder Said', and in particular the nightmare vision of lines 377–84.

The colours in these lines repeat and modify the 'violet air' (372) and are prevailingly funereal: 'black hair' (377), 'violet light' (379), 'blackened wall' (381). The sounds too are funereal: 'tolling' bells which 'kept the hours' (383) recalling the 'dead sound' (68) of Saint Mary Woolnoth. The focus is a woman whose 'hair' (377) reminds us of the women of both the hyacinth garden and 'A Game of Chess'. 'Bats with baby faces' (379) suggests a perverse birth ('crawled head downward down a blackened wall' – 381). The 'empty' cisterns and 'exhausted' wells accentuate depletion and loss, and the total inversion of the passage marks it as the nadir of the poem.

In the two sequences which precede this (lines 359–76), hallucination has opened out to a prophetic vision of some clarity:

> hooded hordes swarming
> Over endless plains, stumbling in cracked earth
> Ringed by the flat horizon only
>
> (368–70)

Apocalypse is not merely declared here: the Speaker questions the identity of the images and the meaning of the vision: 'Who . . . What . . . Who . . . What'. The 'hooded hordes' represent – if we pay attention to the notes – the most recent breaking-point of civilisation as perceived by Eliot, the 'present decay of Eastern Europe'. The telling phrase 'present decay', like the 'road' and the 'approach', places the event within the moment of crisis. (One is reminded of Lawrence's 'long process' of 'dissolution'.) But the urbanity of the note is belied by the dramatic fervour of the poetic articulation. The hordes are in the desert, now 'cracked earth' (compare the 'mudcracked houses' of line 345, which house hostility) and 'endless plains' (compare 'arid plain' – 424). These 'endless plains' (369), 'Ringed by the flat horizon only' (370), extend forever. These people, in marked contrast to the impassive crowd on London Bridge, display a feverish activity: 'swarming', 'stumbling'. Yet, despite the active pressure, the adjectival, generic quality of the present participles again retracts any reached destination. The hordes are 'endlessly' going nowhere, and this is a vision of apocalypse as *perpetuum mobile* and permanent crisis.

The apocalyptic vision extends over the mountains to reintroduce the city, and the urban apocalypse[31] of *The Waste Land*:

> What is the city over the mountains
> Cracks and reforms and bursts in the violet air
>
> (371–2)

This is marked by an unusual density of active present-tense verbs: the impression is of violent non-human fracturing, even in fact of explosion. '. . . bursts' connects with the lexical set of 'broken', which signifies a completed, irreversible change of state (the completion, in fact, of 'Cracks' and 'Falling'). It was a later and more forceful substitution for the word 'breaks', which still appears in the draft version.[32] The line taken as a whole carries an aural and visual association with a bombing-raid, rather like the explosive pyrotechnics of Lawrence's descriptions in 'Moony'. Here again, it seems, is an oblique rendering of the war of 1914–18, which might also make us think again about those swarming, stumbling hordes.

The urban apocalypse is a nightmare 'memory' of the smash of empires, represented in their ruling cities, in a vision of many pasts simultaneously present:

> Falling towers
> Jerusalem Athens Alexandria
> Vienna London
>
> (373–5)

The collapse of 'Falling towers' is at the same time irreversible yet continuous and recurring. 'Falling towers' picks up the 'White towers' (289) – the Tower of London: it will be restated in the surreal sequence as 'towers / Tolling reminiscent bells' (382–3); and, finally, in the tag from the nursery-rhyme 'London Bridge is falling down falling down falling down' (426). This final restatement, and indeed the entire concluding sequence of the poem, distils once more the mode of crisis, the poem's promised end and withheld apocalypse. These towers, and London Bridge, have already fallen, an irretrievable catastrophe: yet apocalypse is both confounded and retracted by the present participle 'falling', which captures the crisis in its process of happening; and the repetition 'falling down falling down falling down' (paralleled – with, I think, a reciprocal irony – by the triple repetition of the consoling 'Shantih' which closes the poem) suggests that such collapse recurs.

The closing section recapitulates the poem's vocabulary, its mode of limited progression, and its apocalyptic motifs: '*la tour abolie* / These fragments I have shored against my ruins' (429–30). This fragment sets up yet again the tantalising ambivalence we have encountered between the spatial and temporal, continuance and completion. 'These' is the poem's final signal of proximacy; but 'I have shored' is ambiguously a completed action or an adjectival use of 'shored' which again makes for an uncertainly situated tense. However, the ambivalence is concentrated in 'against my ruins'. Visually, we have an image of 'stony rubbish' (20) heaped against the ruined tower to buttress or 'shore' it up, reading 'against' in a spatial, and 'ruins' in a physical sense. But we may also read 'against' as equivalent to 'in the event of', 'so that these at least may survive', as an insurance against total cultural collapse. The ruin may not yet be in ruins. This coda is a summative statement of the imminence and recurrence of catastrophe: *The Waste Land* presents crisis as a continuous present.

Between these two framing visions of apocalypse is 'What the Thunder Said', as Eliot turns to the calm wisdom of the Upanishads in a set of injunctions which translate as 'give, sympathise, control'. The Thunder has the force of a divine pronouncement or intervention, and we might compare it with the divine nemesis which Hector Hushabye calls down on Heartbreak House, or with the evolutionary elimination posited in *Women in Love*. Both of these, we found, were warnings, an 'unless' which was exhortatory. The same might be said of Eliot's Thunder; but it is also the equivalent, in *The Waste Land*, of the Zeppelin or bombing-raids, although Eliot did not use air raids in his poetry until the *Four Quartets*. (There, in 'Little Gidding', we find an image curiously close to Lawrence's interpretation of the Zeppelin as the Holy Ghost, in the 'dark dove with the flickering tongue' – 81.) The title 'What the Thunder Said' is ironically framed: the injunctions are contained by the poem, and, however regrettably, do not materially affect its apocalypse. What the Thunder Said does not provide a *deus ex machina* solution.

But what does the Thunder say? It may be helpful to recall the fable. The gods asked their father for a word, and he gave them DA, which they interpreted as *Damyata* (control). He gave the same answer to men, who interpreted it as *Datta* (give): the demons interpreted the same answer as *Dayadhvam* (sympathise). In *The Waste Land* each answer generates a reflective passage with an elegiac quality, significantly dominated by the past tense, which places the entire passage in the non-proximate area of the experience of the poem. The memories registered here connect with the motif of death. All three sections connect specifically with motifs, vocabulary or allusions which occur elsewhere: so the second (*Dayadhvam*) anticipates a subsequent reference to Dante's account of Count Ugolino dying in his tower-prison; the third

(*Damyata*) takes us back to the quotations from *Tristan und Isolde*, and to 'Death by Water'.

The 'we' of the first section (*Datta*), which divides in later sections into 'I' and 'you', is very intimate. This is the climactic moment of intimate, shared reflection, concerned with the meaning of death, both to the dead, and to the bereaved, left with objectifications such as obituaries or wills. What is questioned, specifically, is the nature or value of the gift:

> *Datta*: what have we given?
> My friend, blood shaking my heart
> The awful daring of a moment's surrender
> Which an age of prudence can never retract
> (401–4)

There are sexual overtones here, reiterating the theme of lust, 'surrender' to the momentary urges of the flesh. But there is too a hint of death, and a reflective post-mortem. Here, it seems, the memory of the war creeps in as well. It is as if the war dead themselves assess what they have 'given' (a common enough euphemism for being killed in war).

Eliot might have had in mind two associations of 'surrender' with death. One is again in Conrad's *Heart of Darkness*, from the rejected epigraph: 'Did he live his life again in every detail of desire, temptation and surrender during that supreme moment of complete knowledge?' The verbal echoes here are strong: the 'detail' of 'surrender' is sexual, but the 'supreme moment' is that of death. The second association occurs in one of Eliot's own poems, 'The Death of Saint Narcissus', which provided some material for *The Waste Land*. The martyr's death, pierced by arrows, suggests a sexual surrender and satisfaction.[33] The satisfaction of death is sexual, as so often the two experiences are fused in poetry. But the predominant experience in the section of *The Waste Land* is surely death, and sexual imagery is a way of expressing violent death. 'Saint Narcissus', written in 1915, is extremely gory as well as erotically charged: the poem could well read alongside those of the War Poets. By analogy, we might see in *The Waste Land* not only an elegiac concern with death, but also a preoccupation with the deaths of the young men who made the ultimate gift of their own lives in a 'moment's surrender' – which might be experienced, and was certainly expressed, in terms of sexual orgasm: going over the top. It is this which 'an age of prudence can never retract'. The intimate directness of 'My friend' (which recalls 'mon frère' at the end of part i) suggests the comradeship of the 1914–18 war.[34] The memory of the war dead here continues in the dusty foray into 'our empty rooms' (409), and the task of the beneficent spider is to spin its web over the naked truth. It is the direct experience only, not the memory, which is of any – and questionable – value: 'By this, and this only, we have existed' (405).

I have, increasingly, suggested that the impact of the Great War informs *The Waste Land*, not always at the level of conscious poetic working. The war seeps into the poem, barely noticed. To draw as much attention as I have to its informing presence is inevitably to distort the effect. However, it does seem to me that Eliot's note on the 'present decay of eastern Europe' does actually obscure the substantial relevance to the poem of the experience of 1914–18. And, however we ascribe it, an elegiac tone pervades the poem. *The Waste Land* is anxious about death, and what may be retrieved from death. It can be read in the literary tradition of the elegy: in that tradition, one such retrieval is art itself.

The Waste Land is anxious, too, about art: indeed the concluding section interweaves the Fisher's reflections with 'fragments' of art. These multi-lingual literary tags serve partly to reiterate the motif of apocalypse (*'la tour abolie'* – 429); but what is also notable is that they are drawn largely from literature which itself focuses on problems of artistic creation, or on a specific artist. So, in the quotation from Dante's *Purgatorio*, the speaker is a poet, Arnaut Daniel. The Philomela legend is restated in a compilation of literary renderings – the *Pervigilium Veneris*, Tennyson's *The Princess* – and, after all, the consequence of the rape was metamorphosis into the nightingale, a song-bird (even more significantly, the 'swallow swallow', sister to Procne, had her tongue cut out). The line (429) from De Nerval's sonnet recalls one of the poet's personae, a nineteenth-century visionary who hanged himself. Hieronymo, in Kyd's *The Spanish Tragedy*, was set on avenging his son's murder: prevented through court corruption from obtaining legal redress, in his role of master of the King's entertainment he produced a play within a play to enact revenge by a reconstruction and mimesis which meshed with actual murder.

'These fragments' then hang together, to express the artist's

anxiety to communicate his vision ('The horror! The horror!').
The impotence of the Fisher King fuses with the self-questioning
of the Speaker in these final lines to suggest the dumb or unheard
artist. The wasteland is metaphor for the impossibility of
communicating the truth (even What the Thunder Said was
subject to varying interpretation). 'These fragments' refers in the
first instance to the literary tags of the immediate context; but, as
with the motif of apocalypse, their juxtaposition ('I can connect
/ Nothing with nothing' – 301–2) gathers up a recurring feature
of the poem – its network of reference to other artists and poets.
The summative experience is that of the artist: this is a reflective
and self-reflexive poem, a meditation on the nature of the poet's
song (hence the relevance of Spenser's refrain). Eliot's notes, far
from 'impersonalising' the poem, mark it as 'his' creation and
oracular utterance. For *The Waste Land* is concerned too with the
artist as prophet: there is Tiresias, 'he who delights in signs'. It
may seem that this figure, who speaks in only a handful of lines,
receives disproportionate attention simply because of Eliot's note:
'What Tiresias *sees*, in fact, is the substance of the poem.' Tiresias
may not be *necessary*, but he *is* relevant. In his role of prophet, he
connects with other 'seers' within the poem or appended to it:
both Marlow and Kurtz from Conrad, the Sibyl, Madame
Sosostris – even, perhaps, 'Gerontion', which Eliot thought of
prefixing to *The Waste Land*.

As we have seen, Eliot's preoccupation with *Heart of Darkness*
impinges on *The Waste Land* at a number of points, and fixes
particularly on the intricacies of narration within narration, and
what these have to say about knowledge, and the communication
of experience. It was with extreme reluctance that Eliot relinquished the original epigraph, the passage from *Heart of Darkness*,
and replaced it by an extract from Petronius. Roughly translated,
this goes, 'For with my own eyes I saw the Sibyl of Cumae hanging
in a bottle, and, when the boys said to her, "Sibyl, what's the
matter?", she answered, "I long to die." ' The Sibyl (whose
prophecies were inscribed on leaves, perhaps analogous to the
'fragments' of *The Waste Land*) is 'suspended' in her bottle between
past and future, memory and desire. There may be a link with the
Bradleyan membrane of private experience in her bottle–prison,
although she can at least reply to the boys who speak to her (and
she herself is perceived and described by a narrator, as with Kurtz
and Marlow). The irony, as far as the epigraph is concerned, is

that from being in the privileged position of seer – in which she requested immortality – she now longs for death, trapped in time, and by her capacity to transcend time by prophetic sight. This is the plight too of Tiresias in *The Waste Land*, the 'lowest of the dead' (246), who must foresuffer all. Tiresias, deathly bisexual voyeur, is the containing consciousness of the poem: he connects with Conrad's Marlow, with the Sibyl, with Madame Sosostris, with St John the Divine (who was the speaker and witness in Pound's deleted line).[35] The substance of the poem, 'What Tiresias *sees*', is an apocalyptic vision, and its crisis is that of the artist–prophet.

In the terms of this book, *The Waste Land* may be read as the culmination of the literature of crisis. It articulates crisis as imminent but suspended apocalypse, by escaping from the constraints of narrative realism into its own poetic method. It both refuses linearity, and tantalisingly refers to it. It posits narrative closure and thematic apocalypse, and leaves both open, suspended in a continuous present. Its controlled contrasts and juxtapositions move the poem through, but not beyond, the wasteland. The poem establishes for us a dimension of crisis, and leaves us locked within it. In *The Waste Land* the literature of crisis achieves a consummate poise.

Yet in achieving such poise, *The Waste Land* becomes the paradigm of modernist poetry. This is not simply a matter of spatial organisation or non-discursive juxtaposition: the 'mythic method'[36] for which Eliot praised Joyce's *Ulysses* was defined as the opposite of narrative method, but there is more to it than that. The use of myth, 'manipulating a continuous parallel between contemporaneity and antiquity', is a way of 'controlling, of ordering, of giving a shape and a significance to the immense panorama of futility and anarchy which is contemporary history'.[37] The mythic method aims, in effect, to dehistoricise crisis. *The Waste Land* proposes, in its movement between past and present and its range of 'Falling towers', that crisis has been repeated, and will be repeated, comprehended in a universal fabric of world experience. And, if the mythic method distances crisis in one direction, the use of Tiresias as containing consciousness does so in the other. This too is a coping mechanism, placing the poem at one remove from the poet. It makes of crisis a private vision: the effect is to internalise the experience of *The Waste Land*, transposing its symbolic landscape into a state of mind. Eliot indeed insisted on referring the genesis of the poem to his own personal crisis, and strenuously denied that he spoke for a whole generation. His disclaimer is not unassailable: a personal crisis might indeed be the 'illusion of being disillusioned' and still speak for a particular generation very well.

Eliot, in *The Waste Land*, both universalises and internalises crisis, doubly withdrawing it from the moment of historical change. He wishes to apprehend crisis as a mode of experience, as an expression of the human condition. Forster, Shaw and, to an extent, Lawrence (who is also drawn to the notion of cyclical historiography) apprehend crisis as event: single, immediate, unique determinant of future events. Eliot's approach is essentially aesthetic, and he significantly writes towards a literary tradition. Nevertheless, what we have seen of these texts moves the others closer to modernism, and at the same time reveals in *The Waste Land* a core of 'cultural statement' of the condition of Europe. This is a two-way comparison.

6 Postscript

'among the ruins'

The claim is not, of course, either that 'literature of crisis' as defined in this book constitutes a unique phenomenon in literary history, wholly specific and exclusive to the period under consideration; or that it offers a definitive and comprehensive characterisation of literary production between 1910 and 1922. Nevertheless, if, as has been suggested in earlier chapters, a measure of this literature is its confrontation of contemporary issues, it would after all be surprising if the grouping could not be extended. A salient feature of the literature of crisis is indeed its engagement with the contemporary situation, even where the immediacy of that engagement is blurred by oblique reference or by an ambivalent posture; and, certainly, many other texts of this period articulate the Condition of England as one of crisis. The familiar motifs recur: social fission, and the split between material power and humane values; sexuality and sterility; madness and hysteria; violence, death, murder and suicide. We find, too, that quality of end-direction which pushes towards a normative configuration, allied to an end-anxiety attaching to narrative closure and to the crisis-in-the-world which the fiction seeks, as it were, to resolve. And, in its most acute form, end-anxiety is found elsewhere to render the terrors of the modern apocalypse.

Fictions other than those already dealt with may then be said to remain in crisis. However, one does not wish to overstate the case, nor to suggest that qualities such as end-direction or end-anxiety may not be discerned in the literature of other periods. As Kermode pointed out, all books must end: that necessity of itself determines the end-anxiety with which a fiction negotiates its progression. In a broad sense every narrative proceeds by meticulously selecting out all 'possible' or impossible progressions. And, of course, the perennial problem of closure is attested to in authors' revisions and discarded endings. When the disclaimers have been made, however, and although it might be said that in a sense every period has its literature of crisis, there may still appear a considerable measure of historical specificity in the conglomerate of features exhibited by these texts: in their literary formulation, that is, of the contemporary situation.

One might suggest, for example, that phenomena such as problematic closure, or sudden shifts of narrative mode into an uneasy symbolism, are particularly pertinent at this historical juncture, with the waning dominance of realism, and the emergence of modernism. Moreover, in forming a conspectus of the period, one might reject a notion of disparate and unconnected developments, or even of a division between the 'contemporary' and the 'modern' (or between realism and modernism, or 'war literature' and modernism), in favour of a holistic model of complex interrelations of diverse articulations of crisis. Such a model would strive to accommodate documentary analysis as well as the poetic image; and the 'mixed discourse' of such popular writers as Wells and Shaw would appear not as marginal or in some way subliterary, but as importantly and centrally focusing the concerns of the period just before the war. Modernism, even in its declared 'objectivity', might be said to embody an impassioned commitment to the dehistoricising of crisis, and thereby to deal – like war poetry – with the problematic situation of the artist in society. Ezra Pound, like Wilfred Owen, is sensitised to the moment of crisis. In *Hugh Selwyn Mauberley*, or even more in the 'Hell group' of the *Cantos* (XIV–XVI), he foregrounds the context against which, in the fullest sense, modernist poets write. Pound can and must interpolate or *include* the war: his insistence on a 'poem including history'[1] begs the question of social responsibility implicitly raised by modernist experimentation, and it is particularly suggestive for a concept of literature of crisis. The direct comparison or contrast is with Eliot's compressed epic, and indeed the *Cantos* rehearse, in a sense, the repeating apocalypse of *The Waste Land*. But Pound, despite the layering of his poem and its density of allusion, does not I think dehistoricise the moment of crisis. Rather more comfortably perhaps than Eliot (although less tidily) he lets in the immediate; the particularised, and the unaccountable.

We turn, then, to other texts which deal with crisis. The object of this postscript is not to provide a checklist of the literature of crisis, but simply to draw attention to a number of texts which may be considered as broadly parallel to those dealt with in preceding chapters. A parallel can be found, to start with, in the socio-historical panorama of Ford Madox Ford's *The Good Soldier*, pervaded by supressed hysteria, madness, suicide and (usually unconsummated) sexual liaisons. This fiction of the decade before the war, concentrated in a group of representative figures, ends in the elimination by death or madness of all except Leonora and the American narrator, and in the latter's 'inheritance' of the English country house Branshaw. As Leonora remarks, it is the end of an era: just ten days after Edward Ashburnham has cut his throat, there are already rabbits on the lawn. But this is not a simple elegy for a lost golden age: the lives of these 'good people' of upper-class society have emerged as a continuing horror of corruption, destructiveness and emotional torment. Ford's narrator, with his delayed revelations and fluctuating stance, refracts the crucial decade with a complex irony. We find we must hold in balance the narrator's double perspective, moving, within two pages, from his characterisation of what has happened as the sudden smash of civilisation – 'Permanence? Stability? I can't believe it's gone. I can't believe that that long, tranquil life, which was just stepping a minuet, vanished in four crashing days at the end of nine years and six weeks'[2] – to the declamation that the civilisation was a veneer: 'No, by God, it is false! It wasn't a minuet that we stepped; it was a prison – a prison full of screaming hysterics. . . .'[3] The narrator is himself implicated in the process he describes, and his final realisation, that he is 'horribly alone',[4] expresses the sense of crisis of the novel's present, in 1913. The book is a retrospective gloss on an age of deceptive stability, and a hint of crisis yet to come, in the apocalyptic recurrence of the fateful date of 4 August. As Ford noted in his Preface, *The Good Soldier* did not appear until the 'darkest days of the War'[5] (by which he meant 1915). By this time the title had been changed (from 'The Saddest Story') and the ironies had multiplied.

The apocalyptic note is also caught in Wells's *Tono-Bungay*, which documents the contemporary (1909) condition of England. Like Ford, Wells presents an aristocracy in decline, as Beatrice, object of George Ponderevo's infatuation and aspiration, proves eventually to be sexually and socially corrupt. But the main focus of *Tono-Bungay* is the social mobility of the lower middle classes over two generations, in its story of the rise and fall of an Edwardian plutocrat. Wells selects appropriate tokens of this mobility, from the Victorian self-help of Uncle Edward Ponderevo's patent medicine, to the 'soaring' of George's flying-machines, and the final 'smash' of both enterprises. The novel closes in a sober and very uncertain present, with George Ponderevo reflecting on the symbolism of his new career of making and launching destroyers: ' "This", it came to me, "is England." '[6] This epiphany is the prevision of a darker age to come, and its note of apocalypse is not retracted. As in *Mr Britling*, the final configuration of the condition of England is constituted in the vision of the central character. But George Ponderevo's conclusion, that we merely make and pass, is markedly different from the progressive evolutionism of Mr Britling in Wells's later book.

For the most vivid and haunting expression of the modern apocalypse we turn to 'The Second Coming'. Yeats's poem is a compressed statement of the certain approach of an uncertain and ambiguous crisis. Here, in lyric form (the poem consists of an octet followed, after a space, by a further fourteen lines, as if it were a restarted sonnet), we find a structural equivalent of the Condition of England fiction. The two sections parallel the twin concerns of the end-directed narrative, in an analysis of society, followed by a prophetic speculation. The imagery of the first section encompasses familiar motifs of dislocation, decline, violence and death. In the second the emphasis shifts from the social to the prophetic, from the immediate to vast, slow historical epochs. Clearly the revelation of this second part is based in myth and religious typology, and the poem as a whole rests – like Lawrence's apocalyptic writing – on a system of cyclical historiography. It might seem that the certainty of a mythical and quasi-historical frame of reference would exclude the poem from the end-anxiety of the literature of crisis. Moreover, although 'The Second Coming' deals with the moment of crisis, it does so with supreme poetic assurance, and in a finely controlled lyric form. To this extent, we might say, it could exhibit end-anxiety in only a limited way. However, the conflation of poetic expectation and dread draws the poem back into the domain of crisis; and, indeed, the essence of the vision is precisely its ambiguous signification. The Second Coming – a pause between two phases or epochs, an End which is also a beginning – does not operate as a consoling myth: the vast image which troubles the sight is not necessarily a positive solution to what is deprecated in the first part of the poem. This is indeed a poem of the End, but one in which the End is dreaded as deeply as it is desired.

What we have, then, is an implied narrative progression ('Surely some revelation is at hand') apparently fulfilled by a vision. But the repeated 'Surely', far from indicating certitude, actually operates as a disclaimer, suggesting a measure of doubt and insecurity. The vision itself is threatening and ambivalent, and the suppressed violence which it generates is not dissipated in the statement which follows. This unrelieved anxiety is encapsulated in the closing lines, where a disjunction of syntax and punctuation disturbs the smooth closure, and the confident assertion of 'now I know' modulates to the ominous question 'And what rough beast. . . ?' That question in part implies its own answer, but the disposition and significance of the beast remain hidden. The beast still 'slouches' towards where it will come to 'at last' (the phrase connotes welcome relief, and dread fatefulness). Moreover, the timing is not certain: the 'Coming' is not yet, the beast is waiting to be born. We are again, as in *The Waste Land*, suspended in expectation, in a continuous present. This suspended crisis has been anticipated by the opening declaration 'Turning and turning', and echoed perhaps in the present participles 'is moving', 'rocking', and by extension 'Second Coming' (the repeated but unfinished apocalypse). This is a poem of 'endless unrelief'.

And, apart from the implications of the sonnet base, the relation between two sections is obscure (because unstated) and complex. The space in the text permits us to infer a sequential relation, or to assume non-sequential juxtaposition, or even transformation. The directness of the opening of the second part may suggest that we are to expect a solution, but as the vision darkens it appears that the poet–seer's revelation may be a product of the 'mere anarchy', or indeed *vice versa*. Each section may read as a gloss on the other, and the statement be turned back on itself (as Birkin's apprehension of dissolution may itself be one of the *fleurs du mal*). And although the poem moves from generalised to more personalised utterance the speaker is not identified: he may be contained by, or contain, the 'vision' of the first section; and the lyric voice may be privileged, or limited and confused. For all its compression and control, the poem thus doubts its own status as fiction or prophetic utterance; and it expresses an acute end-anxiety. It is exactly of a piece with what we found in earlier chapters: 'The Second Coming' might well have been taken as a central text for this book.

The literature of crisis did not come to an end at 1922. The remainder of this postscript will extend the time-span to refer to four texts which appeared a few years later, and in which the features we have discussed are repeated or modified. In these texts – *Mrs Dalloway*, *Lady Chatterley's Lover*, *Point Counter Point* and *The Silver Tassie* – the line of the Condition of England fiction is continued, in critiques of contemporary society which exhibit a marked satiric temper. Those narratives are also retrospective, as they must be in depicting life after the Zeppelin, enclosing the memory of war, and detecting dislocation as well as continuity. In 1925 or 1928 we have a fresh site of crisis, but one which necessarily registers the aftermath of the Great War. These texts may be seen in the context of the spate of war fictions and memoirs which showered Europe in the mid twenties, with an *annus mirabilis* in 1928. Yet memory is not the primary motivating spirit of the narratives: it is there because memory persists in the present, and because to live modernly is to live among the ruins. These are elegies, as well as contemporary satires: they must be the one in being the other. They strive less, perhaps, for a normative (that is a positive) configuration, although their endings confirm a vision or tableau, and the plot motifs of sex, procreation and death again determine that tableau; but there is still anxiety over the End. All share in what Malcolm Bradbury has called the 'double cataclysm' of modern literature,[7] more sharply apprehended in *Lady Chatterley* and *Point Counter Point*, poised between the Great War, which they clearly remember, and the anxiety of another: it is the double awareness that 'The cataclysm has happened, we are among the ruins', and yet that 'There's a bad time coming, boys'.[8] End-anxiety is still felt, even where apocalypse is retracted into a self-deprecating irony. Moreover, the narrative unease which we found in the earlier texts persists, not only in closure, but in the interpolation of symbolic episodes and figures. The suicide of Septimus Smith, the importance of Sir Clifford trapped in his bathchair, Harry Heegan paralysed by a war wound – all have similar functions in novel or play; and, similarly, they operate to disturb as well as to focus and unify. What we may miss, however, in these later texts, is that anxiety over narrative closure expressed as a pun on finality: how is it all to end?

Mrs Dalloway delineates the condition of contemporary London society in a group of figures which suggest City and Empire, government and palace: Peter Walsh and Lady Bruton, both with the 'thought of Empire' at hand; Richard Dalloway, sentimentally patriotic and conventionally limited; and Hugh Whitbread, 'all that was most detestable in British middle-class life'.[9] Royalty is felt to be close, and the Prime Minister actually appears: the latter's attendance at Clarissa's party seals its establishment significance. But the representative power-figures do not indicate national vigour: it is on the whole an aging and sterile gathering. The elegiac feeling of the book is summed up in the memory of Lady Bexborough, opening a bazaar with a war telegram in her hand: here lay the integrity, strength and waning power of the English aristocracy. And Clarissa's Uncle William, who knew a lady by her shoes and gloves, turned on his bed and died one morning in the middle of the war. Clarissa herself is of the ruling classes (she has seen all the great houses lit up once); she is used as the register of change, comparing life before and after the war: all is in a sense restored, but all has changed. Her memories are crucial, as a personal focus of the collective quality of life, 'there being no more marrying, no more bearing of children now'. Clarissa attempts to provide a positive counter to decline; she seeks to connect, to make things whole. Her party is the equivalent of the work of art in *To the Lighthouse*, 'matches struck unexpectedly in the dark';[10] for Woolf, the artist's imagination and the aesthetic object may redeem time, flux and death. Clarissa's 'offering' (which is the main destination of the narrative) will enact such a retrieval.

But Clarissa stands between the representative figures of English society, who act in the present and remember the past as time past, and Septimus Warren Smith, whose past experience pervades and supersedes the present. The figure of the dying ex-soldier weaves in and out of the ongoing preparation for the party, the two main narrative lines merging in a final epiphany. *Mrs Dalloway* is, in 1925, a fiction of the Great War. The memory and meaning of the war are articulated in the consciousness of Septimus, which is agonisingly held, suspended, in the historical moment of crisis. His breakdown came about when his friend Evans was killed – not because of the acute suffering this caused him, but paradoxically because he could not feel. The horror of war is here registered as numbness and emotional atrophy, a moral anaesthesia for which Septimus accepts guilt. When he sees Bradshaw he is impelled to confess, yet cannot remember his crime. He feels, that is, all the non-specific, free-floating guilt of his generation: it is as if he bears all the sins of the world. In the aftermath of war, those sins are perceived by Septimus as concerned with sex. The fact of copulation distresses him, and he is relieved at the possibility of severance from marriage (importantly, his death means that he and Lucrezia will not have a child).

Guilt and prophetic anxiety remove Septimus from the world of everyday social transactions. Instead, he communes with death: like the ex-soldiers of part I of *The Waste Land*, or like Harry Heegan, he is one of the walking dead. So he lives in an alternative reality which impinges on the experience of the other characters, but which is fatally incompatible with it. The plane which flies overhead signals his destiny; a dog is horribly metamorphosed into a man. His vision of Evans (actually Peter Walsh) is the apogee of his alienated perception, as he sees the ghost of war. The vision of Evans is reminiscent of the obscure complicity of the speakers in 'The Burial of the Dead', their secret intimacy darkly associated with the war. We may also recall the ambiguity of death and birth in Eliot's poem (Septimus is about to join Evans in death, but will triumph over it through Clarissa's transforming vision).

The party which Clarissa has shaped is interrupted by the news of his suicide: 'in the middle of my party, here's death, she thought'.[11] Death is a threat to her achieved vision, her solution, but one which she can apparently transcend. She has speculated earlier as to the possibility of recovery or survival in death, and now interprets Septimus's death as an attempt to communicate. Drawing apart in meditative retreat, she achieves an 'extraordinary night' of communion and identification with Septimus. As Septimus has 'seen' Evans walking, so Clarissa now sees and recovers his suicide. This recovery might well have closed the novel; but there is a further stage, in a coda which transfers emphasis to Sally and Peter Walsh. Finally Clarissa herself is perceived in epiphany by Peter Walsh: in the last sentence of *Mrs*

Dalloway she becomes object, to his subjective experience. 'For there she was':[12] the recognition is that of a somewhat discredited witness, but we must I think take it as synthesis and transfigura-tion. Clarissa is finally perfected and finished in her party.

Nevertheless, the perfected Clarissa has communed with and absorbed Septimus Smith; the appropriateness of this narrative resolution must be assessed. We may consider that the figure of Septimus is too resonant, too numinous to be thus absorbed. And, after all, what are we to make of a book which places Clarissa at its centre, and treats Septimus as deranged object? The difficulty is that the consciousness limited and clouded by insanity is actually that which comprehends – contains – the sublimated guilt and anxiety of all the rest. Septimus is the fragmented conscience of this society, his death a messianic sacrifice atoning for their guilt. The problem here is in part one of narrative mode: the multiple symbolism of the figure of Septimus does not wholly mesh with the social comedy, and the symbolism shifts and expands. First, he is representative of his class, an aspiring clerk; then, shell-shocked war veteran; then, in his suicide, scapegoat for a lost generation; and, finally, a haunting symbol which encompasses the generalised madness and latent horror of contemporary society. On the positive side, the insistent juxtaposition of Septimus's deranged vision and social normality is brilliantly disturbing: his misperception of Peter Walsh and 'Evans walking' is not merely a comedy of mistaken identity, but creates a montage of discrete yet congruent meanings. But there is, still, some uncertainty of authorial stance, and we may be aware of a similar awkwardness here to the treatment of Leonard Bast. The careers and aspira-tions of the two characters have common features, and both are patronised in their desire to buy culture. Like Leonard, Septimus is a pathetic figure, who just misses heroism: like Leonard, too, he is a scapegoat, for war-guilt rather than Edwardian money-guilt. Leonard, Septimus and, for that matter, Boss Mangan enact a communal death-wish, hounded by the establishment. The elimination of each of them disturbs the narrative closure. The best analogy with Septimus is, however, Harry Heegan in *The Silver Tassie*: there too the wretched survivor is a crippling embarrassment to post-war society. We may conclude that the power of *Mrs Dalloway* derives, in part intentionally, from a centre of unresolved violence in the social comedy. The text grasps at the centrality of Septimus's derangement and suicide, only to 'sur-

vive' them first through Clarissa's imaginative embrace, and then
by the oblique apprehension of Peter Walsh. The crisis is
negotiated by this double accommodation of Septimus, and of his
memory of Evans and of the war; but we are left with an
ambiguity, as to whether the war is thereby enshrined in the
contemporary consciousness and the contemporary process, or
rather exorcised and dismissed.

In *Lady Chatterley's Lover* (1928) Lawrence again maps out for us
the socio-economic, political and emotional territory. The themes
and concerns of *Women in Love* persist: the industrial machine, and
the sterility of personal relationships in a society gone dead. Here,
ten years on, the war which was obliquely rendered in the earlier
novel is recorded as history. But history interacts with contemporary life in a critique which, like *Mrs Dalloway*, is necessarily
retrospective: Sir Clifford and Connie Chatterley are remnants of
the Great War, crippled survivors living among the ruins. The
forward impetus of the novel is imbued with the end-anxiety of a
double cataclysm, of another 'bad time coming'. *Lady Chattlerley*
sets its face against that further apocalypse, attempting to
displace the materialism of Sir Clifford in favour of the organic
and productive relationship of Connie and Mellors. However, the
narrative hesitates finally to place the lovers in a definitive or
positive configuration, and, wavering in its hope of redemption,
may to that extent actually be seen to confirm Sir Clifford's
position.

Lawrence's successive rewritings steadily gave more weight to
the country-house motif, increasing its capacity to focus the
Condition of England and express the hegemony of the ruling
class.[13] The final version of the novel includes a house party of
figures whose main function is to discuss the Condition of
England: Tommy Dukes, the most articulate, is a choric centre of
the vision of a doomed civilisation: coolly aware of the disparity
between what he believes of sex and what he can actually achieve
in a relationship. Besides voicing the issues, these figures reveal,
in the sexual and emotional paucity of their lives, what Connie
fears to be 'the incipient insanity of the whole civilised species'.[14]
They supply a sexual and a social context in which Sir Clifford's
impulse to dominate, and Connie's passivity and submissiveness,
may assume a representative historical and contemporary
significance.

Sir Clifford Chatterley himself embodies an escalating and

progressively dehumanised post-war industrial power, compensating by tyranny for his physical and emotional damage. As with Boss Mangan in *Heartbreak House*, the characterisation makes an implicit indictment of capitalism and industrialism by combining material power with emotional impoverishment, symbolic emasculation and infantilism. Clifford Chatterley forms a physical and emotional dependency on Mrs Bolton, exploring her breasts and being bathed like an infant. Mangan and Gerald Crich were similarly enthralled by a mothering tyranny, but, whereas those two were eliminated, Clifford survives. Moreover, he survives to persist in this quasi-sexual relationship, a grimly symbolic union which must be integrated in the final configuration. Mrs Bolton feels she has taken Lady Chatterley's place, and the relationship sustains and strengthens Sir Clifford, enabling him to remain at Wragby after his wife has been 'expelled'.

The figure who dies is here Sir Geoffrey – of chagrin at his son's inability to produce an heir for Wragby. The motif of inheritance is central: like *Howards End* this is a quest for an heir to the normative environment of England, a search for continuity and regeneration. The quest is thwarted, redirected and finally unfulfilled. With Sir Geoffrey dies the old stable order (and that death is significantly associated with the watershed of the Great War); Clifford is impotent; and, as Mrs Bolton observes, a child of Connie and Mellors would 'put a Tevershall baby in the Wragby cradle'.[15] As it happens, a connection between Tevershall and Wragby is the only accommodation of division which the narrative envisages in both Connie's child and the liaison of Clifford and Mrs Bolton.

This accommodation is not necessarily a positive solution, and in fact the novel specifically rejects Wragby Hall, leaving Sir Clifford in possession, but with Connie having left her home, and without the prospect of a permanent alternative. Moreover, having thus consolidated yet rejected the hegemony of its normative environment, the novel fails, despite Connie's pregnancy, to ratify an heir, perhaps because the inheritance is itself now uncertain. The positive value of her pregnancy is undercut by the depressed reaction of Mellors ('It's the future');[16] and Connie is emphatic that her child will not be the heir to Wragby or Sir Clifford. The fathering of her baby has been an issue from the start, as Clifford speculates on the paternity of his heir; but a child by any man other than Mellors is clearly rejected (the nominal paternity of Duncan Forbes is posited only to be dropped). Connie's negative decisions leave the configuration, and the narrative quest, in limbo. The child is not yet born; as in *The Waste Land*, the affirmative event is still awaited. But what is in suspense is not the birth so much as the status of the child: we cannot know whether Connie will succeed in denying Clifford paternal rights and claiming the child solely as her own. And, unless Clifford grants her a divorce, she will be unable to marry Mellors. The continuation of this central relationship is not guaranteed.

If there is a final configuration, it is then one of non-resolution, waiting, doubt and expectation. Mellors's letter suggests a resolution, but his pastoral vision awaits confirmation: 'they would have to wait till spring was in, till the baby was born, till the early summer came round again'.[17] Clifford and Mrs Bolton are together at Wragby Hall, Connie and Mellors separated in a chaste exile: the narrative has enacted a sexual renunciation as well as a homeleaving. We may conclude that the negative narrative decisions, the rejection and separation, are in effect its desired solution; but there is, surely, some retraction of the affirmative relationship. The book closes with Mellors's farewell: 'John Thomas says good-night to Lady Jane, a little droopingly, but with a hopeful heart.'[18] This validation, combining 'hopeful' expectancy with detumescence, is a pause in the regenerative movement. It suggests, but does not guarantee, continuity in a relationship that will be resumed. There is some intimation ('a little droopingly') of change and decline. Moreover, the coy reference to the class-implications of the sexual contract (with perhaps an undertone of mock courtly love) throws into some doubt the validity of that contract. These two have 'fucked a flame into being',[19] but the narrative decisions reduce the affirmative conviction of that intercourse. The pastoral interlude may not survive the greenwood.

It is not only the affirmative relationship which causes unease. Of perhaps greater interest is the melange of narrative styles, the fluent discursiveness of sexual description joining with the compression and clarity of social satire or with apocalyptic revelation. The iconography of the novel is perhaps at its clearest in the scene in chapter 13 where Mellors wheels Sir Clifford in his bathchair, Connie looking on. Here the pastoral is invaded and threatened by the man in the machine. The scene is in some ways a triumph of emblematic economy, rather like the completed sign of Leonard Bast's death. It is a *tableau vivant*, an epiphany of the central triangle and of the novel's dialectic. But Lawrence here draws together figures which elsewhere in the novel exist discretely: elsewhere, the representative characterisation of Sir Clifford tells differently (and perhaps more convincingly) than the passional spontaneity of the sexual relationship. Moreover, a multiple but somewhat rigid symbolism is operating, in the pastoral setting, the emblem of the bathchair, its damage, Sir Clifford's crippled state, his present anger, and so on; but each element signifies singly and separately, without the suppleness which would permit a unified and subtly suggestive texture. And yet this is after all a strikingly effective episode: the figure of Sir Clifford is as disruptive as that of Septimus Smith, bringing death to *Mrs Dalloway*, or Harry Heegan at the dance in *The Silver Tassie*. Similarly, an anger and violence latent in the novel are here explosively concentrated in the figure of Sir Clifford: the episode functions as a moment of crisis for the novel, yoking realism and symbolism uneasily together.

Point Counter Point (1928), Huxley's satiric portrait of the 'wearisome condition of humanity', vividly and often acidly ranges over the author's contemporaries, thinly disguised. The brilliance and the disgust of the novel are integral to the cultural statement it makes of contemporary England. This is a post-war society whose trivialisation of sex and science, of the emotions and the intellect, is allied to the feeling of a double cataclysm articulated by the self-conscious and often politically active characters. As the characters – like those in *Heartbreak House*, *Women in Love* or *Mrs Dalloway* – discuss the meaning and direction of their lives, the book displays and juxtaposes discrete visions of the Condition of England and the state of civilisation. Their points of view present a spectrum of political commitment, fascist, liberal and communist, and of philosophical positions, from progressive evolutionism to apocalyptic pessimism. So, for example, the painter Mark Rampion deplores the 'inward decay . . . infantilism, and degeneracy' of modern life.[20] Rampion attributes the decline to industrialism and, like Lawrence, advocates the natural as against the mechanistic. But the destination will be the same whatever the political belief: all are inevitably bound for hell and social collapse. Rampion undercuts his own gloom by describing himself as a 'worry-about-the-bloody-old-world pervert'; but Philip Quarles agrees at least that they are probably moving towards the 'bottomless pit'.[21] The range of eccentricity and fanaticism also includes Lord Edward Tantamout, crippled aristocrat and natural scientist, who believes that global destruction will follow from a lack of phosphorus. Everard Webley, leader of the British Freemen, foresees imminent revolution arising from class-conflict, and determines to suppress the masses from the abyss. Against Webley's right-wing extremism is set the communism of Spandrell and Illidge, a doctrine based in envy and hatred. Illidge is imbued with social envy, another Leonard Bast but without Leonard's positive vision or his courage, a weak accomplice in assassination. Spandrell's political hatred is more profoundly expressive of inner decay; he feels the slimy growth of fungus and mildew in his soul. Sinister and cadaverous, Spandrell is the agent of whatever measure of tragedy or deliverance we find in the novel.

The End-anxiety expressed by such characters is endorsed by events. *Point Counter Point* is another end-directed fiction which seeks to identify and eliminate the enemy, and whose plot strives to achieve a definitive configuration by means of symbolic births, deaths and sexual relationships. But, in tune with the non-affirmative disillusion of the novel, illicit liaisons replace marriages as the significant relationships contracted in the course of the action. In the first chapter Walter Bidlake, already estranged from his wife, is about to desert his pregnant mistress for the quixotic Lucy Tantamount. Lucy, to whom 'living modernly's living quickly',[22] prefers casual connection to a continuing relationship: she doesn't want to pick up any baggage. Another extramarital relationship is formed by Elinor Quarles and Everard Webley. Elinor gradually yields to Webley's seduction, no longer physically repulsed by him; but she will be 'punished' for her fall by Webley's death, and even more that of her son Phil. Elinor is in fact a linking figure in the novel, drawing together the several deaths.

The farcical and undignified affair of Gladys and Sidney Charles results in a pregnancy: yet another misconceived child comically infiltrates the upper-middle-class bastion, as Gladys hysterically bursts into her house to make her melodramatic announcement. This is the closest the novel gets to a regenerative motif; there is little positive sexuality in *Point Counter Point*: in fact the main sexual connection celebrated in the narrative is that of Denis Burlap and Beatrice. The latter's name ironically recalls the courtly ideal; but Burlap is a wholly cynical seducer, and Beatrice an elderly virgin. As they cuddle and bathe together, in the concluding tableau, we witness that infantilism which Rampion berated and which we have seen recur in several texts. The debased sexuality of Beatrice and Burlap is crucial in that, unlike the liaisons of Lucy and Walter, or Elinor and Webley, we have no reason to infer its end. It will, as far as we know, continue. This sexual infantilism is the culminating communion of the novel and its continuing crisis, the 'Kingdom of Heaven'[23] and the inner decay of modern life. In it the narrative reaches its 'normative' or satiric tableau.

The deaths which occur in the novel are both violent and natural. The enemy is eliminated by the violent deaths of Webley and of his murderer Spandrell, the latter in an elaborately contrived 'suicide'. Spandrell plans to prove to Rampion and Mary the existence of God by the music of Beethoven and arranges this revelation to coincide with his own death at the hands of Webley's followers. Violent death destroys the beatific vision: 'A deafening explosion, a shout, another explosion and another, suddenly shattered the paradise of sound.'[24] This purging of criminal fanaticism might be thought to confirm a positive solution; but the configuration is complicated by the 'natural' deaths of John Bidlake and little Phil, the past of England and its future. Bidlake's cancer is anticipated early on, and the progress of the disease provides a commentary on events. It runs parallel, in particular, to the acute illness of Phil: Bidlake revives when the child apparently makes a recovery, only to feel again the ominous pain as the boy lies dying. Bidlake lingers on; but with him will die a generation and a way of life. Phil dies prematurely and horribly of meningitis, and the 'natural event', graphically depicted, is deprived of tragic meaning: to his father, Philip Charles, the novelist in the novel, 'It was a peculiarly gratuitous horror.'[25] The death is not a redemptive sacrifice: it merely reinforces and darkens the overall picture of loss and decline. The carefully orchestrated finale of multiple deaths is in fact 'redeemed' only by the epiphany of the infantilism and degeneracy of Burlap and Beatrice, an alternative revelation of heaven to succeed Spandrell's violent paradise of sound. The 'disturbance' of this close is overt, but to speak of disturbance is not in this case to suggest authorial uncertainty. Huxley's juxtapositions are finely judged, presenting without resolving the crisis of faith, identity and personal relationships of a society in search of apocalypse or millennium. *Point Counter Point* has been compared to *The Waste Land*;[26] certainly it can be read alongside the literature of crisis.

Also in 1928, O'Casey wrote *The Silver Tassie* to counter the 'false effrontery' of R. C. Sherriff's account of the Great War in *Journey's End*. In order to distil the essence of the war he 'broke away from realism',[27] interpolating an expressionistic second Act which owes much to the influence of such playwrights as Wedekind, but which may equally be compared with *The Waste Land* and the poetry of Owen and Sassoon. Act II is set *'In the war zone: a scene of jagged and lacerated ruin of what was once a monastery.'*[28] Its symbolic surreal landscape juxtaposes religious and military iconography: a broken crucifix, a soldier crucified on a gunwheel, a howitzer to which the soldiers pray. The weird figure of the Croucher, described as a death's head, presides over the scene: he intones a biblical passage, and chanting alternates with war jingles. The soldiers are hardly differentiated, and barely recognisable from the individualised characters of the preceding Act. They are sharply contrasted with the ignorance and prejudice caricatured in officials such as the Visitor, with his jingoistic slogan 'The uniform, the cause, boys, the corps.'[29] Act II of *The Silver Tassie* is more than an exposure of the day to day reality of warfare: it is concerned, in its montage of imagery, styles and characters, with the meaning of war – 'wy'r we 'ere'[30] – and with the construction of that meaning by religion and ideology. Detached from its context it is impressive enough; but experienced in the dramatic progression it has profoundly disturbing implications for the impact of war on civilian life. In particular, it threatens to invalidate the experience and ethic of the hero, Harry Heegan. The gulf between soldier and non-combatant is marked by the shift into expressionism, but that shift does more than dislocate temporarily the realistic dramatic action: it triggers an unease which is not resolved.

In Act I Harry Heegan, footballer, soldier and local hero, wins the trophy – the Silver Tassie – for his home town before going back up the line. In Act III he lies wounded in hospital: in Act IV, paralysed in a wheelchair, he attends a dance to celebrate the end of the war, only to find his fiancée, Jessie Taite, involved with another man. This apparently straightforward scenario, of the hero tragically cut down in his youth, is complicated by Harry's

unsympathetic and unheroic behaviour, and by suggestive interrelations with the imagery deployed in Act II. For one thing, the
values Harry embodies are seen to fail. Act I anticipates the
religious and ritualistic feeling of the second Act when Harry raises
the Tassie as if it were a chalice, to drink from it in a symbolic
communion which suggests Christian redemption and sacrifice.
In addition, his role as footballer suggests an analogy between
football and war as the great game which is a test of courage and
must be played to win. But concepts of patriotism, heroism and
sacrifice are invalidated, first by the anonymity and futility of war
as depicted in Act II; then by Harry's impotent and bitter hatred
and anger in the wheelchair, his personality damaged as well as
his body paralysed (O'Casey based the plot on Wilfred Owen's
poem 'Disabled'). Moreover, the community rejects his
behaviour: the 'Armistice' release of the celebratory dance in Act
IV is a purgation of the war, which must purge Harry as well. He
and the blinded Teddy Foran have 'gone to live their own way in
another world'.[31] Like Septimus Smith, their experience and
vision is incompatible with a post-war society; their alienation
and separateness are stylistically emphasised in a ritualistic
litany. The final configuration of *The Silver Tassie* is a sexual
affirmation of continuity and survival, achieved by eliminating
not the enemy, but the hero. Indeed Harry, a 'life on the ebb',[32]
has become the enemy whose presence is a violent threat to the
community.

The presence of Harry patently disturbs the closing scene, and
the final Act as a whole does not quite hang together as a coherent
dramatic action. The problem of drawing back from the expressionism of Act II seems to me secondary, although it is worth
noting that the earlier non-realistic action more easily accommodates a mixture of tragic poetry and satiric caricature. Act IV
uneasily combines low-key realism, farce and symbolic material:
even more, it radically divides our sympathies. Harry's pain is too
intense to be tolerated, and he is paralysed and fixed in a heroism
which has proved to be false; but Jessie Taite's callous assertion of
sexuality is at least equally alienating. The action and dialogue do
not run smoothly here, and there is no easy dramatic resolution.
The discomfort thus generated makes of *The Silver Tassie* a play of
crisis: in a sense, the crisis which is thereby enacted is that of the
meaning of the war, concentrated and clarified in Act II, but
dispersed and still pervasive in the surrounding action. In *The*

Silver Tassie O'Casey explicitly manipulates and foregrounds stylistic disjuncture in order to articulate an ideological crisis, that of post-war society's construction of its own history. Nevertheless, his play does in the end exhibit a certain assurance and finality, and its judgement is not suspended. There is, moreover, no sense here of a double cataclysm: by the close of the play the war has receded, and with it all trace of end-anxiety.

With *The Silver Tassie* this study has moved beyond the compass of literature of crisis, although without having exhausted the usefulness of the concept. We might, for example, turn next to Ford Madox Ford's *Parade's End*. This mammoth novel, written over several years in the 1920s, was confirmed as a tetralogy only when Ford added, almost as an afterthought, *The Last Post* (1928). It centres on 1917, and on the experiences in the trenches of Christopher Tietjens, the representative hero maimed mentally and emotionally by the war; but its broad span covers an entire society in crisis, with a line of continuity in the protracted domestic warfare of Tietjens and his wife Sylvia. The third volume, *A Man Could Stand Up*, closes with an Armistice night dance, reminiscent of *The Silver Tassie*, and equivocally celebratory of the end of war and the illicit union of Christopher with Valentine Wallop. *The Last Post* constitutes an alternative and happier ending, with the heir to Groby legitimised and the union of Christopher and Valentine redeemed from incest. To an extent, then, this coda provides for finality and consolation (although not without loss: Mark Tietjens, a kind of Fisher King, dies). But *The Last Post* may read as an oblique recapitulation, and as separate and distinct from the earlier books; and Ford claimed to have appended it solely to show 'how things turned out'.[33] The suggestion here of an ambiguous status might lead us back into the preceding volumes, and to the articulation of a crisis which was focused but not fully resolved by the bacchanalian finale of *A Man Could Stand Up*.

Notes

ABBREVIATIONS

FACHH   *Heartbreak House: A Facsimile of the Revised Typescript*, with an Introduction by Stanley Weintraub and Anne Wright, in the series *Bernard Shaw Early Texts: Play Manuscripts in Facsimile*, general editor Dan H. Laurence (New York and London, Garland Publishing Inc., 1981).

FACWL   T. S. Eliot, *The Waste Land: A Facsimile and Transcript of the Original Drafts*, ed. Valerie Eliot (1971).

Note: place of publication London unless otherwise stated.

NOTES TO CHAPTER ONE: TOWARDS A LITERATURE OF CRISIS

1. It is also the period which marks, in the title of a work by Robert H. Ross, *The Georgian Revolt: Rise and Fall of a Poetic Ideal 1910–22* (1967). Ross distinguishes between 'revolt' and 'revival', with the First World War as the point of demarcation. His account provides a valuable amplification of literary production in the period, alongside the growth of modernism.
2. See, for example, in relation to *Heartbreak House*, S. Weintraub, *Bernard Shaw 1914–1918: Journey to Heartbreak* (1973); in relation to *Women in Love*, P. Delaney, *D. H. Lawrence's Nightmare: The Writer and his Circle in the Years of the Great War* (Hassocks, Sussex, 1979), and Scott Sanders, *D. H. Lawrence: The World of the Major Novels* (1973); and, for *The Waste Land*, S. Spender, *Eliot* (1975), and P. Fussell, *The Great War and Modern Memory* (1975).
3. D. H. Lawrence, *Women in Love*, ch. 5: 'In the Train'; p. 67 in the Penguin edn. (Harmondsworth, 1960). Subsequent references to *Women in Love* are also to the Penguin edn, the Cambridge edn being unpublished at the time this book went to press.
4. Sanders, *Lawrence*, ch. 3: '*Women in Love*: Study in a Dying Culture', p. 99.
5. This phrase was deleted from Act II of Shaw's draft typescript. See *FACHH*, p. 138.
6. For a full treatment of this theme see M. Bradbury, *The Social Context of Modern English Literature* (Oxford, 1971); R. Gill, *Happy Rural Seat: The English Country House and the Literary Imagination* (1972); and R. Williams, *The Country and the City* (1973).
7. G. Hough, *The Dark Sun: A Study of D. H. Lawrence* (1956) p. 12.
8. See T. Eagleton, *Criticism and Ideology* (1976) p. 89.
9. F. Kermode, *The Sense of an Ending: Studies in the Theory of Fiction* (New York, 1967). Contrary to Professor Kermode's misgivings, as recently expressed in *Essays on Fiction 1971–1982* (1983), that his book 'became antediluvian almost

on publication' (p. 3), *The Sense of an Ending* remains an immensely valuable
study, to be read alongside subsequent developments in narrative theory.
10. Ibid., p. 25.
11. Ibid., p. 5.
12. Ibid., p. 18.
13. Ibid., p. 6.
14. Ibid., p. 16.
15. Ibid., p. 3.
16. Ibid., p. 23.
17. Eagleton, *Criticism and Ideology*, p. 87.
18. Kermode, *The Sense of an Ending*, p. 101.
19. Ibid., p. 124.
20. H. G. Wells, *Mr Britling Sees It Through* (1916) p. 206. Subsequent page-references are inserted in the text.
21. R. Wohl, *The Generation of 1914* (1980), discusses the idea of a lost generation as it appears in English war writing, and queries its historical accuracy.

NOTES TO CHAPTER TWO: 'HOWARDS END'

1. For an account of the persistence of the Condition of England novel into this century see J. Colmer, *Coleridge to Catch-22: Images of Society* (1978), and esp. ch. 10: 'The Modern "Condition of England" Novel'.
2. Peter Widdowson traces this connection in ch. 2 of his *E. M. Forster's Howards End: Fiction as History* (1977).
3. O. Stallybrass, *The Manuscripts of Howards End* (1973), appendix A: Working Notes, p. 355.
4. C. F. G. Masterman, *The Condition of England* (1909) p. 34.
5. *Howards End*, ch. 12, p. 101 in the Abinger edn. This definitive edition (1973) is used throughout. The phrase is reused and echoed by several characters, but first voiced by Helen.
6. Williams, *The Country and the City*, p. 298 (discussing the fiction of Henry James).
7. See D. Read, *Edwardian England 1901–15: Society and Politics* (1972) p. 32.
8. Ibid., p. 33.
9. In Aldous Huxley's *Point Counter Point* (1928) ch. 15.
10. See P. Thompson, *The Edwardians: The Remaking of British Society* (1977) p. 38.
11. *FACWL*, p. 43.
12. *Richard II*, II.i.46: 'This precious stone set in the silver sea'.
13. *Heartbreak House, The Bodley Head Bernard Shaw: Collected Plays with their Prefaces* (1972) vol. v, pp. 167, 156.
14. See Editor's Introduction to *Howards End*, p. vii.
15. I am indebted here to the hospitality and conversation of Miss Elizabeth Poston.
16. See *Into Unknown England 1866–1913: Selections from the Social Explorers*, ed. P. Keating (1976) pp. 24–7.
17. Wilfrid Stone deals with money and guilt in *Howards End* in ch. 10 of *The Cave and the Mountain* (Stanford, Calif., 1966).
18. *Marianne Thornton, 1797–1887: A Domestic Biography* (1956) p. 289.

19. See *D. H. Lawrence: Collected Letters*, ed. H. T. Moore (New York, 1962) vol. II, p. 716.
20. See Thompson, *The Edwardians*, pp. 42–3.
21. *Into Unknown England*, p. 21.
22. See P. N. Furbank, *E. M. Forster: A Life* (1977) vol. I: *The Growth of a Novelist (1879–1914)* p. 187.
23. May 1958. Quoted ibid., p. 190.

NOTES TO CHAPTER THREE: 'HEARTBREAK HOUSE'

1. *Heartbreak House*, *The Bodley Head Bernard Shaw: Collected Plays with their Prefaces* (1972) vol. V, p. 177. This definitive edition is used throughout, with subsequent citations inserted in the text.
2. The dates '1913–16' which Shaw placed below the title in the first published edition refer to the span of the action rather than to the play's composition. Shaw gave several accounts of the genesis of *Heartbreak House*, some relating to events of 1913; but, even if he conceived the germinal idea then, there is no evidence that he actually started writing until 1916.
3. A. J. P. Taylor, *The First World War: An Illustrated History*, Penguin edn (1966) pp. 24–5, 140.
4. For a full account of Shaw's life and writing in the war years, see Weintraub.
5. 'Fabianism and the War', typescript dated 1 Jan 1917, in the Humanities Research Center, University of Texas, Austin.
6. Letter held in Humanities Research Center, University of Texas, Austin.
7. Letter of 5 Oct 1916, quoted in A. Henderson, *George Bernard Shaw: Man of the Century* (New York, 1956) p. 378.
8. Quoted in Grey's autobiography, *Twenty-Five Years 1892–1916* (1928) vol. II, p. 223.
9. See Earl Jellicoe, *The Submarine Peril* (1934), for an account of submarine warfare.
10. See A. J. P. Taylor, *English History 1914–1945* (Oxford, 1965) p. 43.
11. *What I Really Wrote about the War*, Standard edn (1931) p. 1.
12. Folio 60 of the draft typescript, which contains the debate between Shotover and Hector over the problems of identifying and eliminating the enemy, has typed on the reverse, 'Shall Roger Casement Hang? To the Editor of the Times'. Shaw's letter, rejected by *The Times*, was printed in the *Manchester Guardian*, 22 July 1916. See *FACHH*, p. 68.
13. Shaw used this idea, probably derived from Proudhon's 'Property is Theft', as early as 1883, to apply to landlords, and later extended it to include shareholders. He progressively used the analogy freely to apply to any profit from capitalist enterprise. See my 'Shaw's Burglars: *Heartbreak House* and *Too True to be Good*', *Shaw Review*, XXIII, no. 1 (Jan 1980) 2–10. Some material from the article is incorporated in the following pages.
14. See *FACHH*, Introduction, p. xvi.
15. Letter of 12 Aug 1918, quoted in L. McCarthy, *Myself and My Friends* (1933) p. 205.
16. See *Lady Gregory's Journals 1916–1930*, ed. Lennox Robinson (1946) p. 202.

17. Letter to Lillah McCarthy, quoted in McCarthy, *Myself and My Friends*, p. 203.
18. See *FACHH*, p. 170 and Introduction, p. xxiv.
19. Margery M. Morgan compares the two plays in respect of this theme in *The Shavian Playground: An Exploration of the Art of George Bernard Shaw* (1972) p. 201.
20. Letter dated 27 July 1917, quoted in *D. H. Lawrence: 'The Rainbow' and 'Women in Love': A Casebook*, ed. C. Clarke (1969) p. 30.
21. *FACHH*, p. 64. The deleted section is indicated by angle brackets (〈〉).
22. Ibid., p. 65.
23. Ibid., p. 65.
24. See *FACHH*, appendix III, p. 210.
25. In the Preface to *Killing for Sport*, ed. Henry Salt (1914).
26. This information was kindly supplied by Dan H. Laurence.
27. See McCarthy, *Myself and My Friends*, p. 203.
28. See L. Crompton, *Shaw the Dramatist: A Study of the Intellectual Background of the Major Plays* (1971) p. 164.
29. For 'Shaw's Dream Play', see Morgan, *The Shavian Playground*, pp. 200–20.
30. *King Lear*, I.iv.288–9.
31. *FACHH*, p. 10.
32. *Sunday Herald*, 23 Oct 1921; repr. in Bodley Head *Heartbreak House*, p. 184.
33. It was earlier called 'The Studio at the Clouds'. See *FACHH*, p. 5.
34. Ibid., p. 177.
35. Shaw revised the opening stage setting for Act III. In the earlier version Hesione and Mangan were simply 'in the background', as opposed to the gloom, the dark void which surrounds the house (see *FACHH*, p. 157). In fact Shaw changed his mind about the time-scale of the entire action, making it proceed from late afternoon into night, instead of from late morning through the heat of the day. The emphasis is thus firmly placed on the light of the weakening sun fading into darkness.
36. The original sketches are held in the Ashley Collection of the British Library (Ashley A 1521, III). Reproduced in *FACHH*, appendix II, p. 208.

NOTES TO CHAPTER FOUR: 'WOMEN IN LOVE'

1. Foreword to *Women in Love*, repr. in *Casebook*, p. 63.
2. For details of stages of composition, see K. Sagar, *D. H. Lawrence: A Calendar of His Works* (Manchester, 1979).
3. For a full account see Delaney, *Lawrence's Nightmare*.
4. Short stories include 'England, My England', 'The Prussian Officer' and 'Samson and Delilah'; essays, notably 'The Crown' and 'The Reality of Peace'. In *Kangaroo*, see esp. ch. 12 ('The Nightmare') and ch. 13 ('Timotheus Cries').
5. Letter to Lady Cynthia Asquith, Aug 1915, in *Lawrence: Collected Letters*, vol. I, p. 358.
6. Letter to Lady Cynthia Asquith, 5 Sep 1915, ibid., p. 364.
7. Letter to Katherine Mansfield, 7 Jan 1916, ibid., p. 411.

8. Letter to J. D. Beresford, 1 Feb 1916, ibid., p. 419.

9. Letter to Catherine Carswell, 10 June 1917, ibid., p. 515.

10. *Kangaroo*, Penguin edn (1950) p. 237.

11. Letter to Catherine Carswell, 7 Nov 1916, in *Lawrence: Collected Letters*, vol. I, p. 482.

12. Letter to Waldo Frank, 27 July 1917, ibid., p. 519.

13. Ibid., p. 366.

14. *Kangaroo*, p. 239.

15. See 'A Study of Thomas Hardy' (1914), in *Phoenix: The Posthumous Papers of D. H. Lawrence*, ed. Edward D. McDonald (1936) esp. pp. 510–13. Also F. Kermode, 'Lawrence and the Apocalyptic Types', in *Casebook*, pp. 203–18.

16. H. M. Tomlinson, 'A Raid Night', in *Waiting for Daylight* (1922) p. 16.

17. *Mr Britling Sees It Through*, p. 249.

18. W. B. Yeats, 'The Second Coming', *Collected Poems* (1933; 2nd edn 1950) p. 211.

19. In the Preface to *Heartbreak House*, p. 22.

20. *Phoenix*, p. 686.

21. P. Fussell, *The Great War and Modern Memory* (1975) p. 301.

22. Fussell (ibid.) points to the contrast between Brooke's 'swimmers' of 1914 and the 'mud-flounderers of the Somme and the Passchendaele'. He relates both to Phlebas the Phoenician, in *The Waste Land*.

23. J. Goode, 'D. H. Lawrence', in *The Twentieth Century*, ed. B. Bergonzi, *Sphere History of Literature in the English Language* (1970) vol. VII, p. 133.

24. For an account of the 'naturism' of Lawrence, see J. Alcorn, *The Nature Novel from Hardy to Lawrence* (1977).

25. 'A ruthless frontiersman of literature', *The Times Higher Education Supplement*, 14 Dec 1979 (reviewing Delaney).

26. Delaney, *Lawrence's Nightmare*, p. 211.

27. See A. Kettle, *An Introduction to the English Novel* (1967) vol. II, p. 100.

28. This is the typescript which I refer to later as 'Typescript I', in the Lawrence Collection, Humanities Research Center, University of Texas, Austin. Quotation from f. 395.

29. J. Kott, *Shakespeare Our Contemporary* (1965) p. 68.

30. Repr. from the *Texas Quarterly*, VI (Spring 1963), in *Casebook*, pp. 43–62.

31. *Hamlet*, V.i.207–8 (slightly misquoted: 'Would' instead of 'Might').

32. The figure of Samson seems to have fascinated Lawrence around this time. In 'The Reality of Peace' he wrote, 'If we cannot cast off the old habitual life, then we bring it down over our heads in a blind frenzy. Once the temple becomes our prison, we drag at the pillars till the roof falls crashing down on top of us and we are obliterated' (*Phoenix*, p. 669). And in 1918 he was writing the short story 'Samson and Delilah' (see Sagar, *Lawrence: Calendar of Works*, p. 254).

33. Goode, in *The Twentieth Century (Sphere History of Literature*, vol. VII), p. 133.

34. Ibid. p. 134.

35. The two typescripts referred to here, and Lawrence's notebook, are in the Humanities Research Center, University of Texas, Austin.

36. The above quotations are from f. 666 of Typescript I (the earlier of the two typescripts in the Humanities Research Center collection).

37. Typescript II, the later of the two typescripts, f. 776.

38. Ibid. The fragment is printed in Sagar, p. 74.
39. Ibid.
40. Ibid.
41. Ibid.
42. Ibid.

NOTES TO CHAPTER FIVE: 'THE WASTE LAND'

1. I. A. Richards, 'The Poetry of T. S. Eliot', in *Principles of Literary Criticism* (1924).
2. F. R. Leavis, *New Bearings in English Poetry*, Penguin edn (1963) p. 77.
3. Ibid., pp. 87–8.
4. *FACWL, p.* 113.
5. See ibid., p. 115.
6. See H. Kenner, 'The Urban Apocalypse', in *Eliot in His Time*, ed. A. Walton Litz (1973) pp. 23–49.
7. See *FACWL*, p. 11.
8. See S. Spender, 'The Temporal City of Total Conditioning', in *Eliot* (1975) pp. 118–19, for a discussion of *The Waste Land* and the Civitas Dei; also Williams, *The Country and the City*, p. 283.
9. For a comparison with Pope's *The Dunciad*, see J. S. Cunningham, 'Pope, Eliot, and "The Mind of Europe" ', *The Waste Land in Different Voices*, ed. A. D. Moody (1974) pp. 67–85.
10. *Heartbreak House*, p. 86.
11. See *FACWL*, p. 5.
12. Ibid., pp. 55–69.
13. See ibid., p. 13.
14. See ibid., p. 45.
15. See ibid., p. 47.
16. See ibid., p. 51.
17. See *The Duchess of Malfi*, III.ii.
18. See *FACWL*, p. 19.
19. Joseph Conrad, *Heart of Darkness*, Penguin edn (1973) pp. 99–100.
20. See *FACWL*, Editorial Notes, p. 125.
21. *Heart of Darkness*, p. 38.
22. Eliot's doctoral thesis (not presented for the degree) was on F. H. Bradley.
23. Conrad, *Heart of Darkness*, p. 38.
24. See *FACWL*, p. 43, for deleted phrases which depict the city population as dazed automata.
25. See ibid., p. 111.
26. See R. Sencourt, *T. S. Eliot: A Memoir* (New York, 1971) pp. 32, 43.
27. Critics who discuss the poem in relation to the war include Fussell; and Cleanth Brooks, Northrop Frye, Kenner, Ellmann and Adams (all in *Eliot in His Time*, ed. Litz).
28. *FACWL*, Editorial Notes, pp. 125–6.
29. The Dog of Eliot's poem has been variously interpreted as denoting sensuality, guilt, humanitarianism, spiritual awareness.
30. See A. E. Waite, *The Pictorial Key to the Tarot* (New York, 1960); and D. Ward,

  T. S. Eliot Between Two Worlds: A Reading of T. S. Eliot's Poetry and Plays (1973) p. 86.
31. See Kenner, in *Eliot in His Time*, p. 42.
32. See *FACWL*, p. 75.
33. See ibid., p. 95.
34. And this was a blood friendship. See ibid., p. 77.
35. See ibid., p. 9.
36. 'Ulysses, Order, and Myth', repr. from *The Dial* in *Selected Prose of T. S. Eliot*, ed. with an introduction by Frank Kermode (1975) p. 178.
37. Ibid., p. 177.

NOTES TO CHAPTER SIX: POSTSCRIPT

1. See H. Kenner, *The Pound Era* (1972) p. 360.
2. Ford Madox Ford, *The Good Soldier: A Tale of Passion*, The Bodley Head Ford Madox Ford, vol. I (1962) p. 17.
3. Ibid., p. 18.
4. Ibid.
5. Dedicatory Letter to Stella Ford.
6. H. G. Wells, *Tono-Bungay*, with an introduction by C. M. Joad, Collins edn (1953) p. 340.
7. M. Bradbury, 'The Novel in the 1920s', in *the Twentieth Century (Sphere History of Literature*, vol. VII) p. 188.
8. D. H. Lawrence, *Lady Chatterley's Lover*, with an introduction by Richard Hoggart, Penguin 2nd edn (1961) pp. 5, 315.
9. Virginia Woolf, *Mrs Dalloway*, Zodiac Press edn (1947) p. 81.
10. Virginia Woolf, *To the Lighthouse*, Granada edn (1977) p. 150.
11. Woolf, *Mrs Dalloway*, p. 201.
12. Ibid., p. 213.
13. The two earlier versions have been published: *The First Lady Chatterley* (first English edn, 1972), and *John Thomas and Lady Jane* (first published in English 1972).
14. Lawrence, *Lady Chatterley's Lover*, p. 114.
15. Ibid., p. 154.
16. Ibid., p. 288.
17. Ibid., p. 313.
18. Ibid., p. 317.
19. Ibid., p. 316.
20. Huxley, *Point Counter Point*, p. 554.
21. Ibid., pp. 564, 416.
22. Ibid., p. 282.
23. Ibid., p. 601.
24. Ibid., p. 599.
25. Ibid., p. 589.
26. See Michael Bell, 'Introduction: Modern Movements in Literature', in *The Context of English Literature 1900–1930*, ed. M. Bell (1980) p. 85.
27. Sean O'Casey, 'Cockadoodle Doo', article published in the *New York Times*, 9

Nov 1958; repr. in *Blasts and Benedictions: Articles and Stories, Selected and Introduced by Ronald Ayling* (1967) p. 143.

28. Sean O'Casey, *The Silver Tassie*, in *Collected Plays*, vol. II (repr. 1964) p. 35.
29. Ibid., p. 41.
30. Ibid., p. 39.
31. Ibid., p. 103.
32. Ibid.
33. Dedicatory letter to Isabel Paterson: see R. Macauley, Introduction to *Parade's End*, Vintage edn (New York, 1979) p. xxi.

Index